Maureen Coop　 ..les more than thirty years of experience as a
professional ed：　 and senior manager in a non-profit organization
with a hands-o　ication in Buddhism. This training enabled her to
manage teams ·　organizations as a practical application of spiritual
values. In 2004　reen founded Awareness in Action, a consultancy
dedicated to t　cular application of mindfulness, meditation and
compassion in　workplace. As part of this work she has designed and
conducted wo：　ps and training programmes worldwide.

If you w　to find out more about Awareness in Action visit
www.awarenessinaction.org,
or contact Maureen on
info@awarenessinaction.org.

THE COMPASSIONATE MIND APPROACH TO REDUCING STRESS

MAUREEN COOPER

ROBINSON
London

Constable & Robinson Ltd
55–56 Russell Square
London WC1B 4HP
www.constablerobinson.com

First published in the UK by Robinson,
an imprint of Constable & Robinson Ltd., 2013

A copy of the British Library Cataloguing in
Publication data is available from the British Library.

Important Note
This book is not intended as a substitute for medical advice or treatment.
Any person with a condition requiring medical attention should consult
a qualified medical practitioner or suitable therapist.

ISBN 978-1-84901-201-0 (paperback)
ISBN 978-1-84901-921-7 (ebook)

Printed and bound in the UK

1 3 5 7 9 10 8 6 4 2

This book is dedicated to everyone who has felt stressed at times in his or her life and who has the wish to do something about it.

May this book be of use to you!

Contents

Part 3
Making Change Happen

ACKNOWLEDGEMENTS

My first thanks must go to Paul Gilbert for asking me to write this book. In all my dealings with him, I experience him as someone who is trying to live a compassionate life rather than just talk about it. Fritha Saunders from Constable and Robinson has been a patient and consistent guide and has taught me a great deal.

This book could not have been written at all without my study and practice of Buddhism, which has been guided over the years by my teacher Sogyal Rinpoche. He has shown me that it is possible to live these extraordinary teachings in the West, in the twenty-first century, with complete authenticity and commitment.

My partner, Bert van Baar, is my fiercest and kindest critic, reading every word I wrote – sometimes several times over. He has selflessly accompanied me through every phase of this project, providing feedback, love and encouragement every step of the way.

My dear friend and colleague in Awareness in Action, Darran Trute, has been an unfailing source of support and inspiration as this book has unfolded and provided me with inspiration when I needed it. His wife Mandy has provided kindness and love throughout.

To my dear friends Susan Burrows, Patrick Gaffney, Astrid and Marc Heijdeman, Nel de Jong, Mireia Pretus, Annemiek Schrijver and Gertie Werner-Baumer – thank you for believing that I could make this book happen and for continuing to talk with me about it as it unfolded.

Finally, my deepest appreciation and thanks go to all the people who attend my workshops and who have provided so much of the material for this book. I continue to learn from every workshop group I encounter.

PREFACE

Stress is associated with a whole range of life's difficulties. Not only can it affect our mood, anxiety and irritability, but also fatigue and general physical wellbeing too. Very few of us will go through life without feeling some degree of stress. In fact, we live in a world of mounting stress in today's increasingly competitive and financially insecure world. Things around us seem to move faster and can feel like they are more unstable. Despite increases in wealth, research suggests that, in general, younger people feel more stressed and less happy than they did thirty years ago.

Many of us are seeking ways to slow down and find points of stability in this increasingly hectic life. In this book, Maureen Cooper brings her many years of experience of working with stress, both at an individual and organizational level, to explore the nature of stress. She outlines how it affects our bodies, minds and relationships but also the way we can find moments of calm through mindfully cultivating a more compassionate attitude to ourselves and others. In fact, it's long been understood that developing the ability to become more kind, encouraging and compassionate towards ourselves, others and life in general, is very conducive to our wellbeing. Indeed, recent advances in scientific studies of mindfulness and compassion have greatly advanced our understanding of how compassion, both from ourselves and from others, can really help us to treat ourselves in ways that are respectful and which increase our sense of wellbeing.

This research tells us that if we learn to be more attentive to the present moment and to what is going on in our minds and bodies, and if we learn to value and respect ourselves and treat ourselves and others with kindness, even when things are going wrong and we are stressed, we are much more likely to be able to cope with setbacks and stress. In this book Maureen Cooper uses her wealth of experience and knowledge of work-related and other forms of stress to guide readers to work with stress in more supportive and beneficial ways. She explores why our evolved brain is now so susceptible to stress and unhappiness in the rushed world we live in, where we quickly feel judged and vulnerable to criticism and even rejected by others for not being good enough.

Key to this approach is understanding our mind better and how it evolved. One of the first steps to achieving mindfulness is to recognize that the way our brain has evolved means that our capacity for thinking, ruminating, planning, anticipating and imagining – although generally very helpful – can also cause us difficulties and make us feel stressed. Unlike other animals, we have a brain that is constantly thinking and judging. Imagine a zebra running away from a lion. Once the zebra has escaped, it will shortly settle down to feed again. However, in a similar scenario, a human is unlikely to immediately relax and easily move on to the next thing; we can spend days ruminating about what would have happened if we had got caught and fantasizing about the most horrible outcomes. Zebras and chimpanzees don't worry about what they're thinking, what they look like or what other chimpanzees might be thinking about them! Humans, on the other hand, do – often very frequently. We look in the mirror and think, 'Oh gosh, is that really me now? How come I have put on so much weight?'

We also think about our internal worlds – fantasies, thoughts and feelings – and we can be critical of those too. Life becomes full of 'shoulds' and 'shouldn'ts', 'oughts' and 'ought nots', or even 'musts' and 'must nots'. Again, no other animal gets stressed because of the way they think, judge, plan, imagine, anticipate and ruminate, but of course humans do all the time.

The more we understand how our own mind is a source of stress for us or likely to keep us feeling stressed, the more opportunities we have to switch our stressed states by using a compassionate and mindful approach. It turns out that kindness has a significant and measurable effect on our brain which help to soothe and calm us and is good for our wellbeing and that of others. By following the steps that Maureen Cooper outlines here, we are given an opportunity to find a peaceful mind that helps us to cope with the stresses of everyday living.

Professor Paul Gilbert PhD FBPsS OBE

April 2013

INTRODUCTION

Quite often we may find ourselves having to drop into our local super-market on the way home from work. If we take the time to look around us as we push our trolleys through the laden shelves, it is not hard to find opportunities to observe many of the ways we human beings experience stress. Consider the middle-aged man in a smart suit buying an easy-to-prepare meal for one – perhaps he is recently divorced, living alone for the first time in years and dealing with the stress of change and upheaval. Spare a thought for the young mother with a baby in a buggy and a toddler clinging round her legs. She looks as if she has not had a proper night's sleep for two or three years. The lounging teenage boy sulking around the soft drinks has an air of aimlessness and boredom about him – maybe because he left school with such high hopes and now does not seem to be able to find any kind of job that lives up to his dreams. Take care as you pass the older woman, walking carefully, who underwent major surgery two months ago and is feeling low and vulnerable as she tries to get her strength back. As we select the items we need to cook our evening meal, perhaps we are rubbing shoulders with people suffering from exam nerves, having relationship problems, shouldering the care of elderly relatives – the list is endless.

Divorce, bereavement, moving house and even going on holiday all rate high on the stress scale. Troubles at work, economic instability and unemployment are also possible sources. We can even feel stress if caught in traffic or standing in a slow-moving queue at the airport. When we worry about our families, our health, our job, our weight, we are creating scenarios in the mind that can create stress. A short-term physical crisis, such as falling over or scalding an arm can be termed stressful, as can longer-term physical challenges like facing chronic illness or disability.

Of course, animals too face the physical eventualities of illness or death but usually, for animals in the wild, a short-term physical emergency will either be resolved quickly or end in death. What is unique to humans is the capacity to imagine and to worry, and it is this capacity that also makes us uniquely vulnerable to stress. For example, we worry over memories of events that have already taken place, and anticipate problems that may never occur. Our imagination can lead us to create scenarios that cause us real concern until we remember that we're daydreaming and bring ourselves back down to earth. Have you ever imagined winning a large sum of money on the lottery? Inevitably you start to think about what you would do with the money and whom you would share it with. Before you know it you're worrying about who might be offended and who might feel left out! Our mind can provide a never-ending stream of potential worries and stressors all by itself. Where animals respond to the world as they experience it, as Professor Paul Gilbert says, 'we humans can respond to the world we have created in our heads'. [1]

The term 'stress' is one that is used so widely and frequently to describe a large variety of situations that it can be hard to arrive at a definition that satisfies everyone. One thing is clear though, when we hear someone describe themselves as 'stressed' we pretty much know what they mean and can identify with what they say. This is not always the case with the idea of 'compassion', which is perhaps not so accessible. Even harder to get a handle on is the idea that we can use compassion as a way of helping ourselves and even reducing our stress.

Compassion can be defined as the wish for everyone to be free from suffering along with having the urge to do something to bring that about. It can be misunderstood as pity, or as some otherworldly notion more in keeping with religious observance than the hustle and bustle of everyday life. It is not uncommon to hear people question how desirable, or even feasible, it is to try and be a compassionate person – isn't there a risk of being taken advantage of, or of seeming gullible? Perhaps many of us feel the struggle of trying to balance caring for our own lives and having a sense of responsibility for the lives of others. Public figures such as Desmond Tutu or the Dalai Lama can be accepted as being compassionate because they are religious figures, seemingly not subject to the demands and pressures of ordinary people. It can be hard to know how we can make a difference. Every day the news bombards us with stories of suffering, cruelty and violence that can seem overwhelming. In such a dog-eat-dog world we may wonder if taking care of number one is not the most advisable course of action. In spite of all this, every day we also come across countless acts of kindness and concern for others that happen quietly in an ordinary and natural way as part of how we live together. Clearly, compassion is fundamental if we are to survive on this planet – we may even discover that it is the most sustainable and effective way of taking care both of number one and everyone else too – but we need to be able to understand it clearly and know how to work with it in our lives in spite of the challenges.

The Compassionate Mind Approach to Reducing Stress is part of The Compassionate Mind series, which is headed up by Professor Paul Gilbert's book, *The Compassionate Mind*. The series as a whole is based on the application of Compassion Focused Therapy, a therapeutic method of using compassion to work with psychological problems developed by Professor Gilbert. In his book on the subject for clinicians, *Compassion Focused Therapy*,[2] Professor Gilbert lists an interest in Buddhism as one of the factors that led him to study compassion in the first place. Although not a Buddhist himself, Gilbert has drawn on its presentation of compassion to develop CFT.

The Compassionate Mind Approach to Reducing Stress is slightly different from the other books in the series in that it is based on Buddhist ideas about compassion, rather than being written from a purely therapeutic perspective. Although Buddhism is considered to be one of the major world religions, people who practise it, particularly in the West, will more often refer to it as a science of mind, because it presents a thorough investigation of how the mind works. The term 'Buddha' means the 'one who is awake' in Sanskrit. In waking up to how his mind worked, the Buddha saw all the ways in which we can limit the potential of our mind with concepts, habits and opinions. His subsequent teachings were practical and experiential descriptions of how these tendencies seem to become part of us, along with clear instructions on how we can uproot these patterns. By cultivating actions that enhance our confidence and peace of mind and avoiding those which cause us anxiety and fear, it is possible to live happier, more complete lives. In short, the Buddha showed a way to overcome suffering through a process of recognition that is a result of training the mind.

I have been a practising Buddhist for almost thirty-five years under the guidance of a Tibetan Buddhist teacher, Sogyal Rinpoche, author of the spiritual classic, *The Tibetan Book of Living and Dying*.[3] From 1993 to 2003 I was fortunate to be part of the executive team that managed Rigpa International, the organization that oversees Rinpoche's work world-wide. In this role I was trained to directly apply the Buddhist teachings to my work, to my interactions with other people and to any difficulties I experienced along the way. It is something I am profoundly grateful for as it helped me to see how practical and effective the teachings can be in every aspect of life. It also sparked my interest in the potential for some of the practices of Buddhism to be useful for people who do not wish to follow the Buddhist path, an interest I have pursued in my professional life with the workshops I deliver to people at work.[4]

This is in keeping with what the Dalai Lama refers to as 'secular ethics'.[5] He draws a distinction between religious teachings, rituals and prayer, and the development of qualities of the human spirit that bring happiness to oneself and others – qualities such as peace and contentment, patience and forgiveness, and love and compassion. Buddhism has a rich resource of guidance on developing mindfulness, meditation and compassion that can be of use to everyone. The Dalai Lama often comments that of the seven billion people on this planet, only one billion follow a religious path – so what about the remaining six billion? With this majority in mind, he has developed this simple, practical way of describing Buddhist ideas in a way that anyone can benefit from, whether or not they know anything about Buddhism, or are interested in religion of any kind. This is the spirit in which this book is written.

As you read this book you will find frequent references to scientific research on the benefits of the practices of mindfulness, meditation and compassionate mind training. For more than twenty-five years the Dalai

Lama[6] has held regular meetings with scientists, psychologists, econo-mists and philosophers under the auspices of the Mind & Life Institute,[7] founded by the Chilean-born neuroscientist Francisco Varela and Adam Engle, an American businessman and entrepreneur. During one of these meetings in 2000 the Dalai Lama made a formal request to the scientists in the room to test techniques such as meditation and compassion practices to determine whether they were beneficial for people and, if they were found to be so, to develop methods of teaching them in a secular way.

Richard Davidson, a pioneer in developing techniques for measuring brain activity, was present at this meeting. He accepted the Dalai Lama's challenge and began to invite experienced meditators to his laboratory to undergo testing there. He is now well known for his work in this area at the Waisman Laboratory for Brain Imaging and Behaviour in Madison, Wisconsin. In 2012 he produced his first book for the general public, *The Emotional Life of your Brain*,[8] based on this research. We will be looking into some of his findings as part of our exploration of using mindfulness, meditation and compassion to help us to reduce our stress.

Using this Book

This book sets out to explore how we can work with one of life's major challenges – stress – by recognizing that it is our attitude towards it that plays a crucial role in how we deal with it. We will explore how we can change our attitude to stress: rather than trying to avoid it and hoping it will go away, we will learn to understand it, work with it and use it to develop compassion. We will see that by practising compassion we can actually reduce our experience of stress.

The word 'stress' is employed as an umbrella term to include all the aspects of life that frustrate our wish to be happy. This is not a book about avoiding stress or eradicating it from our lives. On the contrary, it acknowledges that stress is an inevitable part of being alive – and one that can provide insight into how we are in ourselves and how we inter-act with other people.

The formula of the book is as follows:

- Define the problem – in our case, stress – and view it from all angles.

- Identify a helpful way of approaching it – applying compassion – and explore it fully.

- Realize that in order to apply compassion we will need to make some changes in our habits.

- Examine how our mind works in order to understand our habits better.

- Engage with mindfulness and meditation as a means to make a space for change and develop discernment, so we can identify which of our habits are helpful and which are unhelpful.

- Learn compassion techniques and how they can help us with our stress – thereby replacing unhelpful habits with helpful ones.

The book is divided into three parts:

Part 1: Our Starting Point

Part 1 of this book is all about exploring what we know about stress and what we know about compassion, and looking into how we experience both. Some of the ideas about stress will be familiar to most people in broad terms, but probably not in this much detail. The point of these chapters is to identify the problem – to give us an idea of how stress works in our bodies and how potentially damaging it can be. This is a good inspiration to do something about it! You could use these chapters as a way of becoming familiar with the stress response, so you can recognize it working in your own body.

We then move on to compassion, and a broad perspective on its use as a remedy for stress. A tendency to compassion is a natural resource, and these chapters demonstrate our capacity to use it to help us with stress. You can use these chapters to help clarify your own thinking about compassion and the place you would like to give it in your life.

As we have already seen, compassion can be defined as the wish for everyone to be free from suffering, along with having the urge to do something to bring that about. So the chapters on happiness and suffering will provide a context for what we have learnt about stress and compassion..As you read them it helps to try and apply what you are reading to yourself as you go along – to make it as personal as you can – so that you can build up a clear picture of how you look for happiness and how you deal with the suffering of stress.

Two important messages stand out from these chapters:

- In terms of happiness we need to look to developing long-term happiness, based on peace of mind and self-awareness, rather than focusing on short-term pleasure.

- In terms of suffering and stress we need to look at our suffering to see how we can learn from it, rather than trying to avoid it.

Part 2: Seeing Where We Want to Change

Part 2 begins by looking at how our mind reacts to the things that happen to us in life and how this relates to the habits we adopt. It is here that the wish to change is stressed as being important. Having decided we want to change, we need to take a step back so we can look at ourselves clearly. We need to develop self-awareness, and take a fresh look at our habits so that we can identify which ones help us and which ones cause us problems. Then we are ready to choose the ones we wish to begin to work with. Mindfulness and meditation help us to be able to do this by beginning the process of quietening and calming the mind, so that we can use our discernment to explore our habits and see how we can replace our unhelpful habits with helpful ones.

First off we look at our habits that cause us stress – both the personality traits we have that can lead to stress, as well as how we cope with it when it happens. It may be worth going back over this chapter several times in order to get a clear understanding of your own habits related to stress. I have written these chapters in such a way that reading them is almost a form of contemplation, so read them slowly and give yourself time to take them in.

Then we look at developing habits based in compassion. These are likely to be less familiar to you than your reactions to stress, so again it is a good idea to read this chapter through a few times in order to familiarize yourself with them. This is an important part of this book, and spending time reflecting on these four chapters will help give you a structure for how you want to work with compassion and how to apply it in your own life. You may need to revisit it from time to time to check your progress as you start working with the techniques.

Part 3: Making Change Happen

Part 3 contains a range of different methods that you can use to train your mind in compassion. We begin by looking at how to develop compassion for ourselves and then extend this to include compassion for others. We complete our investigation by looking at compassion from the big perspective of universal responsibility.

Practical points

Summaries

The summaries that you'll find at the end of each chapter provide a thread through the book. If you need to refresh your memory about a certain point the summary is a good place to start. You may like to re-read the summary of your favourite chapter in the morning before you start your day, or at the end of the day before you go to bed.

Exercises

The exercises come in three places:

- The main exercises come within the chapters and are explained in detail.

- At the end of each chapter are a series of exercises to help you apply what you have learnt in the chapter to everyday life situations.

- There are some additional exercises in an appendix at the back of the book.

You may wish to keep a notebook and pen handy to record your responses to these exercises. By the end of the book, the complete set of exercises represents a simple way of following the thread of the book as well as a practical working method for applying what you have learnt.

Part 1

Our Starting Point

We begin by looking into stress and examining how and why it can be a problem for us. In this book we will use compassion in order to reduce our stress, so having looked at the historical development of stress and how it operates in our bodies, we will go on to explore our understanding of compassion and how it too has a biological basis. Sometimes when we feel stressed we just want to distract ourselves from it in order to feel better and so we try to find ways to make ourselves happier and to avoid the uncomfortable feelings stress can bring up. This often means we go for a quick-fix, such as shopping, eating foods that are delicious but not so good for us or spending a lot of time on the internet. At the end of this section of the book, we will look at ideas about happiness – both this kind of short-term, fleeting happiness, or pleasure, as well as longer term happiness, or contentment. We will learn how suffering and stress can actually be useful for us if we learn to work with it instead of trying to avoid it.

1 What is Stress?

If you have no stress in your life you are dead.

Hans Selye

A Historical Perspective on Stress

When I think back to living with my parents as a child, I do not have any memory of them ever saying they felt stressed, although my father's job was very demanding and my mother left a large family in Ireland when she moved to England to marry, and never quite got over missing them. No doubt they experienced feelings of being pushed to their limits from time to time, but that generation who lived through the Second World War would never have labelled such feelings as stress. For us, nowadays, the term stress is used to describe a huge variety of experiences and interactions – some critics would say that the term has become so widespread as to be almost meaningless. So, perhaps a helpful place to begin this examination of stress is by examining how our use and understanding of the term has evolved as our lifestyles and priorities have changed over time. Beginning from quite a limited picture of what stress is, due to the insight and vision of particular pioneers in the field we now have a considerable body of research and a wide range of tools to approach it. Exploring how society's understanding has grown over the last 400 years can help us to understand what stress is and how it affects each one of us.

Robert Hooke

Early ideas about stress were based on engineering terms, and saw the body as operating like a machine. For example, in Hooke's Law of Elasticity (formulated by prominent physicist-biologist Robert Hooke in 1678) the term 'load' is used to describe the demand placed on a mechanism, 'stress' is the demand placed upon a structure and 'strain' is the change in form that results from the interaction between load and stress. If we take the example of constructing a bridge, which needs to carry heavy loads without collapsing – the 'load' would be the weight the bridge needs to carry; 'stress' is the area of the bridge's structure over which the load is applied and 'strain' is the deformation of the structure produced by the interplay of load and stress. This was the basis of the idea that, just as a machine is subject to wear and tear, so the body is subject to the wear and tear of life. Although nowadays stress is not seen as something just affecting the body, even this early description has influenced how we describe our experience of stress today. We often speak of feeling 'loaded down' by worry or pressure and it is common to hear people describing themselves as 'strained'.

Neurasthenia

Just as a machine needs energy to run, so does the body, and this was thought to be provided by the nervous system. So, to explain the circumstances under which the body might fail to renew its energy, scientists began to speak of nervous depletion, or disorders of the nerves. By the eighteenth century this idea had taken a firm hold and 'nerves' were frequently cited as the cause of many and various diseases. The character of Mrs Bennet, whom Jane Austen described with such penetrating humour in her novel *Pride and Prejudice* (published in 1813), is an excellent example of someone living at the mercy of her nerves and ensuring that all around her are too!

The second half of the nineteenth century saw what has been called a second Industrial Revolution, with a marked increase in the growth of factories and use of mechanized transport. It was increasingly believed that the very pace of modern life, with its rapidly accelerating pace and complexity was proving too much for the human nervous system to cope with – a theme that may sound very familiar to us today. This led George Beard (1839–83), an American physician specializing in diseases of the nervous system, to identify a condition that he called 'neurasthenia'.

Patients suffering from this condition experienced a weakness of the nervous system, or nervous exhaustion. Symptoms included anxiety, fatigue, generalized aches and pains and a fear of not being able to meet the demands of daily life.

Neurasthenia enjoyed a lot of attention until the end of the nineteenth century when it began to lose validity as a diagnosis. It is no longer used in Western medicine although it is still referred to in traditional Chinese medicine. An interesting footnote is that some modern researchers regard MCS (Multiple Chemical Sensitivity) as a twentieth-century version of neurasthenia. Although neurasthenia fell out of fashion, Beard's work had introduced ideas that have become an integral part of our modern understanding of stress. Having a working definition of neurasthenia meant that a patient's struggles to cope could be seen within a purely scientific context without any sense of judgement or criticism of their behaviour. In addition, Beard saw a direct correlation between the increase in the number of people experiencing mental exhaustion and the speed of change in nineteenth-century society. His attempt to understand this connection foreshadows research being carried out nowadays on the relationship between the individual and their quality of life.

However, in spite of the emerging field of psychology, the close of the century saw the scientific approach to understanding stress remaining dominant. Any approach that was more concerned with the unique characteristics of an individual was considered 'unscientific' because it strayed into areas that could not be scientifically analysed and was therefore suspect. The scientific view remained firmly based in trying to establish general laws of functioning. Part of the unfolding story of research into stress concerns the way that this division broke down and was replaced by a more organic idea of how stress works.

Walter Cannon

There was a hint of this new approach in the early decades of the twentieth century when the 'psychosomatic medicine movement' began to develop. Unlike previous studies, it included the impact of social, psychological and behavioural factors on physical health and quality of life. Furthermore, it was interested in drawing attention to the previously neglected area of the role of the mind in physical diseases and, by challenging the view of a person as a machine, in reintroducing the human element into medicine. The work of Walter Cannon (1871–1945) paved the way for this approach. A respected physiologist and neurologist, and professor and Chairman of the Department of Physiology at Harvard Medical School, his work can be said to be the starting point of understanding how stress occurs. Two of his main contributions to this understanding are the use of the term 'fight-or-flight response',[1] which you may well have come across, and the less common concept of 'homeostasis'.[2] Homeostasis refers to the tendency of the body to try to regulate its internal conditions so as to maintain health and functioning, regardless of outside conditions – for example, the clotting of blood if you're bleeding, or the cooling and warming of the body in order to maintain our optimal body temperature. In this model, a *stressor* is anything that knocks the body out of homeostatic balance and the *stress response* is what the body does to try and restore that balance.

Cannon was interested in how mental and emotional states affect how the body works. He noticed that the animals that he was experimenting on suffered digestive problems when they were anxious or frightened. Further investigation showed that the major emotions stimulate the sympathetic nervous system. This in turn leads to many changes in the body – such as increased secretion of adrenaline, increased heart rate, blood pressure and perspiration, and reduced stomach function. This is why we feel such powerful responses in the body when we are in the grip of strong emotion – for instance feeling nauseous or having an increased desire to go to the toilet when we are feeling 'stressed' or nervous. Cannon saw these natural responses as having been honed over a long period of evolution for the very purpose of increasing our chances of survival.

Furthermore he saw a relationship between specific emotions and reactions. For example, anger and fear have always been used as a preparation for action – anger is used for standing one's ground to attack and fight, and fear for escaping. Hence this reaction came to be known as the 'fight-or-flight response'.

Cannon's work on homeostasis builds on the previous work of Claude Bernard (1813–78) who studied what he called the *'milieu interieur'*. This is a term he used to describe the internal environment in which the cells of the body are nourished and maintained in a state of equilibrium. As we already saw, homeostasis is the body's process of maintaining the required stability in the functioning of bodily systems so that life and health can continue. So, health can be understood as a dynamic process of successfully adapting and maintaining this kind of balance in the midst of ever-changing conditions. When this balance is overwhelmed by change then stress and illness can result. For many researchers who came later, these two concepts – the fight-or-flight response and homeo-stasis – came to describe the starting point for how stress occurs.

Hans Selye

The work of Hungarian-born Hans Selye[3] (1907–82) spanned more than sixty years. He is generally credited with bringing the concept of 'stress' into the mainstream. In the 1930s Selye was a young assistant professor doing research into the functions of hormones, which necessitated his injecting rats on a daily basis. It seems that Selye was not skilled in hand-ling laboratory rats, frequently dropping the poor things and having to chase them around the laboratory. When he examined the rats after a couple of months of this kind of treatment he discovered that they had peptic ulcers, greatly enlarged adrenal glands and shrunken immune tis-sues. Thinking this was a result of the injections he had administered he ran a control group to check his findings. Although only injected with saline, these rats experienced the same daily trauma of being injected, dropped and chased and in time exhibited exactly the same range of conditions as the non-control group. Realizing that the rats' symptoms were not related to the substance with which they were injected, Selye tried to ascertain what else both groups had in common and came to the conclusion that the unpleasantness and discomfort of the life of a rat in his laboratory was in some way contributing to the symptoms they were experiencing. To test this theory, Selye devised more challenges for the long-suffering rats, exposing them to extremes of hot and cold, forcing exercise on them and so on. In all cases the symptoms were the same. In order to describe the range of unpleasant factors that the rats were experiencing, Selye said they were suffering from 'stress'. This was no longer simply a reference to nervous stress but the nonspecific response of the body to any demand made upon it.

It was not until after the Second World War that Selye's ideas were to receive proper attention. Not surprisingly, the experience of the war had led to increased discussion of 'nervous tension', 'war nerves' and the 'stresses of war' and before long talking about stress became part of everyday language. Both during and after the war, because of the role it had to play in understanding these conditions, psychology gained in importance and influence and increasingly psychologists joined in the discussion of stress. According to Selye, the basic point to grasp about stress is that the organism undergoes a range of physiological responses in its efforts to adapt to whatever demands and pressures it experiences. We will see this more clearly in the next chapter when we look at how stress affects the body.

The essence of Selye's view on stress was that there are many ways for the body to respond to it, rather than a specific formula that is the same for everyone. He pointed out that all demands on the body have one thing in common – they make it necessary for the body to adapt in order to be able deal with them and this adaptation is non-specific.

The General Adaptation Syndrome

In 1946 Selye formulated these ideas as the 'General Adaptation Syndrome', in which the body passes through three stages of coping – alarm, resistance and exhaustion. The initial response of the alarm stage is the 'fight-or-flight' response as described by Walter Cannon. Selye's addition was the understanding that no animal, or human, can sustain this level of excitement indefinitely, so if it survives the first stage the second stage of resistance occurs. In the second stage, resistance to persistent stress is built up either as successful adjustment, or, if it goes on too long, as tissue damage and the beginnings of disease. If the stress goes on even longer the animal or human enters the third phase – exhaustion. Selye claimed that by this point the stores of hormones released during the initial fight-or-flight response have been used up. This means there are no defences left to deal with the threat, which can result in illness and even death. We shall see later that current research into the stress response challenges this view. As Robert Sapolsky explains in his book, *Why Zebras Don't Get Ulcers*:

> It is not so much that the stress response runs out, but rather, with sufficient activation, that *the stress-response can become more damaging than the stressor itself.*[4]

This is important for us to take on board as we consider our own stress. We will see throughout this book that in modern times we experience stress more frequently than our forebears – more frequently than our systems were designed to deal with. Because we experience stress from so many and such varied causes we exist in a state of constant arousal, just like a pot simmering on a stove. Therefore, as Sapolsky points out in this quote, rather than the stress response being used up and running out during times of persistent stress, as Selye claimed, in fact, it is possible that our stress response itself, rather than enabling us to cope better, actually becomes a cause of damage in itself as our system registers the strain.

Selye considered stress to be a natural part of life that cannot be avoided and can only end when life itself ends. He divided the stress experience into four different kinds of stress: good stress (sometimes referred to as 'eustress'); bad stress or 'distress'; overstress (sometimes referred to as 'hyperstress') and understress (or 'hypostress'). Drawing on the work of Bernard and Cannon, Selye saw the goal as the maintenance of a healthy balance within the body and an increase in the amount of good stress as opposed to the other three. For him, therefore, the biological purpose of the General Adaptation Syndrome was the body's attempt to maintain a steady state in the face of stress.

Even at the time he was developing his work, Selye experienced difficulties in defining stress that foreshadowed many of the challenges we face today. He chose to define stress as a *response* and conceived the term 'stressor' to describe whatever triggered the stress response – for example, hearing a noise outside when you are all alone in the house at night. However, at various stages of his work he also defined stress as a stimulus, as a response and as the interaction between stimulus and response (in other words, stressor and stress response). He claimed that this merely emphasized that stress was the result of all these interactions, but this lack of precision was considered by many to be confusing.

By 1979 Selye was defining it in his written work as 'the body's non-specific response to any demand'. The language was deliberately more inclusive to include the growing list of stressors, which would eventually include both psychological and physical agents. As we have seen, much of the early research on stress was carried out on animals and did not distinguish between a psychological and physiological manifestation of stress. Critics of Selye's work point out that if a rat is distressed by being injected, its distress could be due to terror of the injection (psychological manifestation) or the pain it causes (physiological manifestation). This may be an academic question in the case of the suffering rat, but in terms of a human seeking to understand how they experience stress it is an important distinction. Although questions of this sort were fertile ground for investigation by psychologists, Selye was mainly interested in the biological stress reaction and remained so throughout his career.

These two strands of interest in stress – the physiological and the psychological – developed independently of each other for some time, but by the 1950s the role of psychology had become firmly established.

Psychosomatic medicine

We saw earlier how the work of Walter Cannon was in sympathy with the development of the study of psychosomatic medicine, which is concerned with the role of the mind as well as the body in the diagnosis of disease. Its popularity ebbed and flowed during the first half of the twentieth century, but by the 1960s psychosomatic medicine had broadened its scope to explore the physical, psychological and social factors that increase our vulnerability to disease, as well as those factors that support how we cope with it. Psychosomatic medicine challenged researchers to look more deeply at the impact of life events, life changes and stressors by focusing on two main issues – the relationship between life events and illness; and the role of individual differences and characteristics of illness based on personality.

During this time, Behavioural Psychology, or Behaviourism, became more popular and quickly came to dominate the psychological scene. Behaviourists claim that all of our behaviours are influenced by our conditioning – our environment, our upbringing and so on – and can be studied systematically. In its most extreme form this led to the belief that there was no need to study the mind at all, as it is a strictly private area and undiscoverable by science – the impenetrable 'black box'. After the Second World War, however, an increasing number of psychologists were finding this approach too narrow and the idea that stress could be understood simply by examining its cause and the body's response, independent of the person who was experiencing it, fell out of favour. Instead there was more openness to exploring the relationship between the cause of stress, the thoughts and conditions of the person experiencing it and their methods of coping. Recognizing that our thoughts about what is happening to us are an important factor in how we experience stress opened the field for study of the mind and how it responds. At the same time there was an increasing interest in a more subjective view of human behaviour that took into account *individual* attitudes, beliefs, expectations, values and motives. In terms of stress, this would mean that both the person and the environment are key players – each needs to be considered in relation to the other, as does the interplay between them.

Richard Lazarus

This shift that took place in the middle of the last century heralded a period of creative study and research, and provided a fitting context for the work of Richard Lazarus[5] (1922–2002) – another giant in stress research whose work spanned half a century. His approach to stress is known as the Transactional Model because it focuses on the interaction, or transaction, between people and their external environment.

In this model stress is defined as:

> A particular relationship between the person and the environment *that is appraised by the person* as taxing or exceeding his or her resources and endangering his or her wellbeing.[6]

With this definition we can see what a leap has been made since the work of Selye. Stress is no longer seen in purely physical terms but now includes the interaction between a person and their environment. Furthermore, how the person experiences that interaction and how they feel about it are also considered important. If someone feels that the demands of a situation they are facing are more than they have the resources to cope with, then they can be said to be experiencing stress. So the manner in which a person perceives a potentially stressful situation is key. For example, one person may view a situation as stressful, whereas another may welcome the same situation as a challenge. If you are a reasonable cook and keep a fairly well-stocked larder you will be pleasantly challenged if you suddenly need to rustle up a meal for some friends who turn up unexpectedly. If you are a poor cook and need to go shopping, such a visit will certainly feel stressful. Lazarus referred to this process as 'appraisal' – the individual's assessment of a situation which determines whether it is experienced as stressful or not. So, even a potentially stressful event cannot be said to cause stress unless it is perceived by the individual to do so. Here we are touching on another major theme of this book – the role that the mind plays in how we view the stress we are faced with. We will pick this up when we look into habits in Part 2.

There are two kinds of appraisal. In the first instance a person judges a potentially stressful situation to be positive or negative and considers how seriously they need to approach it. Next they think about whether or not they have the resources to deal with the stressor, in other words, the situation that is causing them stress. It is at this point that they begin to look at their coping strategies – how they are going to manage the situation. Perhaps you are like me and have a dread of visiting the dentist? Whenever I need to go, my initial appraisal of the situation is very negative, but then I think back to previous visits to the dentist and realize that, in spite of everything, experience shows me that I will survive. Then I bring to mind how I have coped in the past – breathing exercises, requesting that the chair is not made too low and so on. By deciding to put these coping strategies in place again, some of my stress diminishes.

Lazarus considered how we cope as fundamental to our understanding of how the stress process works. He defined coping as:

> Constantly changing cognitive and behavioural efforts to manage specific external and/or internal demands that are appraised as taxing or exceeding the resources of the person.[7]

So, going back to my visit to the dentist: preparing myself to go by remembering what has happened during previous occasions and requesting certain things that will make the experience easier for me (for example, asking the dentist to ensure the chair is not too low) enables me to manage. In this way I can anticipate the visit will be one that taxes my resources rather than exceeds them. It follows then that when we are able to cope effectively, our stress is usually controlled; when we are not able to cope, stress mounts and can get out of control. We will look at how 'out of control' stress can manifest itself in the next chapter.

Lazarus's legacy, the Berkeley Stress and Coping Project, which he established, is still influential today more than twenty years since it ended. It spanned more than thirty years of study, of which the period dating from the late 1970s is thought to be the most important. During this time, Lazarus's theories of the strategies of appraisal and coping came to fruition and shifted the focus for the study of stress from the laboratory to the arena of real life. It is also worth noting that it was at the same period that Lazarus's work began to shift from a focus on psychological stress to working with emotions. He felt that simply asking people to place themselves on a scale with minor stress at one end and considerable stress at the other was limiting and did not take into account the wide variety of emotions that stress actually produces. Instead, he saw individual emotions linked to the ways in which people perceive stress. We will be exploring working with emotions as part of applying compassion to our reactions to stress later on in this book.

The work of Lazarus and his colleagues in the Berkeley Project inspired supporters and critics alike, and remains at the heart of our understanding of stress today.

Challenges in Defining Stress

Hans Selye is often credited with popularizing the term stress, but later on, in 1976, he wrote that he thought he had confused the terms 'stress' and 'strain' because of weaknesses in his use of the English language. If this is the case, it is ironic, because since Selye's use of the term there has been intense debate over the difficulties in defining stress, which in turn has led to problems in measuring it. Of course, even before it was named as 'stress', there was always interest in how we adapt to the struggles of life – sociologists, anthropologists, physiologists, psychologists and social workers had used a range of different terms. Once the term 'stress' was in the public domain, however, concepts such as conflict, frustration, trauma, alienation, anxiety and emotional distress were brought together under the same label, and it became a sort of umbrella term for a wide range of ideas.

As we have seen, the early 'mechanical' approaches to stress focused on how an animal or human responds to pressure from the outside, whereas Selye's approach was concerned with our body's response to stress and the internal pressures that can result. The 'psychological' view that came later favoured the study of the dynamic relationship between the outside causes of stress and the responses we have to it – thus combining all three elements of the body's response to stress, the internal pressures that can result from that stress and the psychological view. The trouble is that in everyday practice the term stress can be used to describe all these different meanings. Someone may describe an unpleasant situation they are exposed to as 'stress' but use the same term to label their reaction to it, such as chest pain, or indeed the end result, which could be an ulcer. We can talk of 'feeling stressed' which indicates our own reaction to an outside pressure, and of 'having a lot of stress', which makes it sound like a simple external factor. In fact, we are talking about the same thing.

As was quoted in the *First Annual Report on Stress* in 1951:

> Stress, in addition to being itself, and the result of itself, is also the cause of itself.

If this sounds confusing, it is because it can be. The confusion over what exactly 'stress' means has led some to suggest that the term has become over-generalized and less useful. Others have even suggested that all of this discussion about 'stress' feeds on itself and has actually increased public awareness of it. The downside of stress becoming less stigmatized might be that people come to view events and emotions as stressful more readily than was common before – in my parents' generation, for example.

However intense the debate about terminology, there is little doubt that the concept of stress has taken a firm hold in our society. There is a wealth of statistics which paint a disturbing picture of how common stress is, particularly in the workplace.

For example, the Sainsbury's Centre for Mental Health states that we lose:

- £8.4 billion a year in sickness absence. The average employee takes seven days off sick each year, of which 40 per cent are for mental health problems. This adds up to 70 million lost working days a year, including one in seven directly caused by a person's work or working conditions.

- £15.1 billion a year in reduced productivity at work. 'Presenteeism' accounts for 1.5 times as much working time lost as absenteeism and costs more to employers because it is more common among higher-paid staff.
- £2.4 billion a year in replacing staff who leave their jobs because of mental ill health.[8]

And the Health and Safety Executive say:

Work-related stress caused workers in Great Britain to lose 10.4 million working days in 2011/12 based on the LFS [Labour Force Survey] data . . . On average, each person suffering from this condition took 24 days off work. This is one of the highest average days lost per case figure amongst the recognised health complaints covered in the LFS.

Both statistics apply to the UK, but there are similar stories to tell about the USA[9] and Australia. Whatever term we use to describe this malaise there is no doubt that it constitutes real suffering for individuals and increasing disruption to society.

As we said at the beginning of the chapter, the starting point of this book is to understand our stress and to recognize its impact on us. Seeing how many ways the term itself can be used can help us to put to one side the aspects that do not apply to us and to hone in on what is important for us and what we can do about it. For the purposes of this book, we will be interpreting stress in the broadest sense, seeing it very much as an umbrella term covering many different levels and facets of human experience. In the next chapter we will begin by taking a look at how the body responds to stress.

KEY POINTS

- Looking at how ideas about stress have changed over time can help us to understand more about what stress is and how it can affect us.

- Understanding how stress affects us, how we perceive it and what we do about it are all important elements in learning how to work with stress, and, specifically, to apply compassion to our experience.

- Early ideas about stress looked on the body as a machine and were concerned with 'wear and tear'.

- Later ideas came to include the understanding of how emotional states affect how the body works.

- Walter Cannon contributed two important ideas to our understanding of stress: the 'fight-or-flight' response and homeostasis: the ability of the body to regulate itself.

- Hans Selye is considered to be the father of stress research. One of his main contributions was the General Adaptation Syndrome.

- Over the years, researchers developed a growing interest in how stress and the mind are connected, and eventually came to explore the relationship between people, their environment and the feelings that they experience as a result of outside forces.

- There is considerable variety in the ways that stress is defined nowadays. Though this may seem confusing, it is helpful to know something about it because it helps us to see what is relevant for us as individuals and what is not.

EXERCISES

Often when we feel stressed we try to distract ourselves by doing something else but, as we will see, it is important to notice our stress so we can do something about it before it becomes a problem.

Try these simple exercises that are designed to help you become aware of your stress in a healthy way.

Exercise 1

Try to pay attention to the times you refer to 'feeling stressed'.

Ask yourself what exactly you mean by 'feeling stressed'.

Is it because of something happening to you?

Is it caused by how you feel?

Is it something to do with your reactions to what is going on around you?

Make a note of what you discover.

Exercise 2

Notice when other people use the term 'stress'.

Ask yourself what you think they mean by it for themselves.

Make a note of what you discover.

Exercise 3

Bring to mind a recent situation where you were with a friend or family member which you experienced as stressful and they did not, for example a traffic jam, waiting in line at the cinema, waiting to be served in a restaurant.

Take some time to explore the difference in perception between yourself and the person you were with.

Why do you think that you were stressed and they were not?

Make a note of what you discover.

Exercise 4

Bring to mind a time recently when you were anticipating a stressful event, for example a job interview, a difficult work meeting, a confrontation with your teenage daughter.

How did you prepare for the stressful event in order to minimize its emotional impact?

Did your coping strategies work?

Is there anything else you could have done?

Make a note of what you discover.

2 The Biology of Stress

> A large body of evidence suggests that stress-related disease emerges, predominantly, out of the fact that we so often activate a physiological system that has evolved for responding to acute physical emergencies, but we turn it on for months on end, worrying about mortgages, relationships, and promotions.
>
> *Robert Sapolsky*[1]

Having spent some time looking back over how our modern ideas of stress have developed, let's now turn our attention to what happens in our bodies as a response to stressful situations. For many of us this will take us into areas we have not thought about much since we were struggling with biology at school! It is worth persevering, however, as it can be surprisingly rewarding to become familiar with how we react to stress and the effects it has on us physically. We don't tend to think about this very much – we just struggle to cope.

As you read this chapter, try to imagine the physical effects I describe happening in your own mind and body over and over again. It could help you to decide that you really do want to deal with stressful events in a different way. However much we may want to change, it is not always easy to do so. The chances are that if you are reading this book you are already thinking about how to reduce the stress you have. Any information we can gather that strengthens our resolve will be a help to us. Becoming familiar with the biology of stress can be another building block in our effort to understand stress more thoroughly.

Humans respond to stress just like other mammals do. Nowadays most people tend to view stress as bad for us and to be avoided when, in fact, the way the body responds to whatever is causing it stress – whether it is an injury, a difficult boss or feeling short of money – has evolved with the sole purpose of protecting us in times of danger and ensuring the survival of our species. Remember in the last chapter when we discussed homeostatis – the capacity of the body to hold itself in balance? The stress response has evolved as a way of returning the body to a state of balance after it has suffered an attack. When we lived as members of tribes of hunter-gatherers on vast savannahs our lives were infinitely less complicated than they are today, and at the same time dramatically more dangerous. Animal predators, unfriendly tribes, the perils of hunting and the demands of a life lived at the mercy of the elements all presented immediate life-or-death situations needing instant action. A gazelle attacked by a cheetah will experience the same set of physiological responses that humans do when feeling threatened, but in the case of the gazelle, the stress response is short-term – lasting either till she outruns the cheetah or the cheetah gets its meal.

The trouble is that in humans this response has not been updated to suit our current lifestyles. In today's complex world, few of us find ourselves chased by a sabre-toothed tiger as our ancestors were, and yet our body's stress response is still geared to deal with exactly this kind of emergency. Our body goes into the same response mode when we are faced with bad traffic, late-running trains and slow service in restaurants but instead of the experience being short-term and relatively infrequent we go through these and similar episodes several times each day. It is this repeated low-grade arousal of the stress response, the sense of a continual simmering of activity, that is the greatest threat to our wellbeing. What makes the picture even more complex is that humans have the capacity to think and stimulate ideas, fantasies and images in the mind, which they then can ruminate on, going over and over them in their mind. This is a very common source of stress so we need to look at it in more detail.

Problems of our Thinking Brain

As Professor Paul Gilbert points out in his book *The Compassionate Mind*, humans have a 'new brain', which is different from that of other animals. This 'new brain' is capable of some amazing achievements – such as advances in medicine and landing people on the moon – but it can also get us into some serious problems with stress. Why is this? About two million years ago pre-humans started to get smart. We evolved the ability to think, ruminate, anticipate, imagine and predict. So whereas the gazelle will calm down quite quickly after it has escaped from the cheetah, we humans are likely to think, 'What would've happened if I'd got caught?' Frightening fantasies and images may come up in our mind as a result. Perhaps we wake up in the night and think, 'What would have happened if I hadn't seen the cheetah? What if I get caught tomorrow? What about letting the children go out – maybe it's too dangerous?' So for us the threat has *not passed away.* We play it over and over in our minds and in this way constantly maintain and stimulate our stress response.

In addition, humans have evolved the ability to understand and think about themselves as individual selves. We can worry about so many things to do with our individual self – such as whether or not people like us, whether our job is secure, whether we will be able to pass our exams and so on. The sense of self gives rise to a constant monitoring of potential threats to our 'self' both now and in the future. We have a capacity to worry about all kinds of things linked to our 'self' identity. So, this thinking brain constantly pulls us away from the present moment into the past and the future.

To put it simply, humans create *loops* in the mind where an emotion or a frightening event can trigger a series of thoughts and attention-focusing, and these in turn maintain and strengthen the emotion. These loops are the basis of many forms of stress and also of mental health difficulties. The reason for this is that people find it very difficult to get out of them – and the greater the threat, the tighter the loop. So people find the mind going back and back and back to the thing that is stressing them, over and over again.

One of the key things that Paul Gilbert points out time and again is that this type of difficulty *is absolutely not our fault*. It is not helpful for us to berate ourselves for falling into the trap of dwelling on things because that will only make us feel worse. Moreover, trying to tell ourselves to stop it doesn't usually work. This is why in this book we are going to set out some exercises that will help you to break up these loops. Although it may not be our fault that these loops work in this way, we do have more choice in how we respond to them than we think. We will see that by using mindfulness, meditation and compassion exercises we can begin to change the way our mind responds to threat and difficulty.

For now, it's important to recognize that our brain has evolved in such a way that loops are very easy to create. It helps to realize that this is actually part of common humanity – all of us struggle with these loops. Our thinking brain, with its sense of an individual self, can be a real advantage when it comes to solving problems and gives rise to culture, art and science but it is also a serious disadvantage when it comes to creating unhelpful patterns of thought.

In fact, we will see later in the book that learning to look more closely into our sense of self can be a valuable way of gaining insight into our responses to stress.

Our Emotional Systems

If our thoughts, imaginations and ruminations playing on our emotions can create loops, then it's quite important to think about what *kinds of emotions* they can play on. Recent studies suggest that we have different types of emotion because they evolved to do different things. There are various ways we can parcel up and think about our different emotions. One way is called *functional analysis* – this means that we think of emotions in terms of their functions. So for example the function of *anxiety* is to alert us to danger and then trigger our 'run away' behaviours; *anger* alerts us to a transgression against us which we might want to do something about; *disgust* alerts us to something toxic that we might want to expel or avoid; *pleasure* invites us to approach something or do something again that's good for us; *love* orientates us to care for and be close to others. Later in this book we will look into how we can work directly with our emotions in order to reduce our stress. In the Compassionate

Mind Approach, it is quite helpful to think of at least three basic types of emotion linked to different functions.

These are:

- The threat and self-protection system (sometimes called the threat-focused regulation system).

- The incentive and resource-seeking system (sometimes called the incentive/resource-focused regulation system).

- The soothing and contentment system (sometimes called the non-wanting/affiliative-focused regulation system).

We will look briefly at each one in turn.

The threat and self-protection system

The first types of emotion are linked to threat, and evolved to help us detect threats quickly, pay attention to them and take defensive action. Typical 'threat' emotions are fear, anxiety, anger and disgust. We will go into more detail about the mechanisms of this system a little later in this chapter. It is useful to think about how the threat system interacts with our other emotions – especially positive emotions. In fact, the threat system is designed to knock out our positive emotions when it is triggered. For example, if you're walking in the forest looking for a nice spot to have lunch and you think you see a tiger, you are going to have to forget lunch, pay very close attention to the tiger and prepare yourself to run quickly. Keeping your attention on how wonderful your lunch is going to be, or where you're going to sit to enjoy the sunshine is absolutely not the thing to do! The moment the potential threat of the tiger appears, all that goes out the window. So threat naturally turns off positive emotions.

However, it does more than this. There are two very important processes that happen in the threat system. The first is that the system itself tends to make mistakes because it uses what is called 'a better safe than sorry' process. How does this work? Imagine you are a rabbit in a field nibbling at a nice lettuce when you hear a sound or see a movement in the bushes. What's the best thing to do? The answer is to run, because although nine times out of ten the sound will be perfectly innocent, occasionally it will be a predator. If you watch birds on the lawn eating your breadcrumbs you will see just how sensitive to threat they are. They will often leave a very good meal of breadcrumbs because they fly away at any hint of danger. The interesting thing is that as we get stressed, this tendency increases, so when under pressure we are even more likely to focus on threats. So here we can see that the threat system can jump to the wrong conclusions, causing us all kinds of trouble.

The second thing the threat system can do is even worse, because it can lead us to think of things that upset and stressed us in the past. Here is an example that Professor Gilbert uses quite often. Imagine you go Christmas shopping. In nine out of ten shops the assistants are very kind, smile at you and show real interest in helping you buy a good present, so you leave the shop really happy. However, in one shop the assistant is talking to her friend and seems very uninterested in serving you, behaving quite rudely, as if you're a bit of a nuisance. Then she tries to sell you a present you don't really want and ends up short changing you. On your way home who is it that sticks in the mind – whom do you tell your partner about when you reach home? It's the rude shop assistant, of course. We've all done it at one time or other – the threat system will make you dwell on the one rude person rather than the other 90 per cent of people who were kind and helpful. Just think about what's going on in your brain and the loop you are getting into. It does not even need to be a recent event because we can ruminate about things that happened months or even years ago and in this way constantly stimulate our brains into stress. In contrast, think about what would happen if you noticed this occurring and made the decision that you didn't want to keep replaying this stressful situation? What do you think would happen in your brain if you deliberately noticed your unhelpful thinking and chose to refocus on the smiling and helpful people? Supposing you replayed again in your mind the real sense of interest the majority of shop assistants had and your own pleasure in the whole experience?

The threat system is like a magnet and it can so easily pull our attention away from a more positive focus if we're not careful. When it does that our mind and our body become more stressed. This is because focusing our attention on threat stimulates the stress system, which plays out in our body. Learning to become aware of when we are doing this is a first step in choosing to react in a different, more positive way.

The incentive and resource-seeking system

Incentive or 'drive' emotions such as enthusiasm, determination and the wish to succeed help us to go out and do things. They create feelings of pleasure and enjoyment from achieving and having; they give a sense of excitement and anticipation. When something really major happens to us we can become very excited, mentally and physically. Imagine for a moment winning the European lottery and being worth €100 million! How would you feel? The chances are you would get a rush of chemicals such as adrenaline and dopamine in your brain and body. These have the effect of making you very stimulated. You would find it hard not to be constantly thinking about your money and what you were going to do with it. In fact, you would probably have a few sleepless nights. This reaction would be perfectly natural, but can be difficult for us to manage.

Interestingly, many scientists now recognize that in our society, 'drive' emotions are often seen as the source of happiness, pushing us to go after what we want. Society encourages us to buy things because that's how our economic system works, and so we are being constantly enticed to do more, have more, try harder. However, as we will see later when we look more deeply into happiness, even the pleasure of winning the lottery doesn't last forever. Within a few months people are often back to where they were in terms of their levels of happiness.

We also know that sometimes people become very driven and high-achieving because underneath the surface they are quite insecure. They are frightened that if they don't achieve things other people won't accept or want them. So for some people the fear of rejection is a reason for constantly trying to prove themselves. People who rely too much on the drive system also run the risk of getting exhausted, burnt out and collapsing. They can even get depressed when they feel they can't achieve enough. Indeed it's not uncommon to find that depressed people have an underlying sense of inferiority which they try to make up for by endlessly trying to prove themselves. As long as they are achieving they feel okay but the moment they can't do so or are forced to slow down, for instance because of illness or incapacity, depression can come.

It can also happen that when people get stuck solely in 'drive' system functioning they run the risk of behaving in quite immoral and unhelpful ways. Recent revelations about the behaviour typified in the banking culture illustrate this.

So 'threat' and 'drive' systems need balancing and it turns out that there is indeed a third emotional system that can do this.

The soothing and contentment system

It's clear that animals – including ourselves – cannot always be running away from threats, or rushing around achieving things. Sometimes animals need to rest and to be in a state of quiescence where they are neither under threat, nor in a state of seeking or achieving – we could say they are in a state of satisfaction or contentment. It used to be thought that these states simply related to the 'threat' and 'drive' systems being turned down for a while, but more recent research is showing that contentment can accompany very profound, positive feelings. It is linked to calmness, peacefulness and wellbeing – very different types of positive emotion from typical 'drive' emotions such as achievement and excitement. These 'soothing' types of emotion are especially linked to the production of endorphins and oxytocin. We will look at this in more detail later on in the book. For now, it is enough to know that the soothing and contentment system is linked to the parasympathetic nervous system, whereas the drive and threat systems tend to be linked to the sympathetic nervous system.

From contentment to attachment and compassion

We will begin to look into compassion in detail in the next chapter but let's take a moment to see how it fits with what we have been talking about here. Compassion is sensitivity to distress – turning towards it and trying to alleviate it, rather than trying to avoid it – but it is also linked to affiliation, or a sense of connection, and friendliness.

There is a fundamental story here that helps us to understand how these 'soothing and contentment' emotions are linked to compassion, and why they have a very powerful influence on our 'threat' system. The moment when mammals evolved to engage in live birth – where the parent, usually the mother, provided care to their offspring – was a very important one in evolutionary terms. It became very helpful for the offspring to spend periods of time in a state of quiet and sleep, out of harm's way. Significantly, the presence of the mother, along with elements such as bodily contact, has the automatic effect on the infant of calming them and stimulating their 'soothing' emotions. As children grow older, the presence of their mother is enough to provide a sense of safeness and calm, which allows for play and explorative behaviour. Commonly, if their mother leaves or moves out of sight of the child its 'threat' system is activated. The return of the mother stimulates the soothing system and deactivates the threat system again. The basic story is that in childhood, access to a loving 'other', such as a parent or carer, plays a very important role in how stressed we feel and how easily we calm down.

Although the full story is complex, we now know that kindness and love operate through specific systems in our brain and have very specific effects on the threat-stress system. So when a baby is distressed, the mother will respond to the distress call and the baby will in turn calm down in response to a cuddle from its mother. Think about this in your own life. If you are distressed, how often do you turn to somebody who you think cares about you and loves you? How much does their ability to listen to you and understand you give you the feeling that they value and care for you? How much does this help you to calm down? We now know that low affection from the parent figure can even affect our genetic make-up as well as how our brain matures – it's that powerful! From the day we are born to the day that we die, the loving kindness of others will have a huge impact on the quality of our lives.

It is not just the kindness of other people but also our own kindness to ourselves that can calm us down. This is because kindness stimulates a very important emotion regulation system in our brain – one that evolved to respond to loving and kindness. This is why people who find it difficult to be kind or compassionate to themselves, but instead are self-critical or even self-disliking, can get into real problems with stress. They find this way of internally calming themselves difficult, or simply don't really know how to be kind to themselves. Indeed, when things go wrong, rather than learning to be gentle with themselves in response to the stress they are experiencing, they increase their own stress with self-criticism and self-blaming. This is another example of our smart brains getting us into serious trouble.

We can depict these three basic emotion systems as three circles that are constantly interacting.[2]

Three Types of Affect Regulation System

Driven, excited, vitality

Content, safe, connected

Incentive/resource-focused

Wanting, pursuing, achieving, consuming

Activating

Non-wanting/affiliative-focused

Safeness-kindness

Soothing

Threat-focused

Protection and safety-seeking

Activating/inhibiting

Anger, anxiety, disgust

From Gilbert, *The Compassionate Mind* (2009), reprinted with permission from Constable & Robinson Ltd

It is not that one system should always dominate, but rather that they should be able to operate in such a way that they feed into each other and balance each other out. The ability to feel anxiety and anger at appropriate times is important, as is the ability to have drive, excitement and ambition, but so too is the ability to be able to calm down and to regulate our behaviour. To rest and to find peace and stability in our own mind is essential; to know how to feel safe in, and calmed by, our relationships with others and ourselves. Many of the exercises in this book will help you to bring these three different emotional regulation systems into balance. To do this will provide you with a greater sense of inner peace and stability.

The Threat–Stress Response

In what follows we're going to explore in more detail the 'threat' system and how stress emerges out of it. Knowing how the effects it can have on us underpins stress, will help us understand how all the exercises in this book can help us calm down, and develop ways and inner resources to help us learn to work with these effects and so care for ourselves in a constructive way.

Imagine that you have enjoyed a pleasant evening out with friends – so good in fact that you lost track of time and missed the last bus home. There are no taxis about and so you find yourself making the journey on foot – it's dark, there are not many people about and you need to pass through some unfriendly looking streets. Suddenly you hear a noise behind you. Your threat and self-protection system is activated – your heart begins to beat a little faster, you become aware that your breathing is more rapid and the meal you so enjoyed a few hours ago now feels heavy in your stomach, but at the same time you feel a surge of energy and a sharpening of your senses.

The first thing you want to know is whether or not the noise represents danger, and the process of working this out requires activities of the brain such as sensation and memory, located in the cerebral cortex, part of the 'new' brain we mentioned earlier. If the noise is indeed considered to be a threat, emotional responses such as fear and anxiety are generated in the limbic system in the brain in order to process the information. The limbic system is part of the evolutionary 'old' brain and is responsible for directing behaviours required for survival such as fear, aggression and sexual reproduction. It includes such areas as the hippocampus, which is located within the temporal lobes and is concerned with memory and detecting threats; and the amygdala (1), which is located near to the hippocampus (2) and is concerned with emotionally charged, or negative stimuli. The amygdala functions like an alarm bell: if the noise behind you sounds a lot like the noise you heard in that scary movie you watched recently, it will pulse a general warning throughout the brain and fast-track signals to your fight-or-flight neural and hormonal systems. In this way the limbic system can activate the hypothalamus (3), which is located just above the brain stem in the middle of the brain and controls the stress response.

The structure of the brain

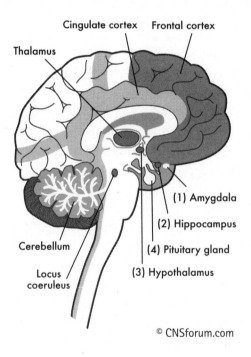

© CNSforum.com

We are accustomed to the beating of our heart, the digestion of lunch, our breathing and blood circulation, the regulation of our temperature all going on without our conscious control. This is the work of the automatic nervous system, which can be thought of as our survival nervous system because without it we would be at best very ill and at worst, dead. It is this system that is activated by the hypothalamus once a threat is identified.

The automatic nervous system consists of two systems: the sympathetic nervous system (SNS) and the parasympathetic nervous system (PNS). As we saw earlier, different emotional states cause different activation of each – feelings of anxiety and stress are associated with the SNS, whereas relaxation is associated with the PNS. So, when that noise behind you gives you a fright on your late night walk home it is the SNS that kicks into action, releasing the neurotransmitter noradrenaline[3] to activate the internal organs. It is responsible for increasing your heart rate, releasing glucose into the blood and slowing digestion in order to prepare your body for action. The PNS will do the opposite – it slows the heart rate, stores the glucose in the liver, and returns the digestion to normal once you feel that the danger has passed.

If the situation seems acute, the hypothalamus activates the adrenal glands to release adrenaline into the bloodstream in order to prepare for fight or flight. This is part of what is known as the 'sympathetic adrenal medullary response system' (SAM). This response system has been likened to striking a match – it takes little effort but its effect does not last long. However we decide to respond to this frightening noise – whether we fight or run – we will need a plentiful supply of energy and oxygen to our brain and muscles in order to meet the challenge and this is exactly what the SAM system is designed to accomplish.

However, if the hypothalamus judges the stress to be chronic and needing sustained attention over time, it stimulates the pituitary gland (4), which puts into process a series of reactions culminating in the production of another hormone, corticosteroid. This enables the body to maintain steady supplies of blood sugar to help cope with prolonged stress. This is known as the 'hypothalamic-pituitary-adrenal axis' (HPA). The image used to describe this stress response system is of lighting a fire – it takes effort to get it going but once it's alight it can remain effective for a long time. The HPA axis is only activated in extreme circumstances. So if we start to quicken our pace in order to get away from the noise behind us but it seems to draw closer however fast we go, our HPA system might kick in. However, this reaction will depend on our own personal threshold for stress – how we react to challenging events. If we are habitually nervous, the noise we are trying to escape will conjure up all kinds of frightening images that could lead to the activation of the HPA axis, but if we are used to long solitary walks in nature we may be more accustomed to unexplained noises and the HPA axis would not kick in. The bottom line is that the more readily the HPA axis is activated the more impact the stress will have on our mental and physical wellbeing.

The downside of the stress response

So our whole stress response system has evolved to help us escape short-term physical emergencies, such as being chased by a sabre-toothed tiger, or attacked by a hostile tribe. In order to survive an event like that our bodies would have needed to respond very fast and work very hard. The main purpose of the stress response is to get energy to our muscles in the quickest and most effective way possible. Our heart rate, blood pressure and breathing rate all increase in order to transport glucose and oxygen to the critical muscles.

The flip side of this is that when the body is mobilizing to face immediate danger it puts a halt on long-term projects which would divert energy from the priority of the moment – to survive. Digestion is a slow process and there is no time to benefit from it, so during times of stress it is shut down. Growth, reproduction, tissue repair and the immune function are also put on hold. All these activities are extremely important for your long-term survival but will not help you if you want to run away from that noise. In addition, our experience of pain is blunted under stress, enabling us to continue to run, or fight, even if we are injured. Various shifts occur in our cognitive and sensory skills, improving our memory and sharpening our senses so that we can draw on memories of similar emergencies and be totally alert to what is going on around us. All our energy is focused on the moment and on staying alive.

Now, in our lives as hunter-gatherers we would not have expected to live for more than thirty-five or forty years, and our encounters with hostile tribes and sabre-toothed tigers, although traumatic, would have been fairly infrequent and short-lived. How different from our lives now when our life expectancy is more than doubled and the causes of stress that we encounter can come in a myriad of forms over and over again. Nowadays, this response is being activated repeatedly and over longer periods of time, so as we have seen, it can be the stress response itself that begins to cause us problems. If we keep mobilizing energy and never store it we will tire easily and put ourselves at risk of some form of diabetes. A cardiovascular system that is frequently overstimulated will result in hardening of the arteries and increase the risk of heart disease. Repeatedly shutting down digestion leads to ulcers, colitis and irritable bowel syndrome. An interrupted reproductive cycle will take longer and longer to regulate itself and can result in amenorrhea (menstruation stopping) and infertility. A suppressed immune system means we are more likely to contract infectious diseases and be less able to fight them.

Repeatedly activating the stress response can therefore have a detrimental effect over time. It is a kind of vicious circle – the more frequently the body responds to stress, the more reactive the amygdala becomes to apparent threats, which in turn increases our tendency to stress, which sensitizes the amygdala still further. This is likely to result in a heightened sense of fear and anxiety. Next time we are out late and hear a noise behind us, we are more likely to treat it as a threat because we have been so recently frightened – the threat system is responding with its 'better safe than sorry' approach. In addition, the same repeated stress activity wears down the hippocampus, which is concerned with keeping clear records of our experience. It is also one of the few regions of the brain that can grow new neurons (nerve cells that receive and send electrical signals over long distances within the body), but steroid hormones, released as part of the long-term stress response, prevent this, impairing the ability of the hippocampus to produce new memories. This means that our memory does not work as well as it used to. Incidentally, the production of dopamine, which has a lot to do with our sense of attention, and feelings of enjoyment and pleasure, is also lowered over time by these hormones. We can see therefore that in a biological sense stress undermines our happiness and threatens our wellbeing.

This has obviously been a simplified account of how the body experiences stress. Those readers who would like to know more could check the bibliography at the back of the book for further reading.

Stress and Illness

The idea that stress can make us ill has taken quite a hold on public opinion, but research is showing that the truth of the matter is more complex and less easily categorized than that. Professor Sapolsky claims that it is not stress itself that makes us sick but rather that it increases our risk of getting diseases that make us sick.[4]

It is clear that different people experience stress in different ways and what leads to illness in one person will not necessarily do so in another. In the same way, one person may recover from illness or disease more quickly than another person. Whether someone is affected by stress, and how long and how severely they are affected, depends on their individual physiological predisposition. However, psychological and social factors can also be important in determining how someone is affected by stress. This may be down to individual personality differences or to environmental factors, such as good medical and advisory care, a person's family and friendship network, or their work situation. Certain characteristics associated with negative emotions, such as anger, have been particularly related to disease. One illustration of this is what has been termed the Type A Personality and its relationship to heart disease.

Type A Personality

In the 1950s two cardiologists in San Francisco, Meyer Friedman and Ray Rosenman, observed that the chairs in their waiting room were wearing out at an alarming rate. Growing tired of frequently replacing them, they sought the advice of a new upholsterer who drew attention to the kind of damage the chairs had suffered. The front area of the seat cushions and the armrests were torn to shreds because the patients in the waiting rooms were literally on the edges of their seats, fidgeting, impatient to be seen, clawing at the armrests. It was not until several years later that the penny dropped and Friedman and Rosenman saw the connection between their waiting room chairs and the term 'Type A Personality' which they had invented to describe people who are competitive, high-powered super achievers, time-pressured, impatient, critical and hostile. 'Type B', on the other hand, is the term they came up with to describe people who do not have these characteristics and who are laid-back, seek harmony, have inner motivation and a creative attitude towards mistakes. In one study that they carried out in the 1970s, a group of 3,000 healthy men were observed over an eight and a half year period. According to the findings twice as many Type A subjects developed heart disease as Type B.

However, Friedman and Rosenman's findings were not confirmed by subsequent studies. For example, a study of 6,000 men starting in 1987 and lasting for six years found no relationship between Type A Personality and heart disease. Critics of the original study questioned how precise it was possible to be in determining personality type, and pointed out that it was not clear which aspects of Type A behaviour were damaging. In addition, the study concerned itself with middle-aged men only and there were no comparable data on women. The impact of social and environmental factors were not fully looked at – for example, it is possible that this kind of person is more likely to drink too much and smoke, and perhaps they have difficulty in benefiting from social support because they are often impatient and have a critical attitude towards others.

By the end of the 1980s it was agreed that although personality traits are more useful in determining whether or not someone is at risk of heart disease among those who have their first heart attack relatively early in life, as we get older a first heart attack is more to do with levels of fat in our bodies and smoking. Later studies identified a high degree of hostility as a more reliable predictor of coronary heart disease and atherosclerosis along with higher rates of mortality with these diseases.[5] More recent studies have shown that hostility is associated with a significant overall increase in mortality across all diseases, not just heart disease.

In this chapter we have traced the stress response as it cascades through the body. We have seen that if it is activated too often, or too readily, the stress we are experiencing is going to have a deeper and more lasting impact. This is what tends to happen with people who have high levels of hostility. A Type A person is going to look on life as a series of provocations and frustrations that they will interpret as requiring immediate and often hostile responses, whereas for other people the same events may well appear as minor irritations. So a Type A Personality's emotion regulation systems will be repeatedly firing on full alert even in such trivial situations as finding oneself in the slowest queue in the supermarket checkout. If we are a Type A person, on our late night walk home, we are more likely to remain irritated, even when we find out that the noise behind us is only a stray cat rummaging among the garbage bins. Even though there is no danger, we keep the stress response going by cursing the cat and our own fearful imaginings. A Type B person is more likely to allow themselves to experience relief and then find some humour in the situation.

The good news is that no one needs to stay as a Type A. If you are a Type A Personality, as soon as you take the vital step of beginning to notice your behaviour and are willing to take steps to change it, you can begin to learn how to reduce your stress levels. We will explore this further when we look into stress habits and look at how developing self-awareness is a good place to start to work with stress.

KEY POINTS

- Understanding how stress affects our body can help us decide to do something about our stress levels.

- Our stress response is the same as that of any other mammal and evolved to help us survive in the demanding conditions of life as a hunter-gatherer several thousand years ago.

- Humans have the capacity to produce ideas, fantasies and images in the mind, which they then can ruminate on. This is a very common source of stress.

- Humans create loops in the mind where a negative emotion or a frightening event can trigger a series of thoughts which in turn maintain and strengthen the emotion.

- In the Compassionate Mind Approach it's helpful to think of at least three basic types of emotion linked to different functions. These are:
  - The threat and self-protection emotion system.
  - The incentive and resource-seeking emotion system.
  - The soothing and contentment emotion system.

- The stress response activates all the emotion systems in our body that are needed to stand and fight, or run away – for example, our heart beats faster, our blood courses through the body more quickly, energy is released into our bloodstream and muscles.

- At the same time, many of our other systems shut down under stress because they are not needed for short-term survival – for example, this can affect digestion, fertility, the immune system and growth and repair of the body.

- However, in modern times we may experience stressful situations several times every day and so the stress response is activated over and over again. Added to this we live much longer than we did as a hunter-gatherer and our bodies can get worn out by the repeated response to stress.

- There is a lot of research into the relationship between stress and illness. It appears that the stress response itself could become a factor in our susceptibility to disease.

- A connection between hostility and heart disease has been firmly established.

- The more we can notice our own behaviour and how we respond to stressful situations, the better we can get a handle on how to work with it.

EXERCISES

As we have seen, the body works hard whenever we experience any kind of stress. Because of this it can provide us with vital clues as to when and how we are stressed – clues that can help us become more self-aware and therefore equipped to tackle the habits that we fall into when we are stressed. We can think of our body as a kind of *stress barometer* that provides evidence to show how we are being affected by stress.

Exercise 1

When you are feeling stressed, pay attention to your body and notice where the stress is making itself felt.

Perhaps it is a tightness in the chest, or a sinking feeling in the stomach?

Has it lodged in your neck, or in frequent headaches?

When you have located the physical feeling associated with stress, firstly just notice it and then try and consciously relax that area.

At the same time, ask yourself if there is another way to respond to the stressful situation and lessen the impact on your body.

Exercise 2

Think about which personality type you identify with most – is it type A, or type B?

3 What is Compassion?

I believe that at the most fundamental level our
nature is compassionate, and that cooperation, not
conflict, lies at the heart of the basic principles that
govern our human existence.

The Dalai Lama[1]

So far we have looked at how our understanding of stress has developed
over time and what our bodies do when they encounter stressful situations. Now it is time to turn our attention to compassion.

Compassion and our World

There is a traditional story that is told in different versions in several
different world religions, including Judaism, Hinduism, Christianity
and Buddhism. A seeker of the truth is curious to know the nature of
heaven and hell, so he requests his guide to show him. The guide leads
him to a large room filled with a table piled high with delicious food
and surrounded by people. Each person is holding a spoon with a long
handle, so long that it is impossible for him or her to put food in his
or her mouth. Everyone is quarrelling and miserable, hungry and desperate. The seeker sighs as he is led away and declares that now he has
seen hell. Next the guide says he will show him heaven and leads him
into another room just like the first one, with people sitting around a
sumptuous banquet holding their long spoons. The astonished and
disappointed seeker declares that this is what he has just seen in hell.
His guide advises him to look more closely, and as he does so he notices
that instead of each person struggling to feed themselves, they are
using the long spoons to reach across and feed each other. Everyone is
getting plenty to eat and is relaxed and happy. 'This is how heaven is,'
the guide explains.

It is easy to see our world as being dominated by people struggling to use their long spoon solely for their own benefit and to miss the numerous instances of people helping each other. Certainly the potential for selfishness, greed and violence exists in all of us, but it sits alongside a core of altruism and kindness that can lead us to perform compassionate acts even for strangers. We can feel overwhelmed by the speed and volume of sad and tragic news pouring into our homes through television and the internet, but amongst this avalanche of suffering come frequent accounts of kindness and bravery on behalf of other people – think of aid workers supporting people afflicted by war and famine, or the older Japanese engineers who volunteered to work on the damaged Fukishima nuclear plant in Japan in order to spare younger men. Human nature is founded in compassion and, although it can be challenging for us, we need to work out some practical understanding of it so that we can apply it in our ordinary lives.

Things were simpler when we lived as members of small tribal communities. Then it was clear to everyone that if a tribe was to survive and flourish it needed to care for its own – the care might have been rough and ready, but the practical necessity of keeping each other together and alive was obvious to everyone in the tribe. As life became more complicated and tribes began to settle into villages and eventually cities, interests multiplied and diversified so that the basic message of 'stick together and survive together' became diluted. Moreover, as civilizations developed and trading opportunities multiplied, wars became more organized, strategic and deadly. Powerful leaders were willing to sacrifice whole regions and all their inhabitants in order to achieve their goals.

Many of the spiritual and religious systems that we are familiar with today emerged as a response to the greed and ruthlessness of such rulers and the devastating wars they were willing to wage. Spiritual thinkers concentrated their efforts on counteracting the short-sighted self-interest of the warring rulers, by showing people how to extend the natural care and concern they felt for their own immediate families to the wider community – to replace self-interest with interest in the welfare of others.

In 70 CE the Jewish uprising against the Romans was brutally put down and Jerusalem was completely destroyed with savage ruthlessness. Only two Jewish sects survived this catastrophe – the Pharisees and the Jesus movement. The rabbis of the Talmudic age were to transform Judaism from a loose conglomeration of competing sects, all focused on temple worship, into one approach based on study of the Torah with compassion at its heart.

Compassion is also at the root of the teachings of Jesus, and the Gospels are full of the stories of practical enactments of his message that we should love our neighbour as ourselves. We see this in his dealings with the sick, prostitutes, and the poor and needy. To become his disciple a person was required to give away their worldly possessions and devote themselves to the service of others.

When Muhammad was born in the late sixth century CE, warfare among the Arab tribes had reached an alarming level. The tribe he was born into, the Quraysh tribe, had left the nomadic life behind and settled around the Kabah, the ancient shrine in the centre of Mecca. They made the area into a sanctuary in which violence was forbidden, and in this more peaceful atmosphere it was possible for trade and commerce to flourish. However, having forsworn tribal warfare the Quraysh became complacent with their new prosperity, which led to greed and self-interest as they consolidated their wealth and left others in poverty. When Muhammad began to receive the revelations that would be collected into what is now known as the Koran, all this began to change. The revelations spoke directly to the conditions in Mecca and encouraged the sharing of wealth, care for the less fortunate, and gentleness and mercy towards all.

Most religions place compassion at the heart of their doctrine, each expressing its own version of what is known as the Golden Rule,[2] or the Ethic of Reciprocity:

> Always treat others as you would wish to be treated yourself.[3]

Perhaps its most common expression is in the words of Jesus Christ:

Do unto others, as you would have them do unto you.[4]

These simple words carry a message of critical importance for the continuation of the human species and as such they constitute the basis of the United Nations Universal Declaration of Human Rights.[5]

When compassion is enshrined in religious doctrine it occupies an elevated position as a quality to aspire to and a way to live a more meaningful life. The trouble is that recent history is rife with examples of the failure of religion to truly safeguard the sacred tenets of an ethical lifestyle and consequently its position in modern society is severely weakened. In addition, religion no longer occupies a central role in the majority of people's lives. So where does this leave compassion? Most of us would recognize it as a quality we would like to see in other people, and would hope to cultivate within ourselves, but in our society there is very little supportive framework to encourage us to overcome the challenges of trying to be truly compassionate. We are left with a slightly wistful and embarrassed feeling of not being quite up to the mark. From there it is an easy step to believe that you need to be a special person to practise compassion – someone of the stature of Mother Teresa or Nelson Mandela – and that, realistically, it cannot be a part of everyday life.

Misunderstanding compassion

This feeling can extend into a concern that in the cut and thrust of modern living we can open ourselves to being taken advantage of, of being 'soft', if we try to bring compassion into our interactions with others. Religious figures, being removed from the daily rough and tumble, may be protected from such considerations, but for the rest of us there is a feeling that as we strive to manage our lives we cannot always count on being able to do so from a compassionate standpoint. People working in the caring professions – medical practitioners, therapists, teachers and so on – are expected to have some idea of compassion, but Wall Street traders, bankers and captains of industry are not. Even our carers are subject to 'compassion fatigue', a sense that their compassion has been so assaulted by the demands of their work that it is exhausted and diminished – worn out, in fact. We appear to have made a disconnect between the benefit compassion brings to the person giving it, the advantages for the recipient and the long-term needs of our society. Rather than view compassion as a natural and vital expression of being human, we have separated it off into particular environments – nursing, teaching, psychology – where it can flourish for a time as long as it is not overused or exploited. There can even be a suggestion of a certain hierarchy in our expression of compassion – those who live comfortably in good circumstances feeling pity for those who live in poverty and hardship.

Moreover, even when we do allow ourselves to feel compassion and put it into action, it is not always consistent or unbiased. Generally we find it easier to feel compassion for people we love and care for, rather than for strangers. When we do extend our concern further, we are more inclined to favour people who we approve of, who appear to share our values and interests. Victims of misfortune tend to be seen as worthy of compassion, whereas the perpetrators are less so. We give or withhold our compassion on the basis of our judgements and opinions. It is hard to imagine going beyond those parameters.

So how does compassion actually work? In this book we will primarily be working with Buddhist ideas about compassion. Central to these ideas is an understanding of compassion *as the ability to feel another person's suffering as if it is your own, to wish for them to be free from it and to be prepared to help them in that endeavour*. It is based on an understanding that all people suffer and that it is not possible for us to maintain an attitude of indifference in the face of this. We will see that developing this kind of understanding has a profound effect on how we experience the difficulties of life and the stress that can result. Training our mind in this way helps to calm the emotional systems that lead to stress and strengthens those that help to alleviate it.

There are several special qualities about the Buddhist approach to compassion. In the first place it is not based on a set of moral guidelines, neither does it rely on a system of belief. Rather it is a step-by-step training of the mind based on logic that combines human feeling with reason. Because of this system of logic and emphasis on reason, it goes hand-in-hand with a modern, scientific approach – as is clearly evident in the Compassionate Mind Approach. We will be looking into some of the findings from Western scientific research as we go along. Moreover, as this approach is not belief-based, people of different religions or people who are not interested in religion at all can practise it.

Taking as its starting point our natural inclination to love and kindness, developing compassion is about learning to consider others as well as yourself. This enables us to engage in a way of living that will bring enormous benefit to ourselves as well as others. Although it may sound surprising, by concerning ourselves with the suffering of others it is possible to find a key to reduce our own suffering. Stress is certainly one of the great sufferings of modern life. One of the things we will learn in this book is how to apply the logic of compassion to our experience of stress, and so try and gain some clues as to how to transform it and reduce our feelings of stress and the impact of stress in our lives.

The Two Psychologies of Compassion

For many thousands of years there has been a clear recognition that helpfulness, friendliness and compassion are central to creating both good relationships between people and happy states of mind within each of us. Recently, compassion has come under the scientific microscope because of the increasing evidence that focusing our minds on compassion and being motivated to be compassionate, both towards ourselves and others, can have a major impact on our bodies, minds and social relationships. There is a growing interest in exploring different aspects of compassion in a practical way and looking at the ways in which it is possible to get the wrong idea about it. We've already seen that it is not about being soft or gullible – in fact, as we shall see, compassion often requires courage.

The word 'compassion' comes from the Latin word *compati*, which means 'to suffer with'. The Buddhist approach to compassion that we just mentioned – the ability to feel another person's suffering as if it is your own, to wish for them to be free from it and to be prepared to help them in that endeavour – includes this idea but goes much further. In his book in this series, *The Compassionate Mind*, Professor Paul Gilbert has taken this definition as a starting point and then pointed out that in reality compassion is two psychologies in one: the first psychology is the *ability to engage with and stay with suffering,* and the second psychology is *the wisdom of alleviation.* His model is based upon the psychology of nurturance and attachment psychology, and also uses many insights from Buddhism. The study of nurturing behaviour has given rise to insights about what motivates us and makes us able to nurture others.

The first psychology of compassion:
Engaging with suffering

The first psychology of compassion is the ability to turn *towards* suffering rather than away from it. Professor Gilbert suggests that engaging with suffering requires of us a number of attributes. Firstly, we need to be motivated to engage with suffering and the causes of suffering. This is important because if we wish people to be free from suffering we need to know something about what it is and how it works. Our tendency is often to turn away, or become overwhelmed by suffering. This is because we are usually too caught in our own drive systems of *achieving* and *doing* to really notice it or be bothered to do anything about it. Even when we think about our own stress we are not always prepared to turn towards it, to really engage with it and get to know it. Secondly, we need to learn to pay attention to suffering, which in this case is the stress that arises within us, and to try to form an emotional connection to it. Many of us really don't do this because it's far easier to crack open a bottle of wine at the end of the day than to try to get to the heart of what is making us feel stressed and to make difficult changes in order to improve our situation. Indeed we say this, don't we: 'I've had such a busy, hard and stressful day I must have a glass of wine!'

When we do manage to connect emotionally with suffering and the sources of suffering, are we able to tolerate it, and make sense of it, or do we close down? In order not to close down, to be able to think about our own feelings and the feelings of other people, we need to develop an empathic understanding of our own minds. Many years ago the famous counsellor Carl Rogers[6] suggested that empathy was the ability to 'walk in the shoes of others'. Many researchers have now pointed out that, in contrast to sympathy (which is automatic – we are immediately moved by seeing pain in others), genuine empathy needs imagination – it requires us to put in some cognitive work. So if we see a beggar in the street we might spend a few moments imagining that we are that beggar – cold and in a state of despair; or caught up in a cycle of drugs, or having some kind of mental illness. It is a process of getting familiar with the mind of another from inside. This is what empathy is – the process by which we come to know the minds of others deeply and, as far as possible, without judgement. So, the *engagement* part of compassion requires us to have certain kinds of abilities.

The second psychology of compassion:
Alleviation of suffering

The second psychology is doing something about alleviating suffering. We could take the example of a doctor when confronted by a new patient. The doctor must first pay attention to the nature of the patient's difficulties, the symptoms and pains, but then his attention needs to switch to relieving the causes of the problem. Alleviating stress through compassion works in a similar way. If we just turn towards pain and try to engage with it empathetically, sooner or later we get burnt out and overwhelmed. The key is to have some insight into what's actively helpful. So we can learn to pay attention to what is helpful, learn to reason in ways that are helpful and also to behave in ways that are helpful. For example, if somebody is agoraphobic then the compassionate thing to do to relieve that source of stress is for them to learn to confront their anxiety and try going out a little further each day. This of course involves *courage*. Compassion is not sitting at home watching television eating chocolate because that seems a nice thing to do! Compassionate behaviour means directly confronting stress and suffering in ourselves and in others, and taking actions to relieve it and its causes.

This also requires us to pay attention to the emotion systems. So in the case of stress, clearly the 'threat' system that we described in chapter 2 is up to its tricks for one reason or another. One of the most helpful emotion systems to get in touch with when confronting stress is our 'soothing' system. Trying to stimulate the soothing system can really help us when we are struggling with stress.

Within the Buddhist tradition there is recognition that the more understanding you have of how your own mind works in relation to experiencing suffering, the more able you are to help others overcome their own. So compassion then requires us to come to understand our minds. As we have seen, the problem is that sometimes when we try to do this we simply get overwhelmed and understandably want to turn away. This is why it's so useful to train our minds so that we can carry out our desire to be compassionate without being so overwhelmed. Engaging with suffering in a helpful way depends on understanding how the mind works and training it, just as a doctor uses knowledge and training to bring a skilful intervention to bear on his patients. The motivation to be helpful is an important start, but is not enough on its own. Training our minds is the road to the understanding that enables us to alleviate stress – it's what this book is all about.

Fundamental Wholeness

When we are feeling overwhelmed by the pressures of life it is not easy to feel fundamentally whole and well but this is another important aspect of Buddhist ideas about compassion and one that can help us as we try to understand both stress and compassion. Picture a jar of water: the nature of the water is clear, but if we add a drop of blue ink to it, then it changes into a blue liquid. If we add red ink then it becomes red. Alternatively, if we drop in some mud and gravel and then shake the whole jar, the water stops being clear and becomes a swirling mass of particles and muddy liquid. If we put the jar down, then all the mud will settle to the bottom and the water will become clear again. This is how it is with us – our mind in itself is calm and clear, but experiences can stir us up and obscure that calmness and clarity to the extent that we hardly remember that it is there. Stress is a major way to 'stir ourselves up'.

It is possible therefore to draw a distinction between a person's fundamental nature and their actions – while this nature is basically 'whole' and well, our actions are subject to confusion, mistaken perception and self-interest. This can make them seem harmful or negative. Making this distinction can bring a tremendous sense of relief, because it removes judgement and brings us and everyone else within the embrace of compassion. How wonderful to realize that however frustrated we can be with ourselves, underneath it all we are perfectly well and whole.

Let's look a bit more closely at what we mean by 'wholeness'. It has three aspects:

- The understanding that ourselves and everything else are interconnected.

- The quality of awareness.

- The natural capacity for compassion.

The understanding that ourselves and everything else are interconnected

This is an idea we will come back to throughout the book, but to get started let's try and break it down a bit.

Probably most of you reading this book will be sitting down on some kind of seat as you read. Consider your seat more closely – the materials that have been gathered to make it, the people who have worked on it, the calculations and arrangements for it to be sold and brought to where you need it to sit on. Your seat cannot exist independently of all these causes and conditions that brought it into being – it depends on them all for its existence.

Now, let's look further at this seat – where is its 'seatness' to be found? Is it in the legs? Is it in the base? If we remove the back is it still a seat, or does it become a stool? These legs, cushion and back are not a seat on their own – they only become one when they are put together. Without the different parts there is no seat, but without the idea of a 'seat' the parts do not make sense.

If we continue to analyse this seat we can see that the notion of 'seatness' is not a continuous, independent one. A child may see a seat as a climbing frame, or a castle. Woodworm see it as food, whereas mice may make their homes in the upholstery. The seat only becomes an object to sit on to work or relax when it is used for that purpose. It does not exist as a seat in and of itself.

We are not used to thinking in this way most of the time, and it is even harder to apply the same sort of perception to ourselves. Try it for a moment. We were born due to the previous meetings of countless ancestors before us. If we change just one of them then we would have been a different person. Ask yourself where your sense of 'self' manifests – is it in your body, in your head? Think of how this body of ours looks to a child, a dog or a visitor from outer space. Consider how it has changed through all the years we have been referring to it as our 'self'. Clearly, we are also not independent and unrelated to our environment and all the people in it.

This way of thinking shows our ordinary perception of the world around us to be limited. Not to take interdependence into account is a form of over-simplification. Thinking about the interdependence of things is not easy: it challenges our tendency to see things as either black or white, desirable or unpleasant. We need to be prepared to question our habitual reactions and accept that we can misperceive things – things that could help us as we try to reduce our stress.

If we begin to apply this new perspective of interconnectedness to our own lives, we can appreciate that compassion is not an optional extra, but the only sane and responsible way to live. Simply for reasons of enlightened self-interest we can see that it benefits us to have compassion for all the other people we share this planet with. The story of people feeding each other with long spoons at the beginning of this chapter is a good example of this. The Dalai Lama sometimes calls this attitude being 'wisely selfish'. We might not be ready yet to put other's interests before our own, but we can start to appreciate that our interests and the interests of other people are intimately related. The world is full of examples of occasions when we have ignored this. For example, we have floating islands of plastic rubbish, and people living in poverty because their leaders have siphoned off the country's resources to ensure their own comfort – anyone reading this book could probably think of several examples of people failing to grasp or ignoring the interconnectedness of us all. In chapter 10, when we look at how to develop new habits of compassion, we will explore this further.

The quality of awareness

This second aspect of 'wholeness' is our capacity to see things clearly, as they are, but without opinion and judgement. This quality of awareness is with us all the time – it is what enables us to know when we are stressed, for example – but most of the time it is buried under layers of thoughts and feelings about what we are experiencing. In spite of this, there are times – when we are by the ocean, perhaps, or enjoying an inspiring view – when we can get a clear glimpse of our own awareness, unencumbered by the limitations imposed on it by the clutter in our minds. This is the awareness that we can learn to develop through meditation, as we shall see in chapter 8.

The example of a crystal can help us to understand this. If we hold a crystal and look into it we can see through it clearly, but if we hold it up against a coloured cloth, then the crystal takes on the colour of the cloth. In other words, it reflects everything – beautiful things and ugly things, things we like and things we don't like. Whatever it reflects, the crystal itself does not change – it stays pure and unaffected. This is how our awareness is. However much stress and anxiety we experience that might appear to cloud our minds, these are external factors, and the basic clarity of our awareness remains unaffected. This is very helpful to remember as we try to work with our stress, as we shall see later in the book.

The natural capacity for compassion

The third aspect that describes our fundamental 'wholeness' is our natural capacity for compassion. The idea here is that compassion is an expression of who we are as human beings, not something we need to acquire from outside. Let's look at some ideas that help to support this.

Firstly, we human beings are social creatures and place a high value on affection. From the moment we are born we rely heavily on the kindness and care of our mother, without whose help we could not survive and grow to maturity. As we progress through life we look for affection in family, friends and partners. We are more readily drawn towards people who are able to express affection towards us. Have you ever noticed how hard it is to be indifferent towards someone who is showing you love and affection? As we grow older and face sickness and reduced energy, we come increasingly to rely on the affection of others, and eventually as the end of our life approaches we will need affection and kindness to support us.

Now think about our natural ability to connect deeply with the suffering of others. It does not matter which culture, religion or country we live in, if we hear a cry of pain, or see a child suffering, our immediate response is a feeling of empathy and concern. Maybe we are not able to do anything with this feeling and it quickly goes away, but this does not undermine its intensity or the reality of the feeling of connection.

Moreover, whoever we are, we are all trying to live happy lives. Our inclination is to seek happiness rather than pain. There are many scientific studies that show that adopting healthy, positive habits as part of our lifestyle has a beneficial effect on our wellbeing, and when we feel emotions such as anger, hatred, jealousy and pride they can have a corresponding detrimental effect. We can experience this directly by observing how we feel when we are in the grip of a powerful negative emotion, as opposed to the peace we feel when we are engaging in acts of kindness or care.

Finally, in order for us to be able to live together on this planet it is necessary for us to cooperate with our neighbours, our national laws and customs, our environment and our global community. We have come this far largely by mutual cooperation and how long we can enjoy life on this planet will be determined by the extent to which this continues.

Training the mind in compassion therefore combines the deep feelings we have for the welfare of others with a chain of reasoning, thereby providing a firm basis for action. In fact, it is said that the Buddhist view is interdependence, and the action this inspires is altruism.

Training the Mind in Compassion

This altruistic action is expressed as the wish that all beings, whoever they are, should be free from suffering and find reliable happiness, combined with the commitment to make every effort to bring this about. For us to be able to contribute the effort required for this, we need to focus on ourselves by training our minds. We will need to understand what suffering is and what it entails, as well as how we can work with it ourselves. We need to develop awareness so that the full capacity of our mind is available to us.[7] When we decide to place compassion at the heart of our lives in this way, it has an immediate effect on how we view ourselves, other people and the world that we share. So, as we begin to use compassion to reduce our own stress, we are starting out on a journey that will lead us to develop the ability to help other people work through their own stressful situations. As we do this, we will find that our own experience of stress is relieved. We will explore this further in Part 3 of the book.

Training the mind in compassion starts from where we are now and leads us through a step-by-step process that gradually reveals our self-focused habits and at the same time provides ways to access our innate compassion. In this way we develop the courage and skills to address any unhelpful habits we may have as we become more aware of them. Personally, I have always found that the training is practical and realistic because it takes into account from the beginning that changing our habits is not always an easy or speedy process, and that we are likely to get sidetracked from our goal and frustrated by our slow progress. The techniques in this book begin at a fairly basic level and gradually become more challenging, but you can work at a pace that suits you. You can work with any of the techniques for as long as it takes and your effort will still have tremendous benefit. It is never too late to begin to train yourself in compassion, and there is no one to judge your progress. The aim is to connect with your own fundamental wholeness, your natural capacity for kindness and affection, and then to extend that feeling in ever-increasing circles until it is universal.

Much of our stress comes from struggling to keep things the way we would like them to be. When we change this perspective to drawing on our sense of wellness and natural kindness, a sense of ease and space opens up. This enables us to gain greater insight into our difficulties and see them not as isolated incidents in our own lives but as part of the pattern of human life, affecting everyone.

The steps in training the mind in compassion are:

- Trying not to cause harm.

- Melting the ice in your heart.

- Seeing other people as just like you.

- Putting yourself in the other person's shoes.

- Seeing others as more important than yourself.

Trying not to cause harm

If compassion is the wish to help everyone become free of suffering, it can seem like a tall order. People often ask how they can relieve other people's suffering. The first step is to focus on what you *can* do rather than trying to aim for seemingly unobtainable goals. Perhaps you do not feel ready to be a force for good, but you can at least try to limit the harm you cause. Hopefully most people reading this book do not set out to cause harm intentionally, but what exactly do we mean by 'harm' in this context? Think about all the small acts of selfishness and irritation we are all prey to in our daily lives – from pushing ahead in the queue at the supermarket to hissing at other drivers who get in our way. Compassion training works at all levels – body, speech and mind – so you need to look at all the things you do, all the words you say and all the thoughts you think. Every time you are able to disarm a self-centred reaction you are managing not to cause harm – to yourself, as well as to others. We will look into this more in chapter 10.

Melting the ice in your heart

The next stage is about accessing our natural capacity for kindness and altruism more deeply, thereby beginning to melt away the self-protective instincts that block our ability to communicate with others. There are four techniques we can use here, traditionally known as the Four Immeasurables – the generation of immeasurable equanimity (or lack of bias), loving kindness, compassion and joy. These Four Immeasurables are important because they help us to strengthen our compassion 'muscles' by giving us the chance to practise showing compassion beyond the range of the people close to us, and the people we like. They help to make our compassion more robust and reliable. You start by applying each technique to yourself and then continue by sharing these feelings with those close to you and then gradually widening the circle until your feeling becomes unlimited and without bias – in other words, immeasurable. We will look at these techniques in more detail in chapter 11 and explore how working in this way can help to reduce our feelings of stress.

Seeing other people as just like you

To understand this step we can begin by remembering that everyone we meet just wants to be happy and not to suffer – and, the truth is, that is exactly the same for us as well. Because our heart has begun to soften with practising the Four Immeasurables, we are more capable of remembering this in a practical way so that we do not always put our own interests and own wellbeing first. We would like to take others along with us and have them share the same things that we want for ourselves. With this step, we take our own concern for our personal welfare and share it with others. We want to do this because we see each person as being just like us – not in the specific details of their lives and circumstances, but in having the same hopes and fears. This step will be explored in chapter 12.

Putting yourself in the other person's shoes

With this step we are ready to go further and actually allow ourselves to imagine what it is like to be another person, to try and experience how they feel, to discover how things are for them. We will look at this further in chapter 13.

Seeing others as more important than yourself

This last step is really the culmination of compassion training from a Buddhist viewpoint. It is a profound step and not easy to do. It requires a deep understanding of interdependence – how we relate to everyone around us – and long meditation experience and so we will just touch on it in this book. However, in order to visualize it, think of the occasions in which people risk their lives to save others, sometimes people that they do not even know. Surely that is at least a willingness to embrace the possibility of seeing others as more important than oneself.

Compassion in Society

We said earlier that with a decrease in religious observance in society, compassion could seem like a specialist virtue. However, there is a move to reintroduce the notion of compassion into our society whether one is religious or not. Here is a brief introduction to four such initiatives.

Compassion Focused Therapy

Professor Paul Gilbert's book in this series, *The Compassionate Mind*, is a superb introduction to Compassion Focused Therapy (CFT). It lays out all the background to the therapy and provides simple and easy-to-follow exercises to try out.

Here is a simple definition:

> Compassion focused therapy is an integrated and multimodal approach that draws from evolutionary, social, developmental and Buddhist psychology, and neuroscience. One of its key concerns is to use compassionate mind training to help people develop and work with experiences of inner warmth, safeness and soothing, via compassion and self-compassion.[8]

Particularly helpful for people working with feelings of shame and self-criticism, CFT trains people to appreciate and apply the healing potential of compassion for themselves and those around them.

Secular ethics

The Dalai Lama's promotion of secular ethics – the application of Buddhist principles in a secular way – was already mentioned in the Introduction. This quote from him explains further.

> My call for a spiritual revolution is not a call for a religious revolution. Nor is it a reference to a way of life that is somehow

other-worldly, still less to something magical or mysterious. Rather it is a call for a radical re-orientation away from our habitual pre-occupation with self, towards concern for the wider community of beings with whom we are connected, and for conduct which recognizes other's interests alongside our own.[9]

By 'spirituality', the Dalai Lama means a concern with those qualities of the human spirit – such as love and compassion, patience, tolerance, forgiveness, contentment, a sense of responsibility, a sense of harmony – which bring happiness to both oneself and others. By 'ethics' he means the universal wish to attain happiness and avoid suffering. An act can be considered to be ethical or not depending on its effect on another's experience or expectation of happiness. An act that harms or does violence to this is potentially an unethical act.

The Charter for Compassion

In 2008 Karen Armstrong, a religious historian and writer, was awarded the TED Prize of $100,000 and the granting of 'One Wish To Change the World'. Karen asked for help in creating, launching and propagating the Charter for Compassion. This is how it is described on its website:

> The Charter for Compassion is a cooperative effort to restore not only compassionate thinking but, more importantly, compassionate action to the center of religious, moral and political life. Compassion is the principled determination to put ourselves in the shoes of the other, and lies at the heart of all religious and ethical systems. One of the most urgent tasks of our generation is to build a global community where men and women of all races, nations and ideologies can live together in peace. In our globalized world, everybody has become our neighbor, and the Golden Rule has become an urgent necessity.
>
> The Charter, crafted by people all over the world and drafted by a multi-faith, multi-national council of thinkers and leaders, seeks to

change the conversation so that compassion becomes a key word in public and private discourse, making it clear that any ideology that breeds hatred or contempt – be it religious or secular – has failed the test of our time. It is not simply a statement of principle; it is above all a summons to creative, practical and sustained action to meet the political, moral, religious, social and cultural problems of our time.[10]

Notice the central position of the Golden Rule!

As well as signing up to the Charter, people are encouraged to engage in compassionate activities – for example, Seattle in the USA became the world's first 'compassionate city' and many others are following its lead.

Truth and Reconciliation Commission

A Truth and Reconciliation Commission is a body set up to discover and reveal past wrongdoing on the part of a government in the hope of resolving conflict left over from the past. South Africa's Truth and Reconciliation Commission, established by President Nelson Mandela after apartheid, is popularly considered a model of truth commissions. Archbishop Desmond Tutu headed the commission and later helped to establish a similar system in Ireland in an attempt to heal the wounds of the era of the Troubles. Commissions have been set up in many places around the world including Brazil, Canada, Kenya, Morocco, Rwanda and the USA. The key feature is restorative justice rather than punishment as a way to heal a society that has been torn apart by war and brutality. Forgiveness is considered the most effective and sustainable way of moving on from these traumas.

As Archbishop Desmond Tutu writes:

> For retribution wounds and divides us from one another. Only restoration can heal us and make us whole. And only forgiveness

enables us to restore trust and compassion to our relationships. If peace is our goal, there can be no future without forgiveness.[11]

This chapter has attempted to answer the question of what compassion is. We've looked at it as lying at the heart of all modern religions and at how it is used as a platform in current secular movements concerned with the quality of life and human development. We've also had an introduction to training the mind in compassion. We will go into this in depth as a sustainable way of understanding and overcoming stress later in the book. Next we will consider the *biology* of compassion. Just as stress has a biological basis, so compassion has its own roots in our physiological make-up.

KEY POINTS

- The Golden Rule: *Always treat others as you would wish to be treated yourself.*

- Compassion is the ability to feel another person's suffering as if it is your own, to wish for them to be free from it and to be prepared to help them in that endeavour.

- There are two psychologies of compassion: the psychology of engagement and the psychology of alleviation.

- Our mind is naturally calm and clear but experience can stir us up and obscure that calmness and clarity to the extent that we hardly remember that it is there.

- Our nature is fundamentally whole and can be said to have three aspects:
  - The understanding that ourselves and everything else are interconnected.
  - The quality of awareness.
  - The natural capacity for compassion.

- When we decide to place compassion at the heart of our lives, it has an immediate effect on how we view ourselves, other people and the world that we share.

- The motivation to work on ourselves in order to help others is fundamental to the development of compassion.

- Training the mind in compassion starts from where we are now and leads us through a step-by-step process that gradually reveals our self-focused habits and at the same time provides methods for accessing our innate compassion.

- The stages are:
    - Trying not to cause harm.
    - Melting the ice in your heart.
    - Seeing other people as just like you.
    - Putting yourself in the other person's shoes.
    - Seeing others as more important than yourself.

EXERCISES

Exercise 1

Try to bring the Golden Rule to mind, *Always treat others as you would wish to be treated yourself,* as you go about your daily activities and check whether or not you are applying it.

Notice when it is difficult to apply it and the means you use to try and justify not doing so.

Exercise 2

Reflect on the idea that we are all fundamentally whole.

How can you apply this to yourself and others as you go through your day?

What changes do you notice in your attitude to people and situations?

What makes it difficult to remember basic goodness?

Exercise 3

Pause during the day to reflect on how inter-connected we all are.

One way to do this is to consider all the people involved in making the cup of coffee that you may be drinking, or in creating and delivering all the books in a bookstore where you are browsing. You'll be able to think of examples that fit your lifestyle.

4 The Biology of Compassion

Something roughly akin to love is needed for proper biological development, and its absence is among the most aching, distorting stressors that we can suffer.

Robert Sapolsky[1]

Competition or Cooperation

We only need to spend some time watching the news on television to feel depressed and hopeless about the state of the world and our fellow human beings. There are the terrible scenes of war and slaughter, imprisonment and torture, and the reckless cruelty of leaders more interested in maintaining their own power than caring for the people for whom they are responsible. Then there are the countless stories of greed and selfishness on the part of some areas of the world and heartbreaking need and lack of resources in other regions. I was amazed recently to read an article on divorce as a booming business. Apparently growing numbers of hedge funds, venture capitalists and high-end lenders are seeking to increase profits by placing large 'bets' on potentially lucrative divorce settlements. It sometimes can seem that not much is off limits when it comes to making money. In the previous chapter we looked at Buddhist ideas about basic *wholeness*, the idea that human beings are fundamentally compassionate and altruistic. Based on what we know of the world there are plenty of people who would argue the opposite case, that people are ruthless and cruel, motivated by self-interest, with powerful passions that are only managed if held in implacable control.

The Dalai Lama often cites the basic human instinct to seek happiness as a proof of the goodness of our true nature. This instinct runs very deep in all of us – we simply wish to be able to live a happy life. Love, affection and the sense of being connected to others are inextricably linked to this search for happiness. When we experience these feelings, we experience happiness and a deep sense of wellness. Anger arises more as a secondary emotion, when our happiness is interfered with and our quest for that happiness is interrupted. Violence and aggression such as that which we see in the news stem from the difficulties that arise when people's plans and projects are obstructed by circumstances, situations and other people's agendas. This is exacerbated by a struggle for survival against a backdrop of limited resources. Life has become more complex, and our requirements for living more demanding. Our ancestors in the grasslands lived very simply, supported by an understanding of their environment that enabled them to live in harmony with it, whereas our complicated cities run into trouble very quickly when there is an oil crisis, or a major strike, or sometimes even a light snowfall!

The Dalai Lama cautions scientists as to the effect their work has on our society and culture and the extent to which it determines our view of life. His own respect for science and his personal interest in it are well known, but he stresses the importance of science and spirituality working *together* to arrive at a more complete understanding of human beings and their intertwined lives. Without this cooperation there is a danger that science could present a more materialistic view than is helpful.

Perhaps this caution could have been applied to what the social Darwinists made of the work of Charles Darwin.[2] His work on evolutionary theory is often summed up in the phrase 'survival of the fittest', and has been repeatedly used as proof of the baseness of human nature. In fact, this phrase is wrongly attributed to Darwin, as it was the political philosopher Herbert Spencer[3] in his *Principles of Biology* who in fact came up with it. There are other sides to Darwin that are less talked about but equally important – his thinking on compassion, altruism and morality and his commitment to the unity of humanity. In 1871 Darwin published one of his lesser-known works, *The Descent of Man and Selection in Relation to Sex*. In this work can be found his thoughts on sympathy or, as we would now call it, empathy. He points to the willingness of animals to come to the aid of others, to our human inclination to relieve the suffering of others, and to how natural selection favours the development of compassion as being vital for the survival of a community.

Evolutionary Theory

We are aware in the back of our minds that our brains are a product of millions of years of evolution, but we don't tend to give this much conscious thought. Let's take some time now to explore how our brain has developed, bearing in mind as we do that evolution is not always a smooth process that can just throw out any previous mistakes and start again! It develops by amending and adapting what is already there. This can lead to tensions and contradictions that we have to find ways to come to terms with.[4]

For example, let's consider the part of our brain that we have inherited from our reptilian ancestors, what is often referred to as the 'old brain'. Consisting of the brain stem and cerebellum – the area that controls motor movement coordination, balance, equilibrium and muscle tone – it controls the body's vital functions such as our heart rate, breathing, body temperature and balance. Now, these reptiles were not complicated creatures – their sole focus was to survive and they were entirely motivated by self-interest. They were concerned with fighting for territory, defeating any challengers, finding enough food to eat and securing a place of safety in order to mate and reproduce. Although reproduction was a priority for reptiles, relationships were not, and after their mating fulfilled its purpose, the animals parted. When they gave birth they had no interest in nurturing their young, not hesitating to eat them if the occasion arose. Not surprisingly, the young that survived were tough and capable of fighting for their lives. We have inherited these characteristics. They are located in the hypothalamus – a key area of the brain in terms of the stress response, as we saw in chapter 2. By preparing us for fight-or-flight this part of the brain helped to ensure our survival.

This mode of life was to change with the advent of mammals that gave birth to offspring who were more vulnerable and needed parental care in order to survive. This departure from the lifestyle of the reptiles represents the first seeds of what would become a biological basis for compassion in humans. The question of survival was still the overriding priority, so these new mammalian instincts did not replace those of the reptile, but existed alongside them. However, the skills required in caring for young, engaging in an increasingly social group and longer-term mating all led to the growth and development of the cerebral cortex – the outer covering of the cerebrum, the layer of the brain often referred to as grey matter. By the time we get to the arrival of humans the area of the 'old brain' was completely enveloped by and buried within it.

The 'new brain' is a part of the cerebral cortex concerned with sight and hearing in mammals, regarded as the most recently evolved part of the cortex. It includes but by no means is restricted to our neocortex and is concerned with the higher functions of reasoning: thought and language, for example. It is altogether more complex, subtle and multi-faceted than the old brain. For the most part the 'new brain' is able to stand back from and regulate the primitive instincts of the 'old brain', but not always. There are times when the old automatic impulses override our more recently acquired skills of reason and discernment and we find ourselves at the mercy of our aggression and self-interest. If you've ever driven home at the end of a long and tiring day and found yourself yelling abuse at another driver for cutting in front of you, then you have experienced what we are talking about here. Worse still is when we employ our new brain skills in the service of old brain interests, for example when someone with a good understanding of finance uses their skills to embezzle the company they work for, thereby being overwhelmed by instincts of greed and self-interest.

Mother's Love

Buddhist teachings on compassion return again and again to the image of a mother caring for her young – offering nourishment as an act of unconditional love without the expectation of anything in return. The mother and the baby are drawn together instinctively in affection and love – the baby's need of love in order to survive matching the instinct that the mother has to care for her offspring.

The Dalai Lama comments:

> What we see . . . is a relationship based on love and mutual tenderness which is totally spontaneous. It is not learned from others, no religion requires it, no law imposes it, no schools have taught it. It arises quite naturally.[5]

As we have seen, what we know of the story of our evolution bears this out. In the case of the earlier mammals, a mother's care was a rough and ready means of keeping her young alive, but over time parental skills developed as parents learnt to engage in behaviour that benefited their children, such as stroking them and teaching them to look after themselves. Human parents also developed the ability not only to protect their young but also to influence their development through the care and support they provide. These increasing skills led to the development of larger and larger brains, which meant that human babies had to be born prematurely in order to navigate the birth canal. Because of this, babies came to need the support and care of the whole community as well as their parents. A human mother had no fur for her baby to hang on to, making it necessary for her to carry it herself. There were times when she had to put the needs of the baby, for example for food and rest, before her own. In this way, the care given to a child developed from an automatic instinct to ensure its survival into something more voluntary, based on feeling. The seeds of compassion were beginning to sprout.

Empathy: The Prelude to Compassionate Action

Along with the need to produce and rear healthy offspring, our ancestors living in small tribes in harsh conditions had a pressing need to cooperate in order for the tribe to survive the challenges of finding food, scaring off unfriendly tribes and protecting themselves from predators. The instinct to care for one's young needed to extend to include the tribe as a whole. This involved the development of empathy, the ability to 'tune into' another person and to share their concerns. It is not hard to see that it was much easier to survive as part of a tightly knit supportive tribal group, rather than trying to keep oneself alive as a lone agent out on the grasslands. Cooperation based on empathy was effective in ensuring the genes for these traits passed on to future generations and so gradually influenced how our brain further evolved. So human beings have developed as intensely social beings that thrive on friendship and close personal networks. Indeed, there is now a lot of research showing that we function at our best and are happiest, with low stress and strong immune systems, when we feel loved and valued (rather than feeling marginalized) and are kind and loving (rather than being indifferent to others or hating them). So to feel part of our social relationships and networks it helps to know that others are concerned for you and will help you (and know how to help you) if you need them to. It also helps that they know you feel the same about them and that you are a reliable and helpful 'friend'. This sharing of our empathic concerns for each other is core to the development of friendship and mutual caring, and has helped make us the species we are today. We will be going into this in more detail when we come to Part 3 of this book, and begin to look at some techniques that we can use to develop compassion.

There are several recent studies that have examined the biological roots of empathy. One study of the brain activity of mothers looking at photos of their babies[6] showed unique activity in the region of the brain associated with positive emotions. A further study[7] monitored brain activity while participants were engaged in helping someone. Activity was found to have been triggered in the areas of the brain that 'turn on' (or, as sometimes described by scientists, 'light up') when people receive awards or experience pleasure, showing that helping others provides us with the same pleasure as when we receive something we like. This will come up again in more detail in chapter 10 when we discuss the benefits of volunteering.

Although we can insulate ourselves from the suffering of others, as we do when we are cruel to people or indifferent to their pain, modern neuroscience is bearing out the fact that our brain does in general react with concern to other people's suffering. When we see someone in distress, circuits are activated in the brain that stimulate us to go and help. For example, when parents hear their child cry, similar circuits in their own brains respond, motivating them to go to the child to comfort it. When we hear a cry for help our instinct is to answer it – this is an empathetic response in the brain that leads to a compassionate action.

Jerome Kagan, a Harvard psychology professor, writes:

> Although humans inherit a biological basis that permits them to feel anger, jealousy, selfishness and envy, and to be rude, aggressive or violent, they inherit an even stronger biological basis for kindness, compassion, cooperation, love and nurture.[8]

The positive emotions of kindness and compassion are part of our biological make-up, just like the negative emotions of anger and aggression. If we focus on training ourselves in compassion, then we can learn to strengthen the aspects of ourselves that are based on kindness and the positive side of our nature.

Research on Compassion

There is an increasing interest among scientists in studying compassion. Some of the findings are very new and still emerging. To understand the biological underpinnings of compassion, it is useful to look into some research projects.

Neuroscience

Of special interest for this book is the work of Richard Davidson. He has carried out extensive research on the changes in the brain that are brought about by training in meditation and compassion techniques. We will be looking into some of these as we go along.

Mirror neurons

In 1996, Giacomo Rizzolatti, a neuroscientist at the University of Parma in Italy, and his team published their findings of research carried out on monkeys. While investigating brain activity related to planning and carrying out movement, the team accidentally discovered that the monkey's brain lit up in just the same way whether it moved itself, or watched the lab technicians moving. When someone returned from lunch with an ice cream and ate it in front of a monkey, its brain fired as if it was moving the ice cream to its own mouth. The brain of the monkey contains a special class of cells, which have come to be termed 'mirror neurons', that fire when the animal sees or hears an action and when the animal carries out the same action on its own.

This discovery was exciting in itself, but even more exciting was the research that followed. It showed that humans have the same kind of cells but more sophisticated, more flexible, smarter, and more highly evolved than those found in monkeys. Before this important discovery, scientists believed that our brain uses logical thought processes to interpret and predict other people's actions. However, this research is giving rise to the belief among researchers that we understand other people not only by thinking, but by feeling as well. If I see someone touch you on your arm, my brain will light up as if I am being touched – the only things that prevent me from thinking it is me being touched are the sense and pain receptors on my skin. In fact, if my arm is anaesthetized so that these sense receptors are not working, then I can actually 'feel' the touch on your arm as if it were my own. These findings are enabling researchers to learn more about how we develop empathy.

Mirror neurons are found in several areas of the brain. They are capable of lighting up in response to perceived intentions, of analysing a scene and of seeming to read minds. That is, if you see me reach towards a bookshelf you will assume that I am going to select a book, even when you cannot see my hand. The neurons will light up when someone kicks a ball, hears a ball being kicked and says or hears the word 'kick'. When we see an action we simulate the action in our own brain because we have a template for that action based on our own movements. In the same way, if you see my eyes fill with tears when I tell you about a distressing incident, your own mirror neurons will mimic my distress. You will automatically feel empathy because you feel what I am feeling. This bears out what we already know about empathy as the ability to 'tune into' another person. One of Rizzolatti's team suggests that we live in a more 'we-centric' space than we realize – one that takes into account the importance of the group – rather than the popular belief that each of us is an island unto ourselves. Understanding mirror neurons is not only changing the idea of how we see others but how we understand ourselves.

The wandering nerve

This is the nickname given to the vagus nerve – *vagus* is the Latin for wandering. It actually consists of two nerves which are the longest in the body, starting in the top of the spinal cord and then meandering through the body to connect the facial muscle tissue, the thorax, and all the major organs of the body – the heart, lungs, kidneys, liver and digestive organs. It plays an important role – influencing the muscle contractions in the stomach that are required to digest food and serving as a natural brake on the heart rate, keeping it relatively low. Recent research has shown that it also has an involvement in monitoring inflammation in the body.

The vagus nerve is sometimes referred to as the 'caretaking nerve' because of its connection with compassion. Dacher Keltner,[9] professor of psychology at the University of California, Berkeley, cites three conclusions that support this description, drawn from studies carried out in his laboratory. Firstly, they found that when people are listening to someone describe an experience of suffering, they give a tiny quarter-second sigh from time to time which acts as an expression of concern and understanding and that in turn comforts and soothes the speaker. This is the work of the vagus nerve, stimulating the muscles of the throat, mouth, face and tongue to make the reassuring sounds. Secondly, the vagus nerve reduces the heart rate from a possible 115 beats per second to an average of 72 beats per minute. This means that when we are alarmed or frightened and our heart races, preparing the body for fight or flight, the vagus nerve acts to calm it, making it more possible for us to respond in a gentle manner. Thirdly, it is believed that the vagus nerve is related to the release of the hormone oxytocin, which is connected to the experience of trust, soothing and love.

It is worth noting that the vagus nerve is unique to mammals. Scientists believe it evolved in order to support the care-giving skills of mammals for their young. It is still early days in terms of understanding the full impact of research into the vagus nerve but indications so far point to it as being an important support for compassionate activity.

Oxytocin

The hormone oxytocin is known to play an important role in relaxing mothers during childbirth and assisting breastfeeding, but recent research indicates that it plays a wider role in our lives. Oxytocin is produced when we are touched, when we are warm and through vibration (such as a good massage). It also acts to calm the stress response – when it is released blood pressure is lowered, which helps us to shift from the muscle-boosting stress arousal state to a restorative mode in which our energy can go into storing nutrients, growth and healing. A surge of oxytocin does not last long, but we can prolong its benefits through loving, stable relationships. Each time we hug, or share an affectionate moment, it causes oxytocin to be released over and over again – which in turn soothes and calms our nervous system. So it is a self-nourishing cycle. As Dacher Keltner writes:

> Being compassionate causes a chemical reaction in the body that motivates us to be even more compassionate.[10]

Ways in which the Biology of Compassion Manifests in Action

Human beings' reluctance to kill

The savagery of war is often cited as evidence to suggest that empathy can only be skin deep. However, the truth is that human beings, for the most part, find it repugnant to kill their fellow humans and there have been several studies that bear this out. During the Second World War, US Army Brigadier General S.L.A. Marshall was asked to set up a study on how soldiers conducted themselves during battle. Marshall was a US Army historian in the Pacific during the Second World War. He had a team of historians working for him and together they carried out research based on individual and group interviews with thousands of soldiers from more than 400 infantry companies immediately after they had been in close combat with German or Japanese troops. The results were a revelation – they showed that only 15 to 20 per cent of American riflemen actually fired their weapons at the enemy. However, those who did not fire did not run away or hide. Instead they risked great danger to rescue comrades, get ammunition or run messages.

These findings were taken seriously by the American military and led to the institution of new training strategies that were designed to enable soldiers to overcome their natural reluctance to kill. These strategies include desensitization, conditioning and denial defence mechanisms. Desensitization works by using language and images that dehumanize the troops of the opposing army, so it is harder to see them as other human beings and easier to see them as an 'enemy'. Troops are encouraged to see killing the enemy as part of their job and to view the enemy as less than human. Instead of learning to shoot using a static target, soldiers dressed in full combat gear stand in a foxhole and fire at human-shaped targets that pop up in front of them. In this way, the soldiers become more conditioned to the act of shooting to kill. Sometimes the targets are filled with red paint to make the experience of 'killing' them even more realistic. Bill Jordan, a career US Border Patrol officer explains:

> There is a natural disinclination to pull the trigger when your weapon is pointed at a human. To aid in overcoming this resistance it is helpful if you can will yourself to think of your opponent as a mere target and not as a human being. In this connection you should go further and pick a spot on your target. This will allow better concentration and further remove the human element from your thinking.[11]

He calls this process 'manufactured contempt' and it describes how denial defence mechanisms work.

Such methods did indeed serve to suppress soldiers' natural empathy towards their opponents, to the extent that by the Korean War 55 per cent of soldiers fired their rifles and by the Vietnam War this proportion had reached 95 per cent. However, the story does not end there – it is well known now that many of the soldiers who returned from Vietnam were severely traumatized by their experiences, with between 28 and 54 per cent suffering from Post-Traumatic Stress Disorder (PTSD).

Modern warfare with its long-range, hands-off methods of killing presents other challenges as it offers even greater opportunity for desensitization. Modern video games with their graphic on-screen violence could also serve as a kind of conditioning and denial mechanism as they tend to view the opponent as a target rather than a human being. We will look into the importance of developing empathy and seeing other people as human beings just like oneself when we come to Part 3 of the book.

Forgiveness

We do not have to look far to uncover examples of people seeking revenge for the hurt they experienced at the hands of another person, but even more powerful, and at least equally common, are the stories of forgiveness and reconciliation. From an evolutionary perspective, revenge may have been a means of deterring further attacks from hostile tribes and punishing freeloaders within one's own tribe. Forgiveness on the other hand would have been an essential element in repairing important relationships that had been damaged by aggression and so deepening the cooperation among tribal members. Now, in the modern world, new research is showing that forgiveness plays a key role in the health of families, communities and nations by enhancing the physical, mental and spiritual health of both those who forgive and those who are forgiven.

If the opposite of forgiveness is bearing a grudge, it transpires that doing so has a damaging effect on our wellbeing. In a study carried out by a psychologist at Hope College, Michigan,[12] participants were asked to recall a grudge they held against someone. Recalling the grudge led to an increase in blood pressure, heart rate and sweating. On an emotional level participants described feeling angry, sad, anxious and less in control of themselves. When they were asked to imagine forgiving the person they held a grudge against, their stress levels fell and the physical symptoms they had experienced subsided. When we consider that hostility plays a large part in maintaining a grudge these results make perfect sense. We touched on Type A Personality and the health issues related to hostile behaviour in chapter 2. When we can forgive other people we are releasing our own hostility as well, so we benefit just as they do.[13]

Elevation

Jonathan Haidt is a professor of psychology at the University of Virginia. Having spent many years studying disgust in human beings, he has now turned his attention to studying what he has termed 'elevation'.[14] This is the good feeling that we experience when we see other people performing unexpected acts of kindness, courage or compassion. The studies he has undertaken have indicated that when people see people helping others they react with as much happiness as if they were receiving the help themselves. Moreover, witnessing such altruism helps enable them to perform similar acts themselves and to turn their attention outwards to the wider community and away from narrow self-interests. Haidt sees this as an indication that, in spite of all the cruelty and injustice in the world, the majority of people simply wish to live in peace and happiness, and experience tremendous satisfaction when they witness others behaving in a way that promotes this. Beyond this, Haidt sees elevation as having possible far-reaching social benefits because of its power to spread and affect the broader community.

It is still relatively early days in terms of research into compassion, but already the findings indicate support for the Buddhist understanding. A predisposition to compassion appears to be built into our physiological design and when we engage in compassionate activity our bodies respond in a healthy way that promotes wellbeing. This is one of the reasons why compassion is a helpful way to work with stress.

A Native American Folk Tale

There is an old Cherokee folk story that I have heard several different versions of. It is a wonderful tale and offers a helpful insight into what we have discussed in this chapter. My favourite version goes like this: an old chief is walking with his grandson, pointing out different features in the landscape and sharing stories. At one point the old man says to the boy, 'You know, most of the time I feel as if I have two wolves living in my heart. One is fierce and wild, a mighty hunter and fearsome fighter, filled with the power to hate, while the other is gentle and tender, filled with the power of love. Sometimes it feels as if these two wolves are doing battle inside me.'

The child asks, 'Grandfather, which wolf will win?'

His grandfather replies, 'Whichever one I feed.'

So it is up to us. We all carry within us the capacity to cause harm to ourselves and others, but we also are built to love and care for ourselves and for other people. We need to see clearly what helps us develop the loving and caring aspect, so we can employ it in healing and transforming the potential for harm.

KEY POINTS

- The instinct to seek happiness runs very deep in all of us – we simply wish to be able to live a happy life. Love, affection and the sense of being connected to others are inextricably linked to this search for happiness. When we are experiencing these feelings we experience happiness and a deep sense of wellness. Anger arises more as a secondary emotion, when our happiness is interfered with and our quest is interrupted.

- Our 'old brain' is concerned with survival – we have inherited it from our reptilian ancestors.

- With the advent of mammals and the need to nurture their young, the first seeds of a biological basis for compassion took root.

- The 'new brain', the neocortex, is concerned with the higher functions – reasoning, thought and language, for example. It is altogether more complex, subtle and multi-faceted than the 'old brain'. For the most part the 'new brain' is able to stand back from and regulate the primitive instincts of the 'old brain'.

- Humans have a natural tendency for empathy – the inability to bear another's suffering without wanting to try to help.

- Current research is coming up with interesting data that show that compassion is part of our physiological make-up and that, when we engage with it, our health and wellbeing improves.

- How we work with ourselves is key in determining whether our capacity for kindness and compassion can become stronger than our instinct to protect ourselves and survive at any cost.

EXERCISES

Exercise 1

The next time someone hurts you – however trivial it may seem – try to practise forgiveness.

Notice how this makes you feel.

Notice the effect on the other person.

How does this help you with any stressful ways in which you may have reacted to the incident?

Exercise 2

Try to identify the two wolves in your own heart and observe what happens to each one when you feed it.

5 The Happiness We Are Seeking

> I believe that the very purpose of our life is to seek happiness. That is clear. Whether one believes in religion or not, whether one believes in this religion or that religion, we are all seeking something better in life. So, I think the very motion of our life is towards happiness.
>
> *The Dalai Lama*[1]

So far we have covered the question of what we understand by stress and compassion, along with their physiological impact. In order to have a complete picture of our starting point in working with stress and compassion it will help us to take a look at what makes us happy as well as what causes us suffering. When we feel happy we feel as light as air, that everything is possible and as if we could fly through space, but when we experience stress we feel so burdened and weighed down that we are like poor Atlas trying to support the whole world on his shoulders. We might conceive of happiness as a stress-free zone – the place that is waiting for us just around the corner when we have managed to overcome all our stress. The truth is that it is rarely that simple. Happiness is trickier than we thought and much less reliable – in fact, trying to be happy can even cause us stress, whereas suffering can present us with challenges that can eventually become beneficial for us.

We all know people who seem to be able to cope with a variety of demands and challenges and still maintain a cheerful attitude, while others, with much less to contend with, are grumpy and hard to please. Recent research is showing that our levels of happiness and wellbeing have wide-reaching effects across many areas of our lives – including on our ability to make satisfying relationships, on our health and even on how long we may live. Previously, conventional wisdom held that if we worked hard we would become successful, and happiness would be our reward in time when all our goals fell into place. Now research findings from the fields of neuroscience and Positive Psychology indicate that it could be the other way around – that happiness fuels success and that the happier we are, the more successful we become.[2] So happiness is not just about feeling good, and the question of what makes us happy becomes increasingly important. Our levels of happiness are not merely haphazard and subject to luck. In fact, if happiness is lifted out of the domain of short-term good feelings and developed as something stable and longer lasting it can become a foundation from which we can learn to cope with stress.

Although the human wish for happiness is deep and sincere, we are often confused as to what constitutes happiness, and our very pursuit of it can lead to all kinds of frustration. A participant in a recent workshop of mine told us how after a highly stressful week she felt debilitated and thought that she deserved a treat, so she bought herself an expensive Louis Vuitton handbag. She said the enjoyment lasted for as long as it took for regret to set in that she had maxed out her credit card. Right there we can see the potential for experiencing stress even when we are trying to achieve happiness. It is so often the case that we feel stressed when our movement towards a desired goal is diverted, interfered with or derailed altogether, and this causes us to suffer.

Compassion, as we said before, is concerned with wanting everyone to be free from suffering and to be willing to support them to become free. There are interesting connections we can explore between happiness and stress. We'll make a beginning in this chapter by examining what constitutes happiness and wellbeing, while exploring whether our ideas about it are in fact reliable or if they can become stress-inducing factors in themselves. In chapter 6 we will explore suffering.

The Complexity of Modern Life

Both as a society and as individuals, we are always looking forward and trying to improve – we would like things to get better and better.

It's undeniable that in terms of improved healthcare and housing, of advances in medical science, and better education, most of us who live in the developed world have much to be thankful for. The technological developments of the last sixty years have changed our lives in ways we could never have imagined, and continue to bring almost weekly innovations – innovations that carry the promise that they will save time and energy so we can accomplish more, with less effort. The question we may ask ourselves is: are these promises being met? Do all our labour-saving devices really save us time, or just lead us to use our time differently? When did we consciously sign up for being available via email and phone twenty-four hours a day? Do we ever stop to wonder what we are doing with all this 'extra time' that's offered to us? Our computers, televisions and phones have graduated from devices that should help us work, relax and communicate, to absorbing multimedia opportunities that have established themselves as essential in our lives. What *did* we do before the iPhone, Facebook and Twitter? As we come to rely more and more on technology, the results of any part of it breaking down and going out of service is highly stressful. Each new device to improve the quality of our life follows so rapidly upon the previous one that there is hardly time to keep up! We've just got our head around our new gadget and it is already out of date. There's no way to update it, so it's better to get the new version, but then how do we choose which is the best? It all starts to feel slightly stressful.

American psychology professor Barry Schwartz, author of *The Paradox of Choice*,[3] claims that the huge amount of choice available to us is in itself a source of worry and stress for two main reasons – firstly, that we can never gather and absorb all the information available in order to make a good decision about which energy plan, digital camera, or holiday option to choose; and secondly, that the moment we make our choice and buy it we have regret that there may be a similar option out there for a much better deal. Schwartz once calculated, on a trip to his local electronics store, that the range of available hi-fi separates – speakers, tuner, amplifier, CD player, tape player – meant that he could construct a possible 6.5 million different stereo systems.[4] A recent article in *Mail Online* entitled

'The tyranny of choice: Do we really need 38 types of milk?' includes the following figures:

> In Tesco it is now possible to buy no fewer than 38 types of milk. Some of it is flavoured with strawberry, banana or Belgian chocolate; some has active bacterial flora; some has extra omega-3 . . . And that's before you get to the aisle with 154 flavours of jam, or the one with 107 varieties of pasta.[5]

So the time we have saved by doing all our shopping under one gigantic roof gets eaten up – quite literally – by our repeated deliberations as to which choice of product to buy.

There is a quandary here: by trying to improve our living standards and make everything happen faster and with less effort we run the risk of creating so many options, possibilities and choices that we expend a lot of energy and worry just trying to manage it all. For example, my Facebook page is a source of delight, but can also be a source of pressure as I struggle to keep up with all the articles and movies that people send me. All this support exists to enable us to feel in touch, and yet it creates this nagging fear of falling behind because there are simply not enough hours in the day to absorb all that there is on offer.

Measuring Happiness and Wellbeing

My neighbour across the road from us is happiest when she has her widescreen TV on all day long, but she has her TV set placed so the constant flickering can be seen through our windows, catching my eye repeatedly during the day. She is happy, I am not. As a rebellious teenager most arguments with my mother ended with her proclamation that she just wanted me to be happy. Like most adolescents in similar situations, I never understood why she just didn't leave me to get on with what I wanted to do – to discover how to be happy myself. Happiness for me meant total freedom, whereas happiness for her meant knowing I was safe. There was a time I was cross-country walking with a friend in Cyprus and we got totally lost, hot and terribly thirsty. Eventually we stumbled on a small cottage and begged a drink. Cool bottles were pulled up from a well and offered to us. I drank mine down in one go – it was absolutely delicious. It was only when my friend pointed out it was beer that I was drinking that I even noticed – I dislike beer and never drink it, and yet at that moment it tasted like nectar. For me at that moment happiness was having a cold drink and whether or not it was beer did not matter one bit! So happiness can clearly mean many different things in different situations to different people, and the clash of those preferences can in itself cause stress.

It's no surprise that the question of what constitutes happiness is one that has occupied philosophers since Aristotle himself. However, it was only as recently as the eighteenth century that the individual's *right* to happiness became an accepted idea, inspiring Thomas Jefferson to enshrine the inalienable right to 'life, liberty and the pursuit of happiness' in the constitution of the fledging American republic. Towards the end of the twentieth century, happiness developed as an area of interest for psychologists. In 1998 Martin Seligman chose his term as president of the American Psychologists Association as an opportunity to launch what is now called Positive Psychology. Along with researchers like Ed Diener, nicknamed 'Dr Happiness' because of his extensive work in this area, and Mihaly Csikszentmihalyi, the architect of the notion of 'flow' (the moments when we are engaged in an activity that is completely absorbing and satisfying for us),[6] Seligman has worked to refocus psychology on nurturing talent and improving life, rather than dealing only with treating mental illness.

In the absence of any universal measurement of happiness and wellbeing, psychologists measure happiness levels through self-reporting in which people answer questionnaires detailing how happy they are. Seligman has created a General Happiness Scale[7] asking people to rate themselves on a score of 1–7 on four questions.[8] An exciting recent development is that scientists can now measure brain activity patterns associated with happiness. We can see that particular moods or emotions are accompanied by distinctive patterns of electrical and chemical activity in various regions of our brain. Brain activity patterns associated with happiness are quite different from those associated with sadness. When subjects are shown images designed to make them happy – such as pictures of a smiling baby – there is heightened activity in the left pre-frontal cortex, which is situated just behind the left eye. When shown upsetting images – such as pictures of a baby in pain – there is a corresponding increase in activity in the right pre-frontal cortex. These differences in left–right brain activity also show up when people are engaged in ordinary activity. 'Left-siders' report more positive thoughts and memories and they smile more, whereas 'right-siders' report the opposite.

The impact of being able to investigate our brain's reactions in this way has elevated happiness studies to a new level. Serious research on happiness and wellbeing is now a growing and productive field. It includes a wide range of interests – brain scientists advancing our understanding of how happiness works, clinicians seeking to help patients avoid depression, social scientists interested in measuring happiness across the globe and economists examining how people choose to spend their money. Since 1960 at least 3,000 studies have been published. There is a World Database of Happiness based in Erasmus University Rotterdam, which collects the findings from current research into happiness.[9] Daniel Kahneman of Princeton University is one of the pioneers of what he calls Hedonic Psychology, the study of what makes experiences in life pleasant or unpleasant.[10] The British economist, Richard Layard, in his groundbreaking book *Happiness: Lessons from a New Science*[11] set out to show that although we may think more money means more happiness, in fact the relationship between our levels of happiness and wellbeing and our standard of living is not straightforward at all. His work draws on psychology, neuroscience, economics, sociology and philosophy. He has been the main instigator of the Improving Access to Psychological Therapies programme (IAPT) in the UK, which has the aim of convincing the government to invest more in mental health services, with particular emphasis on increasing access to therapists. In his book he describes mental illness as the 'greatest source of misery in the west',[12] and suggests that this issue needs to be addressed as a matter of urgency for the wellbeing of society.

Gross National Happiness

In the small Himalayan country of Bhutan there is another initiative to turn these research results to practical use by supporting its citizens' pursuit of happiness in a sustainable way. In 1972, His Majesty Jigme Singye Wangchuck, who was the king at that time, first used the term Gross National Happiness (GNH) as a means of measuring the development of his country in terms of the happiness of its people. It's an alternative to the more commonly used economic measurement gross national product (GNP). Dasho Meghraj Gurung, former ambassador and director of Bhutan Post and the Royal Institute of Management, describes it as an ideology that reflects Bhutan's vision of the purpose of human life – to put the individual's self-development and wellbeing at the centre of the nation's developmental goals.[13]

Bhutan is a Buddhist country, and the idea of Gross National Happiness is built around the central idea that the ultimate purpose of life is to cultivate inner happiness. This provides a strong common view and understanding among the Bhutanese people and makes a national policy of this kind possible. In spite of the encroaching realities of global economics, it has become a model and inspiration for other governments, including those in the West, and several international conferences[14] have been held to explore it further. The most prestigious so far has been the first ever United Nations Conference on Happiness, which was held in April 2012. Inspired by the example of Bhutan, 600 delegates attended.

What the Happiness Research Shows Us

Although it seems that an increasing number of people consider happiness as an important factor in our lives, we can see that the plans we make in order to promote that happiness do not always turn out successfully. This disappointment can bring its own stress. In addition, we do not all seek happiness in the same places and our wishes may conflict with those of other people – think of my neighbour and her TV. A picture emerges that provides clues for how we might approach our own individual quest for happiness and wellbeing as a way of coping with stress. We could start by questioning some of the ways in which we have assumed we can be happy. In order to understand more clearly how unreliable happiness can be, let's start by looking more closely at some of the main research findings that explore this.

Happiness and the pursuit of stuff

One of the key findings highlighted by Richard Layard in his book, *Happiness: Lessons from a New Science* is that over the last fifty years, the standard of living in the US and western Europe has roughly doubled, while levels of happiness have stayed the same. When we consider the effort involved in doubling our standard of living – the compromises in work–life balance, the increase in the number of families where the only way to manage is for both parents to work, the stress of the increase in pace and variety of the modern workplace – then it is shocking to find no increase in our basic level of wellbeing. We can only exclaim, like the super-stressed executive Charles Grodin played in the 1990 movie, *Filofax*, 'But I worked hard to work this hard!' Psychologists describe us as being on a hedonic treadmill,[15] running hard to get somewhere that we never reach. As Harvard psychology professor Daniel Gilbert comments in his book, *Stumbling on Happiness*,[16]

> Regardless of what we achieve in the pursuit of stuff, it's never going to bring about an enduring state of happiness.

What it does do is to keep the wheels of the global economy turning, producing more material goods that we are convinced we cannot do without, while longer-lasting possibilities for happiness, such as volunteering, or spending time with friends, get sidetracked because we lack time.

Adaptation

An on-going social survey carried out in the United States[17] on a cross-section of Americans monitored the choice of items that people considered necessary for a good life. Participants were asked to list what they considered their 'essential' items and then tick the ones they already possessed. The list of items included things like a house, a car, a TV and a holiday home. The survey was repeated with the same group sixteen years later. During this time people went from possessing, on average, 1.7 to 3.1 of the items on their list, whereas the items deemed necessary for the good life increased from 4.4 items to 5.6 items. So, revealingly, people considered that their circumstances fell as far short of the good life as they always had. Our chances of winning the lottery may be pretty small but even if we do, the effect could be disappointing. In fact, one of the most startling results to emerge from research into happiness is that big lottery winners, after experiencing an initial period of euphoria, tend to return to their normal levels of happiness within a year. The huge rise in their financial and then material resources is not enough to lift their happiness levels long term. The trouble is that we adapt to what we have and so become used to it, and when the gloss of having it fades we want something more.

The process of adaptation we experience with material possessions seems to work in the same way for life experiences – so career moves, lifestyle changes or new relationships, rather than transporting us to new levels of happiness, eventually settle down until they become simply part of our normal pattern of happiness. The good news is that this also seems to hold true for many things we would wish to avoid – redundancy, accident and romantic disaster. This is something it would be helpful to remember when we are in the thick of anxiety about a job interview or the high of a new love affair.

Martin Seligman gives a clue as to why this might be:

> Remarkably, the evidence shows that when positive and nega-tive events happen, there is a temporary burst of mood in the right direction. But usually over a short time, mood settles back into its set range. This tells us that emotions, left to themselves, will dissipate. Their energy seeps out through the membrane, and by 'emotional osmosis' the person returns in time to his or her

baseline condition. Expressed and dwelt upon, though, emotions multiply and imprison you in a vicious cycle of dealing fruitlessly with past wrongs.[18]

The very emotions we use in order to make choices are themselves unreliable and transient, and yet each time they occur we behave as if this time they must be for real and so we make the same miscalculations all over again. Emotions are a key weapon of stress, and understanding them is an important element in learning to apply compassion to our responses to stress. It is hard to be compassionate to oneself or to other people when one's emotions are running wild. We will be looking at emotions in more depth in Part 2 of this book.

Comparison

Along with adapting to what we have in life, we also suffer from comparing our lives with other people's – your new car may be satisfying while no one else in the street has a better one, but as soon as someone turns up with a newer model then you become less satisfied. We're pleased with our pay rise as long as we're the only person to receive one, or if our rise is greater than anyone else's. Students at Harvard University were asked which of two imaginary worlds they would prefer to live in: the first was one in which they would earn $50,000 per year while everyone else earned $25,000; the second was one in which they would earn $100,000 a year and everyone else $250,000. Most people preferred the first choice and opted for a lower actual income that was still higher than most other people's.[19] We compare ourselves with our peers, people with roughly similar lifestyles – the lives of the super-rich are far beyond our reach, while many of us feel comfortably far away from the very poor. Studies of Olympic medallists show that bronze medallists tend to be happier with their medals than silver medallists because they compare themselves to people who did not get a medal at all, while silver medallists believe they just missed a gold.[20] Changing one's point of reference from comparing one's situation to someone less well-off to someone more well-off can be quite stressful. One illustration of this is the case of East Germany. The standard of living for East Germans improved considerably after re-unification in 1990, but happiness levels fell, because instead of comparing their standard of living with other members of the former Soviet Bloc, people compared themselves with the more prosperous West Germans. Previously they had been able to see themselves as better off than their neighbours, but after unification they themselves were the poor neighbours by comparison. Richard Layard sums this up:

> The things we get used to the most easily and take for granted are our material possessions . . . Advertisers understand this and invite us to *feed our addiction* with more and more spending . . . If we do not foresee that we get used to our material possessions, we shall over invest in acquiring them, at the expense of our leisure . . . As a result, our life can get distorted towards working and making money, and away from other pursuits.[21]

We could interpret 'leisure' here to include time for reflection on what we actually want out of life, while we work out the connections between how much we struggle to acquire more possessions and our stress levels. Perhaps working so hard to gain a certain standard of living exacts such a high price from us that it is hard to actually appreciate and enjoy the fruits of our labour.

Remembering and forecasting happiness

So there is evidence to show that when we look at our material circumstances, in other words the things we think we need in order to be happy, we are not skilled at seeing things objectively, or in proportion to their long-term effect on our wellbeing. Do we fare better when we contemplate how things have been for us in the past, or when we try and gauge our needs in the future? Ideally we should be able to accurately review how our past experience has been in order to reasonably predict which choices to make in the future, but a growing body of research is showing that this is not the case. We know, of course, that the future has not happened yet and all we have to go on is our present circumstances with our current likes and dislikes. The trouble is that we rarely take into account how our preferences or circumstances may change – we don't consider that our future selves may see things differently from how we do now.

I have a Danish friend who became a Buddhist nun some years ago. Whenever it's too hot to wear socks I have the treat of seeing a tall, slender woman in long, maroon robes with a tattoo of an iguana coiling up her left ankle. The frisky young woman who, some years back, thought this tattoo would be an addition to her image, apparently did not envisage the possibility of herself as a nun in the future.

A friend of mine worked for an independent company that was taken over by a multi-national. He was in middle management and was one of the people from the old company that the new bosses considered worth keeping on and promoting. He was very anxious to get the job – both for his family's security and for his own career path – and was sure that it would bring him happiness. After a period of anxious waiting he was offered a two-year contract at a higher level of management than before. He had been so worried about the outcome that the relief of getting the job was almost an anti-climax. Now, several months later, he is working longer and longer hours in an increasingly competitive and unfriendly environment and struggles to find a level of satisfaction in his work. He is plagued by the fear of not being able to maintain the pace and style of the 'new' company, even though he does not feel in sympathy with much of their approach. In his old role, he was one of a group of middle managers who supported each other, whereas now he is more senior and alone, with only the top bosses to compare himself to – so he is constantly trying to keep up. His belief that the new job would bring him happiness is an example of how poorly my friend was able to predict how it would turn out for him. We've said several times that happiness can be unpredictable and tricky – and indeed my friend did not accurately predict what would bring him happiness; instead, he adapted very quickly to the desired outcome when it arrived and now suffers from comparing his situation with people in seemingly better ones.

In remembering the past, the way we experience how things end seems to be particularly tricky. Psychologist Daniel Kahneman, who we mentioned earlier, conducted an experiment in which participants were asked to place their hands in cold water. For one group the water was at 14°C and the experience lasted 60 seconds. For the second group the water was at 14°C for 60 seconds and then the experience continued for an additional 30 seconds with the temperature of the water raised to 15°C. When asked which trial people wanted to repeat, the majority chose the second one – the one with a longer period of discomfort.[22] People chose more pain over less because their experience was defined by its ending – in this case, the water becoming marginally warmer. In terms of everyday experience we could equate this with a pleasant evening out with a friend – a delicious meal, good conversation, a great movie, but when we go to collect our car we discover we have been given a parking ticket. The unpleasantness of the parking ticket will override the positive experience and colour our whole recollection of the evening. In our memory it will become, 'that evening I got a parking ticket'. In addition, as we saw in chapter 2, we are programmed to remember negative experiences longer than positive ones because from an evolutionary perspective this helps us to survive. However, if we get caught up in this pattern it can be a painful source of stress.

Happiness, resilience and longevity

In April 2006 the BBC presented a series of six programmes on what they termed the Happiness Formula.[23] As part of their investigation they set up what they termed 'a happy lab' to run various experiments. In one experiment they asked people whose happiness levels they had already tested to see how long they could keep their hands in ice-cold water. (It seems that happiness researchers have a thing about cold water!) At one end of the scale was a young man whose happiness score had been quite low and who managed thirty seconds with his hand in the water. One of the women who had scored highest on the happiness questionnaire still had her hand in the water after six minutes when the tester asked her to take it out. This simple experiment provided convincing evidence of what research is showing – that people with a higher level of happiness and wellbeing have greater resilience and more staying power than their less happy counterparts. We also know that happier people have lower levels of the stress hormone cortisol, high levels of which are linked to type 2 diabetes and hypertension.

So, not surprisingly our wellbeing and health are linked. Perhaps even more remarkable is the relationship between happiness and wellbeing, and longevity. An intake of nuns into a nunnery in Milwaukee in the USA during the 1930s was the subject of a now-famous study. The nuns were asked to write a journal of their lives up until they entered the convent. Some of the journals were joyful and optimistic, others less so. The researchers counted the number of times each nun used a positive or negative word and on the basis of their score divided the nuns into 'happy nuns' and 'not so happy nuns'. After joining the order their lives were almost exactly the same – same food, same work, same routine, but not the same life expectancy. Among the less-positive nuns, two-thirds died before their eighty-fifth birthday, whereas 90 per cent of the happy nuns were still alive. On average the happy nuns lived nine years longer than the not so happy nuns. In an interview on the BBC's *The Happiness Formula*, Ed Diener, a positive psychologist, points out that smoking one packet of cigarettes a day takes on average three years off your life. Discovering this has transformed how we treat cigarette smoking in society, yet with happiness levels we are talking about a difference of nine years.

The presenter of *The Happiness Formula* travelled to visit the nunnery and to attend the 102nd birthday party of Sister Helena, one of the happy nuns. When she was asked for the secret of her long life her answer was this: 'Be accepting of everything that comes to you.' In this simple statement she summed up an attitude of patience and contentment. She was less vulnerable to the vicissitudes of hope and fear that for many of us dominate our interactions with the world. Here is a clue as to the kind of happiness which is worth cultivating and has the potential to act as a basis for reducing stress.

The happiness set point

There is an on-going discussion about what is called the 'happiness set point'.[24] This is a sort of genetic baseline for our level of happiness and wellbeing that we slip over and under as we go through different experiences throughout our lives. We inherit this set point from our parents and it has an influence on how we handle happiness in our lives, but not on our overall capacity for happiness. The theory states that only 50 per cent of our happiness levels are determined by this set point, and 10 per cent by life circumstances. That leaves the remaining 40 per cent within our power to change – so there is plenty of room for manoeuvre. This research gives scientific endorsement to the notion that we have a considerable role to play in deciding on our own level of wellbeing, and consequently on how we manage stress.

Wandering mind and unhappiness

Our tendency to remember events inaccurately and to wrongly anticipate the future has a lot to do with our habit of not paying full attention to what we are doing, but rather going through the motions on a kind of automatic pilot. If we are not fully paying attention in the present then it is going to be hard to gather all the clues we need to make decisions for the future, or to remember clearly enough to assess the past accurately. A recent research programme contributed startling evidence of the link between this habit of allowing the mind to wander and dissatisfaction. Towards the end of 2010 Daniel Gilbert carried out a research study with his doctoral student, Matthew Killingsworth, at Harvard University. Killingsworth designed an iPhone app that contacted 2,250 volunteers over an age range of 18–88 from a variety of socio-economic backgrounds. At random intervals during the day people were asked the following four questions:

– How happy they were at that moment.

– What activity they were engaged in.

– If they were thinking about their current activity.

– If they were thinking about something else that was pleasant, neutral or unpleasant.

The results showed that for almost half their time, the volunteers were thinking about something different from the activity they were engaged with. The study concluded that people spend 46.9 per cent of their waking hours thinking about something other than what they are doing, and this mind wandering typically makes them unhappy. If we think about this in terms of our own lives it means we are missing almost half of our experience on a regular basis – quite an extraordinary statistic.

Killingsworth and Gilbert write,

> A human mind is a wandering mind, and a wandering mind is an unhappy mind. The ability to think about what is not happening is a cognitive achievement that comes at an emotional cost.[25]

Although the human mind has this capacity to wander, it is capable of much more. The habit of wandering can be addressed by using mindfulness and meditation, which have the effect of enabling the mind to calm down and settle. When this happens the mind's capacity to see clearly is enhanced, increasing discernment and leading to a greater degree of self-awareness. With increased self-awareness we are able to see our habits more clearly and make better choices as to how we wish to behave. This is one of the first steps towards self-compassion.

During an interview for the magazine *Shambhala Sun*,[26] Gilbert was asked how we could become more accurate in our assessments of what would make us happy, and develop more self-awareness. He replied that to be really self-aware, a person would have to see their experience clearly at the time of the experience, and they would also have to remember correctly. It is possible to perceive an experience clearly, but then later on get muddled as to what actually happened. We will look into developing self-awareness when we explore mindfulness and meditation in chapter 8.

Exercise: The wandering mind experiment

Try out the wandering mind experiment for yourself.

Set your watch, mobile phone or computer to set off a buzzer at random times during a twelve-hour period and have a notebook ready to record your responses.

When the buzzer goes ask yourself these questions from the study:

Am I happy at the moment? (You could set a scale of 1–10)

What am I doing?

Am I thinking about what I am doing?

Write your responses in your notebook each time.

At the end of the day count up:

How many times you asked yourself these questions.

How many of the times you were happy.

How many of the times you were thinking about something else apart from what you were doing.

Calculate:

How much of the time you were focused on what you were doing.

How much of the time you were happy.

Notice the relationship between the two.

Notice which activities you were paying full attention to.

Notice when you were happy and when you were not.

Pleasure and Happiness

In evolutionary terms, pleasure acts as an incentive for keeping us alive. Most people would list sex and food among their main sources of pleasure – both activities cause the brain to release the chemical dopamine that make us feel happy. While eating keeps us alive, sex ensures our species will continue. This search for good feeling has helped to keep the human race going, but these feelings were designed to be temporary. If we only mated once and never needed to again, we would see a startling fall in the birth rate. So pleasure is something that is so enjoyable that we want to experience it again and again, but it starts out as a temporary state with a specific purpose, not something that will last forever. Sadly, we often seem to find this hard to accept, and our search for wellbeing and happiness can become narrowed down to the pursuit of pleasure and the attempt to hold on to it once we get it – or at least to repeat it as often as we can. There is nothing wrong with enjoying pleasure – we can see how good it can be for us – but grasping on to it is another thing entirely.

Unfortunately, when advertising and peer pressure hook into our delight in pleasure things can turn sour. Instead of increasing our wellbeing, the search for pleasure can become a source of worry and even stress as we strive for the perfection dangled in front of us but always just out of reach, or attempt to hold too tightly to what we already have. A simple experiment illustrates this point. Participants were given a choice between a mug and a sum of money. They were asked to say how much money they would need in order to prefer the cash to the mug. They agreed on a sum of $3.50. Then the participants were given the mug to keep and asked how much money they would need to give it up – the average went up to $7.12.[27] Once we feel something belongs to us, is 'ours', then we place a much greater value on it and want to hold on to it.

The trouble is that we so often mistake transient pleasurable experience for lasting happiness that we can neglect our human capacity for something deeper and more fulfilling. We are no longer functioning at the level where our happiness is based on survival alone, and yet we so often settle for the quick fix, pleasure-based route to happiness, without taking into account the full range of potential effects. Perhaps we feel a bit low, so we surf the internet for a bit, then drink a coffee and check out the news channels on TV. Instead of examining the low feeling, our impulse is to distract ourselves from it – it's as if we are aiming to run our life as a series of good moments, with as few bad ones as possible to interfere with our final score.

Much of the happiness research that has been described in this chapter bears out the temporary nature of pleasure and how this differs from our expectations. Most of us work hard in order to service our needs, but the question is clear: do we really need all that we think we do in order to be

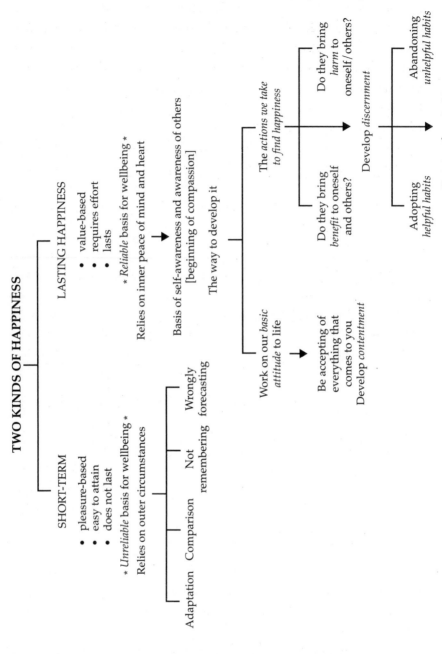

TWO KINDS OF HAPPINESS

SHORT-TERM

- pleasure-based
- easy to attain
- does not last

* *Unreliable* basis for wellbeing *
Relies on outer circumstances

Adaptation   Comparison   Not remembering   Wrongly forecasting

LASTING HAPPINESS

- value-based
- requires effort
- lasts

* *Reliable* basis for wellbeing *
Relies on inner peace of mind and heart

Basis of self-awareness and awareness of others [beginning of compassion]

The way to develop it

Work on our *basic attitude* to life

Be accepting of everything that comes to you
Develop *contentment*

The *actions we take to find happiness*

Do they bring *benefit* to oneself and others?

Do they bring *harm* to oneself/others?

Develop *discernment*

Adopting *helpful habits*

Abandoning *unhelpful habits*

Training the mind in *meditation and compassion*

happy? The research shows that as our lifestyle improves, we set the bar higher in terms of what we want to achieve, often adding to our stress and rarely feeling deeply satisfied. The pleasure of attaining a goal does not last and is undermined by how we view the achievements of other people. What we think will bring happiness often only brings short-term pleasure and too infrequently adds to a deeper feeling of contentment. Our habit of distraction means we are not sufficiently skilled in learning from our experience, or foreseeing how to be happy in the future. However, the research also shows that happiness is important for our wellbeing – our resilience to difficulties such as stress – and even impacts on our longevity. We need to make a shift away from short-term, quick-fix solutions to achieving happiness and instead take a look at a more enduring state of mind.

Lasting Happiness

We've seen that pleasure is based on external circumstances, such as our job, where we live, what we like to eat, and although the benefits are short-term we can often mistake this for happiness, overlooking the possibility of something more reliable. A more helpful view is to say that there are two kinds of happiness: the short-term, pleasure-based experience and a more lasting happiness. The first kind is much easier to attain than the deeper happiness, which requires effort but once established serves as a reliable basis for wellbeing. Although in seeking short-term pleasure we are trying to improve our lives, ironically the fruits of this search often have adverse effects because repeatedly we are let down by the results. For example, perhaps we have our heart set on moving to the country-side and when we actually manage to bring it about, we find we miss the city and are lonely and isolated from our friends. Stress can occur easily when we feel that our aspirations are thwarted and undermined – so we work harder in order to obtain more possessions, have better holidays and wear the latest fashions. Sadly, the harder we try, the tighter the spiral of effort–disappointment–stress–renewed-effort becomes. The trouble is that initially our strategy works – as the research shows, short-term happiness does give us a rush of pleasure. This is the trap that we fall into again and again. Developing lasting happiness is much harder – there is rarely an initial flood of pleasure, although there can often be a sense of relief that at last we have found something we can count on. However, we need to work at it regularly and over the longer term. On occasion it can seem beyond our ability to sustain this feeling, and then it is so much easier to simply go and buy the latest gadget in order to feel better about life. Giving ourselves the time and space to explore and develop this lasting happiness is one of the deepest acts of self-compassion we can engage in and marks the first step in using compassion to reduce stress.

So how do we access this deeper kind of happiness? Firstly, we need to recognize that it is not about looking outwards, but depends on having an inner peace of mind and heart. This is the basis for self-awareness and the awareness of others – the foundation of compassion – that enables us to view our actions and those of other people with greater clarity. It can be developed by working with both our basic attitude and with the actions we take while trying to be happy.

To start with, take our basic attitude to life. This is going to be influenced by our happiness set point, but remember there is 40 per cent room for manoeuvre. Recall what the 102-year-old nun Sister Helena advised: '*Be accepting of everything that comes to you.*' She is describing a kind of contentment that could be seen as a basic attitude to life that enables us to deal with patience and a favourable outlook with everything that comes. This is not about being a doormat, but about developing a willingness to engage with life as it comes, rather than trying to insist that it somehow be different. We could say it is the foundation of peace of mind and heart, and the more we can cultivate it, the more reliable it becomes. It has the potential to be a safeguard against stress.

Next we can begin to look closely at the actions we take in order to be happy. There is a simple question we can use here as a measure of whether or not our actions will be a source of lasting happiness: *do they bring real benefit to oneself and others, or not?* Actions that bring benefit automatically result in happiness and, as we will see later, are important elements in training our compassion. We need to develop a clear sense of discernment to enable us to analyse our actions clearly in the light of this question, and to identify the habits that lead us away from lasting happiness even if they initially seem to bring pleasure.

This is the way to start the process of training our own mind to become more useful to us. It is the first step in learning to become compassionate towards ourselves, and the first step towards coping with stress. In fact, as we increase our ability to discern in this way we begin to cut through our normal responses to stress. This is because we learn to recognize that such responses are not useful for us, or for others. We may not be able to achieve this all in one go but we can learn to notice our responses more and more often and to remember them more quickly. This is what training the mind is – abandoning unhelpful habits and adopting new, more helpful ones. This brings us back to self-awareness, which we will come to in chapter 8.

As we learn how to work with our mind to understand our own happiness, the next natural step is to increase our understanding of other people and their wish for happiness. We are all hoping for happiness, but at the same time fearing that we may not be able to achieve it, or hold on to it. It is this tension – between hoping for happiness and fearing its loss – that leads us to stress, as we shall explore in the next chapter.

KEY POINTS

- Everyone wants to be happy and to avoid pain and suffering, but how we go about trying to be happy does not always bring the results we hope for and can even result in stress.

- Happiness is trickier than we thought and much less reliable – hoping for it can even be a source of stress – whereas suffering can present us with challenges that can in the end be beneficial.

- Recently scientists have discovered how to 'measure' happiness by monitoring blood flow to the emotional centres of the brain.

- Current research into happiness shows us that:
  - Technology has not resulted in giving us more free time.
  - The amount of choice we have can be overwhelming.
  - Improvements in our standard of living do not necessarily lead to an increase in happiness.
  - We adapt to what we have and then want more.
  - We compare what we have to what others have.
  - We remember causes of happiness inaccurately and are not good at forecasting what will make us happy in the future.
  - 40 per cent of our potential for happiness is in our own hands.
  - Happiness can improve our resilience and even our chances of living longer.
  - 46.9 per cent of the time we are not focused on what we are doing and this makes us dissatisfied.

- There are two kinds of happiness:
  - Short-term, easily attained, pleasure-based.
  - Lasting happiness, requires effort, value-based.

- Lasting happiness can be developed through peace of mind and heart, and self-awareness.
  - It is a powerful source of self-compassion and a starting point for compassion for other people.
  - Contentment is a good starting point.

EXERCISES

Exercise 1: Everybody wants happiness and to avoid suffering

As you go about your daily life try to bring this phrase to mind whenever you are with other people. What effect does it have on how you view them?

Note down what you experience.

Exercise 2: Be accepting of everything that comes to you

Choose one day in the week and take this statement as a focus for your day.

What difficulties do you experience in trying to do this?

What effect does it have on your levels of stress?

Note down what you experience.

Exercise 3: Adaptation

Notice how you adapt to each new possession in your life, for example a new piece of clothing, a new car, a new sound system.

What does this tell you?

Exercise 4: Comparison

Observe whenever you find yourself comparing your situation with that of other people.

Do not judge your reaction, just notice it.

How does it make you feel?

Exercise 5: Anticipating what will make us happy

Think of a time when you were planning an event that was designed to make you happy, for example a holiday, an outing, a party, decorating your bedroom. Try to remember:

What worked and what did not.

What went according to plan and what did not.

What was better than you hoped.

What was worse than you hoped.

Were there any surprises?

What can you learn from this in terms of planning for happiness?

6 The Suffering We Wish to Avoid

It may seem strange that some people's first move into compassion is through their rage at and sense of injustice about the suffering of life.

Professor Paul Gilbert[1]

Knowing that We Suffer

Our investigation of happiness in the last chapter shows clearly that however much we may wish for happiness, it is not as easy to find, nor as reliable as we may have thought. Although our wish is to find happiness and avoid pain, life just does not work like that. Difficult things can happen to us at any time, and even the good things may have an undertone of sadness because we know they cannot last forever.[2] However, it is not easy to look at your life and admit that suffering is a deep thread that runs through it. A friend of mine spent time in Sydney, Australia recently and he commented on what a wonderful lifestyle people there seem to have – great beaches, fun cafés and an amazing climate. How can people like that ever be unhappy? It is an important question and one that demands a great deal of thought because there is a lot to learn from the answer.

The big sources of pain and distress in our lives are not hard to spot because they stare us in the face. From the moment we are born our bodies are on a conveyor belt of change, growth and eventual disintegration. No sooner are we 'grown up' and able to enjoy the independence of adulthood, than our bodies start to age and develop unwanted wrinkles, extra bulk and various aches and pains. Unfortunately, most of us will face serious illness at some time in our lives and, as we all know, at some point our time will run out and we will die. Depending on where we live, natural disasters can strike at any time – floods, earthquakes and drought affect large areas of the planet. In some parts of the world, people live under the burden of famine, war and social unrest. Throughout our lives we will be subject to a number of sources of unhappiness rooted in the society we live in – economic collapse, political upheaval, crime and violence. Then there are mishaps and accidents – things we try to avoid do happen, things we don't want to be taken from us are lost. For example, we may fail an important exam even though we worked hard for it; our car may come off the road on a foggy night; the promotion we've planned for may be given to someone else and the friend we love dearly may go to live in another country. All of this is the backdrop to our lives. We hope it will never happen to us but we know it could – or if not to us, then to someone we care about. This lends a sense of insecurity to everything we do. Perhaps many of us are familiar with the feeling that life is just not that easy to get a handle on, and people and situations can change in ways one never imagined. It is possible that this feeling increases with experience when we have been hurt, failed to take up certain opportunities, or carry regrets and memories tinged with sadness. It is no wonder that we can feel stressed from time to time, and that in modern times stress has become one of the most widespread manifestations of suffering.

Added to this, we also experience all kinds of everyday, small travails that in themselves do not seem to amount to much but which, when we add up all the wear and tear they impose on us, can also be sources of stress. Whether you live in the sun in Australia, or in the chillier climate of northern Europe, you still need to wake up, shower, dress and get to work most days. Food does not arrive prepared and nicely served on the plate – we need to shop and cook and, even worse, wash up! Only a small minority of people get their houses cleaned for them, or their clothes ironed. We may look at someone else and think that their lifestyle has to be easier, or happier or less stressful than our own. Often that is just not the case.

The problem is – we fear suffering, and because we are afraid of it we try and pretend it is not there. We focus on pursuing happiness. That way we never get to the bottom of what might be causing us pain, never mind trying to do something about it. As we heard in chapter 3, this tendency is increased by our 'drive' system, which leads us to turn away from suffering and try to ignore it. The importance of developing self-awareness is one of the central themes of this book. As our self-awareness increases we can see our unhelpful or unhealthy habits more clearly and so gain insight into the actions we take that are useful for us, and the actions which in fact undermine ourselves. This opens up the possibility for change – self-awareness is transformative. It is hard to help ourselves if we cannot see our difficulties clearly. So to examine our pain and our stress is not, ultimately, a depressing task. If we can try to look at our lives realistically and see our suffering clearly – with tenderness and a gentle humour – then we have the possibility to learn some important things about how we live and what changes we need to make in order to reduce our stress levels. Our pain can become an inspiration to make changes.

The realization that everyone is in the same situation – everyone has their own kinds of suffering and stress, whoever they are, however they live – can also be helpful to us. Realizing that we are not the only ones to suffer is one of the foundation stones of compassion. When we are able to see suffering and stress as an inevitable part of life and so learn to take it less personally, then we are able to relax to some extent – we see that things are not all calculated to make life difficult just for us! In that relaxation comes an easing of our focus on ourselves and so there is room to see how things are for other people and how, to a large extent, we are all in the same boat. Realizing this can touch a deep tenderness in us, as we see how pervasive suffering is. Just as we wish not to suffer ourselves, we are moved to want to help relieve other people from their suffering – remember in chapter 3 we talked about this as the essence of compassion. When we are in the grip of stress it may seem unlikely that we would have the time or inclination to spare a thought for the stress of others. However, as Professor Gilbert suggests in the quote at the beginning of this chapter, one of the surprises of training the mind in compassion is how an understanding of our own suffering can lead to more understanding of and concern for the suffering of others, and that in this there is a seed for our own relief. We will look into how this happens in chapter 12.

The thing to remember is that it is hard to truly care about how other people suffer if we are not able to look at our own difficulties in the first place. If we are tightly focused on avoiding recognizing and understanding pain and simply want to feel good about life, then we are creating an unrealistic worldview that closes off our capacity for compassion. Sadly, instead of protecting us, as we imagine it will, it prevents us both from healing our own pain and at the same time distances us from others.

An additional benefit of developing this awareness of other people's struggles is that it helps us to see our own in a different light and to feel less critical of ourselves. If everyone is going through similar experiences then we do not need to feel bad about having difficulties of our own.

Understanding What Causes Suffering

In chapter 3 we looked at how interdependence underpins the whole logic of compassion and how often we are not aware of its full extent. Nowhere is this more the case than when we look at our self. When we consider the person we believe ourselves to be, we tend to think in terms of our job, our family history, our nationality, our gender, our education and so on, and yet these are only the outer circumstances of who we are that have come together at various times in our life and are subject to change. If we go deeper we may describe our *feelings* about our self, our *hopes* and our *aspirations,* but again this is a description of our thoughts and emotions rather than of our *self.* The person we were when we were ten years old is not the same person that we are now. Not only do we look very different, with altered life circumstances and interests – the kind of toys we choose to play with have certainly changed – but the physical make-up of our body has almost completely altered as well. In fact the person that we were yesterday does not have all the experience of the person we are today – even the last twenty-four hours will have brought a wealth of thoughts, feelings, impressions and activities that have moved us on from where we were this time yesterday. How we are at home is rarely exactly the same as the person we are at work. When we are in a parent role we are not the same as when we are with our own parents, or with our lover, or friends. This self that we see as 'me' or 'myself', that in my case carries the label 'Maureen', is in fact not one single independent entity but a mass of interconnected elements that are themselves interconnected to other sets of elements and so on.

Some time ago, a friend of mine left his home to do some shopping. While he was out he suffered a mild stroke that affected the parts of his brain to do with comprehension. One moment he was in his car driving to the supermarket, and the next he was by the side of the road not knowing what he was doing or how he got there. For a few days he had no idea of who he was and how he fitted into the world around him. It must have been so profoundly frightening that it is hard to imagine. It brought home to me with renewed intensity the reality of change and interdependence – my friend left his house as 'himself' and returned not knowing who he was. He could not even call on his home environment to help him piece his notion of himself back together. It is so easy to assume that this self, this 'Maureen', is a constant entity moving along through life rather than a combination of ever-changing facets that shift every moment in relation to a variety of other shifting and changing people and circumstances.

Our inability to view life in this way is the basis of suffering. We all do it. The point is not to feel bad about it but to realize what we're doing and try something different. Lacking awareness of the way that we are connected to circumstances and to other people, and avoiding the reality of impermanence and change, means that we assume things are one way when they are in fact quite different. Because we don't acknowledge the constant flow of change throughout life, we try to hold on to our position by going after the things we think will strengthen us and by avoiding the things we think will harm us, or cause us stress. Even though life constantly moves and changes we are not able to see this as the natural course of events but tend to see it as threatening, and so we tighten our grip even further, which limits our compassion. So instead of taking things as we find them without judgement, which we find painful, we develop increasingly sophisticated habits in order to avoid facing reality. These habits then cause us further suffering as they limit us more and more.

When we are faced with stressful circumstances, it becomes all too easy to strike out in protest rather than see such events as an inevitable part of life that affects us all. It is extremely hard work to maintain this limited attitude (that refuses to acknowledge interdependence and impermanence) in the face of all the evidence of real life. It exhausts us and leads to all kinds of stressful reactions, which undermine our ability to feel contented. Becoming aware of the habits we learn in a misguided attempt to keep ourselves safe, and understanding that they cause us pain, are the first steps in learning how to change them.

Transforming our Suffering

If our limited view of the nature of things is one of the causes of suffering, then it follows that changing this view will help reduce stress. This ties back into one of our central themes – the importance of awareness. We saw in chapter 3 how awareness is an element in our fundamental 'wholeness' and a crucial element in our wellbeing, but we need to develop it, to bring it out. We can develop our awareness through meditation.

By practising meditation we can uncover the ways our mind overlooks change and impermanence, interconnectedness and interdependence, and all the patterns we fall into because of this. In the last chapter we learnt that research carried out on distraction and the wandering mind has revealed that for almost half of our waking hours we are not paying full attention to what we are doing. When we are distracted in this way we miss what is going on around us because our mind is not settled enough to see clearly and understand events. However, our mind has a need to keep the narrative of our lives constant, and to fill in any gaps, so that these lapses in concentration are filled in with assumption rather than fact. These assumptions build up as further layers of misperception, clouding our awareness and leading to more unhelpful habits of thought.

Imagine having an argument with someone at work who frequently annoys you. Perhaps your colleague is late for a deadline and this is going to put you in a tight spot. This is not the first time this has happened in fact, you think the person is a pretty lazy worker and gets too

UNDERSTANDING WHAT CAUSES SUFFERING

ROOT CAUSE: Our mistaken belief that things are independent and permanent

RESULT: We misperceive how things really are

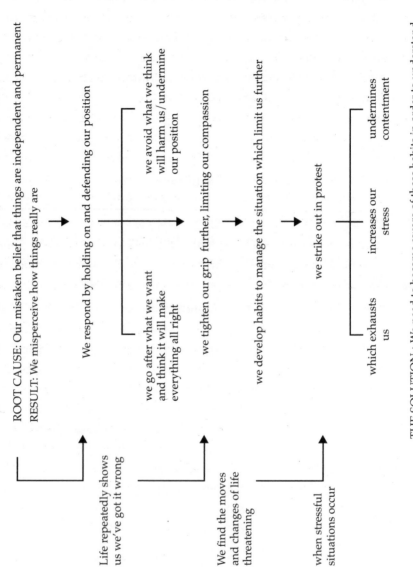

We respond by holding on and defending our position

we avoid what we think will harm us / undermine our position

we go after what we want and think it will make everything all right

we tighten our grip further, limiting our compassion

we develop habits to manage the situation which limit us further

we strike out in protest

undermines contentment

increases our stress

which exhausts us

Life repeatedly shows us we've got it wrong

We find the moves and changes of life threatening

when stressful situations occur

THE SOLUTION * We need to become aware of these habits in order to understand why we suffer and learn to replace them with useful habits * much leeway from your joint boss. As your colleague tries to explain to you that they are late with their piece of work because they were up all night with their daughter being sick, your mind is whirring with feelings of resentment and irritation. Because of all these thoughts and emotions, you do not really listen to what they are saying and miss the chance to express sympathy and work out a solution to the problem together. Our tendency, however, is not to realize we are doing this. We do not recognize that we have failed to pay attention to the full situation, and instead are indulging in a stream of judgement. In this case, this means that the relationship between you and your colleague deteriorates further, having missed an opportunity to come closer. It means that the next time there is a misunderstanding between you, you will remember how resentful you felt and your colleague will remember how unsympathetic you were. You have both been pushed further apart and your negative opinions of each other have taken a firmer hold.

In meditation, our mind calms down and begins to settle, so it becomes possible to see what is going on with us, and around us, more clearly. In this state, we are more likely to recognize that some of the habits that we have developed as a means of self-protection are not only useless to us but sometimes even harmful. Our self-imposed limitations are unnecessary and obstructive. Meditation allows our mind to settle into its natural state of awareness. It has been found to be one of the most effective and sustainable ways of reducing stress – in other words, once we learn to meditate we have a technique to hand which can help us to address stress as it happens. As a means of helping us develop peace of mind, meditation is also a way to develop lasting happiness. Because of this, learning to meditate is one of the most profound acts of self-compassion possible. We will look at how to meditate in more detail in chapter 8.

Tools to Help Us

In meditation practice and compassion training we can find a series of methods that can help us reduce the suffering of stress and transform our attitude to it. Too often, we are not in the habit of using our mind to achieve contentment, but it is possible to learn how to do this and the tools exist to enable us to do so.

As we have discussed in this chapter, firstly we need to be able to see our problems clearly from the basis of a peaceful mind and compassionate heart. Furthermore, we need to see that the causes of these problems are in part connected to our own emotions and that how we react to the situations we get into is connected to our inner state of mind. In the example of the work colleague we just looked at, we can see that there was an emotional reaction that triggered an exaggerated reaction, which made the situation worse. How we react to particular situations will help determine how they turn out. If we wish to work with difficult circumstances then we need to work on what is going on inside us – our emotional reactions and opinions about what is happening to us. The good news is that we are not hardwired into our habits. We can reduce stress because we have the ability to transform our thought processes. As we shall see when we look into neuroplasticity in later chapters, our brain is malleable and can change in relation to our experience. It is possible to change how we respond to what life throws at us and therefore to change how we feel. We can use meditation and training the mind in compassion to make this happen.

Paul was a CEO of an organization supporting the homeless in the UK. He had been hired to turn it around after a period of poor management and loss of volunteer support. He was passionate about his work and cared deeply about the people his organization was set up to help. However, instead of this being inspirational for his staff, he often came over as judgemental, hard to please and a poor listener. Paul was not able to communicate his own inspiration because his enthusiasm made him feel vulnerable to accusations of naivety, and yet he badly wanted to succeed. Instead of engaging his staff in his vision for the organization, he adopted a top-down management style based on his word as law. After his first six months in the job, several of his staff were sufficiently frustrated to think about looking for new jobs and the volunteer numbers were not improving. Unable to see the connection between his style of leadership and the behaviour of his staff, Paul was ready to let them go and hire replacements but at this point his deputy Martin intervened.

Martin had attended a training course on communication skills for managers that included meditation and compassion training. Plucking up his courage, he went to see Paul and during a long and difficult meeting managed to broach the topic of Paul's negative style of communication. Martin tried to get Paul to see that by not opening up to his staff about his vision for the organization he appeared not to trust them and that by being so bossy and judgemental he was undermining their self-confidence. Paul was shocked. He had been so caught up in his passion to help the homeless, his feelings of vulnerability and his fear of failure that he had not realized the effect his behaviour had on others. He had not seen the extent of his own stress in striving to succeed and he certainly had not seen that *his* stress was *causing* stress to his staff. Martin helped Paul to see that there was a problem in the first place, and then he gave him an insight into how his own state of mind and emotional habits were a factor in the disappointing results he was getting from the staff and volunteers. Slowly Paul was able to see that what he thought was a straightforward lack of enthusiasm on the part of his staff was in fact the result of a combination of his own hopes and fears and those of his staff. The staff just wanted a boss who would guide them creatively and enable them to do a good job but in his very wish to do a good job himself, Paul was stifling enthusiasm and causing himself stress.

After his initial conversation with Martin had broken the ice, Paul took him into his confidence and asked him to share with him some of the techniques of communication he had learnt on his course. Then Paul spent quiet time at home over a weekend trying to identify the habits he had fallen into which had proven to be so unhelpful. He recognized that it would help him and others if he was able to talk to his staff about his vision in an inspiring way without fear of feeling exposed. He thought about delegating more work and adopting a more consensual form of decision-making. He even tried a bit of the meditation technique that Martin had shared with him and was surprised to find that it helped him to relax more and to sleep better at night. Furthermore, he came to see that he and his staff were engaged in a joint venture to help the homeless and that if he could not express some empathy for the people he worked with, he was not going to be of much use to their clients.

Like many of us, Paul needed help to recognize that there was a problem, but once he saw it he was able to accept his part in it. Having done that he took time to work out the causes of the problem and the part his habits had played in it. He decided on steps to try and improve things and was open to new methods such as meditation to help him to do this effectively.

Perceiving Suffering

Last year a friend of mine was diagnosed with cancer. Fortunately it was in its early stages and treatable but, still, the experience of having cancer is intense, frightening and sometimes lonely. She had surgery, which went well, and was then prescribed radiotherapy. She described to me what it was like to be a patient in a radiology outpatients' department of a large, busy hospital. Having been through several weeks of convalescence, suddenly she found herself part of a community of people all undergoing the same kind of treatment. Her own treatment consisted of twenty-eight daily visits excluding weekends. Over the course of this she often ran into the same people having their daily session and saw that there was a sense of everyone going through something together. She told me that being with people who were recovering from cancer, just as she was, was a profoundly moving experience. There were people there she felt she could have made friends with and there were others with whom she felt little in common except the experience of this illness. The patients were from all kinds of cultural backgrounds and social classes. There were people older than her and some younger. Some people came with their sons or daughters, others with their husbands or wives. All these differences faded into insignificance, she said, as each was joined by the experience of going through cancer. Each person was facing their own fears and anxieties about their illness and the changes in their lives. No one wanted to be in the hospital and yet, faced with the necessity of treatment, each person was facing it with their own courage and fortitude.[3]

Suffering is an inevitable part of life, and our circumstances and who we are change all the time. It is natural to long for happiness and wish to avoid pain but in the process we can find ourselves mistakenly grasping at happiness and trying to push away any suffering we encounter, increasing its power to hurt us as well as depriving ourselves of the opportunity to learn something about ourselves. Every circumstance has a cause and effect – some actions will lead to happiness, others to unhappiness. It is by working with these causes that we will learn to transform the suffering of stress. At the same time, the way in which we perceive the difficulties that come our way determines how we deal with them and the effect they have on us. If we take them personally and feel that our troubles are worse than anyone else's, then we are shutting ourselves off from being able to change our reactions. Stress is one way to respond to suffering but it is only one of a range of responses that we can draw on. The trouble is that we can get into the habit of getting stressed. It is helpful to be able to see how this happens so that we can try a different approach.

My mother contracted breast cancer in her seventies – a disease she had particularly feared all her life. She was angry and confused by what was happening to her and seemed unable to draw on her Christian faith to support her. In one conversation we shared I tentatively suggested that thinking of all the women who were suffering as she was could possibly help her to have a different perspective. I was concerned that she would think me unfeeling but I will never forget the change that came over her at my words – she relaxed and gave the sweetest smile as she told me that she had already been thinking of them each day in her prayers and that wishing them well helped her very much indeed. It was a living example for me of how thinking of others with compassion helps in coping with one's own suffering and pain.

KEY POINTS

- Recognizing and understanding the causes of our suffering will help us to change it.

- Stress is a manifestation of suffering.

- Recognizing that suffering is an inevitable part of life touches a deep tenderness in us which is the basis of compassion.

- Suffering is caused by our misperception of how things are – we think things are independent – in other words, capable of standing alone and never going to change – when the opposite is true.

- We can address this misperception by developing our quality of awareness through the practice of meditation.

- Meditation is one of the most effective ways to work with stress and is an act of self-compassion.

EXERCISES

Exercise 1: Seeing our pain as it is, is a tremendous help

Spend time reflecting on this statement.

Can you relate to it in a positive way?

Make a note of what you experience.

Exercise 2

As you go about your daily life try to notice when you attempt to avoid discomfort, uncertainty, anxiety.

Does it work?

Can you think of a different approach?

Make a note of what you experience.

Exercise 3

Try to remember how everything is changing as you go about your daily life.

How does this make you feel?

Does this change your perspective on what is happening? How?

Make a note of what you experience.

Conclusion to Part 1

In Part 1 of this book, we have looked at what we understand by 'stress' and 'compassion' and learnt how our physical make-up is related to both. We have seen that as we go through life we tend to hope for happiness and fear suffering, but that happiness is both more important and more elusive than we think it is and that suffering is an inevitable part of life. We experience stress when our pursuit of happiness is interrupted and the suffering that we do not want comes to us anyway. However, there are other options open to us apart from a stress response and in Parts 2 and 3 we will look at what those are.

PART 2

Seeing Where We Want to Change

This is the part of the book where we begin to look at how we want to change. We've seen the reality of stress and how it can affect us, and we have seen how working more closely with compassion can help us on many levels. However, the ways in which we experience both stress and compassion will depend on how our mind reacts to situations that we face, and so it is useful to spend some time looking at how our mind works. If we are going to make changes in how we deal with stress we are going to have to drop the habits we have that increase our stress, and look at replacing them with habits that help us reduce those feelings – such as Compassionate Mind techniques. In chapter 7 we will examine how our mind works and look at what we understand by 'habits' and how to go about changing them. Chapter 8 introduces mindfulness and meditation techniques and explains how these techniques can help us use our mind in ways that are more useful for us, and help us to change our unhelpful habits. In chapter 9 we will look more closely at the unhelpful habits we need to let go of and chapter 10 will look at the new habits we need to adopt in their place – the habits of compassion.

7 Taking a Fresh Look at our Habits

Mind is its own place and in itself
Can make a heaven of hell and a hell of heaven.

John Milton[1]

The Mind that Experiences Stress and Compassion

So far, we have talked about understanding, working with and even train-ing the mind. How our mind reacts is an important factor determining how we are affected by the suffering that life can throw our way as well as the stressful situations that we all have to face occasionally. We have already glimpsed the importance of the mind in working to reduce stress and to develop compassion. This is a fundamental theme in using compassion as a means of reducing stress – in order to really get to grips with our stress and develop compassion we need to be aware of and ready to change how our mind responds to our experience. It is more than likely that we have all had experiences that bear out the quotation above from the poet John Milton. Perhaps we may call it our 'mood' but we know that if we are in a positive frame of mind we feel that we can handle more or less anything that comes along, whereas if we are feeling down, even going out for a birthday treat can seem like nothing more than an obligation. How our mind reacts will determine how we will engage in whatever we are doing, but for the most part we rarely realize this and look to factors *outside* our-selves as the causes of whatever mood we may find ourselves in. In this chapter we will start to look at ways of working with our mind more sys-tematically before moving on to meditation techniques in the next chapter.

Accepting that our mind needs training is a process in itself. After all, we use our mind all the time and it seems to more or less keep up with everything we require of it – why bother to ask it to do more? In order to answer this question, let's begin with a simple exercise.

Exercise: 'Watching' our mind

Take a moment now to look up from the page and 'watch' your mind – just observe its movement and activity.

If you like you could break it down into three steps:

First, connect with your *body* and allow yourself to 'check in' with it, to become aware of how it is feeling.

Do you have any discomfort, any tightness? Perhaps you feel hungry, or a little tired, or just simply relaxed.

Just notice these feelings without judgement if you can.

Next, check in on your *mood*.

Is it relaxed, or a little tense?

Just notice the emotions that move through your awareness.

Finally, notice the *thoughts* that come and go in your mind.

It could go something like this: perhaps you start out by thinking about my asking you to do this and form an intention to try and go along with it, but maybe also random thoughts come into your mind. You might start thinking about what you are going to do this evening, for example, if you need to go shopping for supper – then you remember that you cooked last night as well but because your partner is working late tonight you offered to cook again. You feel a bit put out about this and then immediately feel guilty because you did offer. At the same time you remember that you are going away for the weekend in the countryside and you spend a few moments reflecting on how much you are looking forward to it – except, oh gosh, you meant to buy a new pair of decent walking shoes, now when can you manage to find the time to go shopping? Just as you are trying to work that out, you notice that your back is aching and that actually you are feeling a bit tired and your mind jumps back to having to cook the supper. You wonder if getting a takeaway would be a good idea and then you remember that your favourite place has closed down and you'd need to try somewhere new – mmm, risky . . .

Do you get the picture?

This exercise shows us that part of the trouble with our mind is that we keep it so occupied there is rarely an opportunity to just let it be. Most of the time our experience of our own mind is covered over with layers of thoughts and feelings and subsequent thoughts about those thoughts and feelings. Then there is sensory information pouring in all the time, such as the noises and smells around us, and this gets caught up in the tumble of activity going on so that the way we process this information can get quite skewed!

We are so used to our mind being hyperactive that we take this state for granted and believe that that is how the mind naturally is, but this is not the case – in fact, it would be more helpful to take a step back and observe our mind. This way we might get some kind of a handle on how our mind behaves and learn to access its innate power and intelligence. As long as we don't do that our mind will run wild. How often do you settle down to a task requiring concentration, only to find yourself day-dreaming, checking your email or making another cup of coffee? We have developed a habit of letting our mind roam around, and we have been perfecting this habit for such a very long time that it seems to be normal. It's as if long ago, in a moment of boredom, we hired an entertainer to keep us always occupied and busy but then he moved in, became one of the family and refused to leave – and now we are stuck with him!

The movement of thoughts and emotions is natural to the mind – there is nothing wrong with it. Remember in chapter 2, when we compared a human getting away from a sabre-toothed tiger to a gazelle, and how we noted that humans are specially evolved to think, image, plan, anticipate and ruminate? Indeed, this is why we need *training* to focus and take control of our attention. Moreover, trouble comes when we treat these thoughts and emotions as solid and real. We have thoughts we like and become attached to, but we also have thoughts we feel bad about or are even frightened by. These are the mental loops we discussed earlier – we all know what it is like to have a worry nagging away in our mind and what it feels like to churn it over and over looking for a solution. Actually we are making it worse by focusing on it more than ever. This gives our thoughts a tremendous power over us – when in fact, they are just *thoughts* that will come and go and be replaced by others, on and on. Rather than identifying with them so strongly and accepting them as *real*, we could even consider watching this parade of thoughts just as we would watch a movie – seeing them unfold before our eyes with a certain tolerance and distance, perhaps even humour!

We mentioned Daniel Kahneman's work on happiness and memory in chapter 5. Part of his work involves research that has led him to con-clude that the mind has two aspects – the 'experiencing' aspect and the 'evaluating' [judging] aspect. Calculating that one moment of awareness is three seconds long, and that each day of our lives contains 20,000 moments of awareness, Kahneman has come to the conclusion that only part of our self relates to this sequence of moments that make up our life. He calls this the 'experiencing self', the aspect of our self that is living in the present – fresh, awake and experiencing each moment as it happens. However, this aspect is mostly overrun by the 'evaluating [judging] self', which is based on memory and concerned with making our life into a continuous story – keeping score and maintaining records.[2] It is here that we go over and over events that have happened in the past, and plan and anticipate events still to come, trying to turn our stream of experiences into a continuous whole in order to make sense of them. In so doing we cover up the individual moments of our experience, numbing our perception and dulling our reactions. We'll find out more about this when we look at mindfulness in the next chapter.

This research is strikingly consistent with Buddhist ideas about the mind, which in simple terms makes a distinction between the busy, distracted aspect of mind and the clear, unobstructed quality of awareness that is the mind's true nature. We are more familiar with Kahneman's evaluating mind – our thoughts and emotions that engage our attention around the clock. However, Kahneman's experiencing mind – we could say the essence of our mind – is how our mind is when it is not stirred up by all these thoughts and emotions. When we were discussing our fundamental wholeness in chapter 3 we used the example of pouring mud into a glass of water and watching how the water first gets cloudy and then, as the glass remains still, settles and becomes clear again. Our essential nature of mind is like the clear water and is the foundation of who we are. In spite of all the activity of our thoughts and emotions, this clear awareness is always available to us and, as we learn to access it, we can learn to tame the activity of our minds.

In order to understand this better let's look at another analogy. Imagine a clear blue sky with the sun shining brightly. Very simply, the mind in its natural state is like this – calm, spacious and limitless like the sky, with a clear, sparkling awareness that could be compared to the sun. We can take the analogy further and say that the rays of the sun are like our capacity for compassion arising from our natural state of awareness. Now imagine a sky that is overcast and pretty cloudy – this is more like how the mind is on a daily basis. The clouds represent our thoughts and emotions, with all our inclination to dwell on our thoughts, our hopes and fears, our habit of wanting one thing and not wanting another and of clinging to the past while also anticipating the future. Just as on a cloudy day we can almost forget there is a clear blue sky above the clouds, so when our mind is occupied with all kinds of thoughts and emotions we can forget what our natural state really is. Some days perhaps we can see quite a bit of sky and there are attractive fluffy clouds moving across it. These are 'good' days for us, when we are not feeling too stressed or busy, and can keep a sense of proportion. However, we all know what a storm sky looks like, with dark, boiling clouds that seem to loom right down on top of us. These are the times of real mental turmoil and distress when our stress levels can seem unmanageable and it feels like there is no way through.

The thing to do here is to change our perspective. Generally speaking we view the sky from the perspective of the ground, whereas when we travel in a plane and look down on the clouds everything looks quite different. A panorama of clouds viewed from above appears quite beautiful and enticing. The cloud cover may be thick but it is lit by the sun and moving in all kinds of fascinating patterns and shapes. It does not look threatening or frightening in any way.

Learning to look at the clouds from the perspective of the sky involves changing our habits and does not happen overnight but, the thing is, once we are able to do it even for a few moments, it brings tremendous benefit and quickly becomes much easier to do. Changing perspective in this way can be compared to observing our mind from the viewpoint of its natural qualities of spaciousness (as represented by the sky) and awareness (as represented by the sun). Instead of restricting the mind with endless activity, this shift in perspective opens up a space that provides the opportunity to change how we react to things. Remembering that there is more to our mind than all this busyness completely changes the possibilities open to us. It starts to seem possible to be able to take that step back in order to look at how our mind is and when we do, to be able to regard our thoughts and emotions as transient, so there is no need to try and hold on to them. Working with our mind immediately seems like a worthwhile, even essential endeavour. We will look at this in a more practical way when we look at the techniques to help us apply compassion to stress in Part 3.

Choosing How to React

Consider for a moment this quote from Viktor Frankl, who was an Austrian neurologist and psychiatrist as well as a Holocaust survivor and author:

> Everything can be taken from a man but one thing: the last of the human freedoms – to choose one's attitude in any given set of circumstances, to choose one's own way.[3]

So often in life we can feel that we have very little choice in the situations that we face and this can make us feel a loss of control, or even a sense of helplessness. Frankl's observation, based on the terrible events he witnessed in the concentration camps of the Second World War, is that whatever we face and however hemmed in we are by our circumstances, we can still choose how we react. The choices we make will depend on our mental state at any given moment – if our mind is suffused with anger and pain we are more likely to respond with aggression, but if our mind is calm and clear, we have the possibility of reacting with compassion. This is not easy, but learning to change our habits gives us the choice as to how we want to react. While we are bound by our habitual ways of reacting to things, we will keep repeating the same old patterns – and the more often we retread the same patterns the more entrenched they become.

When we feel stressed our response is often to turn away from the feeling by trying to suppress it, by denying it, or by trying to distract ourselves from it and comfort ourselves. How often have you gone shopping or switched on the TV to distract yourself from feeling stressed? These are classic responses and there is nothing wrong with them in the short term. Sometimes taking a short break from our stress can help to give us perspective. However, if distraction is our main strategy for dealing with stress then it is a different story. Continuously trying to avoid the issue and provide ourselves with short-term comfort can reduce our ability to choose how we truly want to react because we are preventing ourselves from seeing clearly what the situation requires. This means we aren't able to be discerning about how we wish to react – we are simply avoiding the problem. So the first step in reducing our stress is to learn to *turn towards our stress*, to face it and to try to see what lessons it is showing us. Just doing this brings about an important change. Although it is likely to be hard to do at first and may show us things about ourselves that we are not very comfortable with, it is a vital first step in learning to use compassion to deal with our stress. After all, we need to diagnose the complaint in order to be able to heal it.

As Christopher Germer, a clinical psychologist who teaches and practises mindfulness-based psychotherapy and self-compassion, writes in his book on self-compassion:

> Leaning into our problems with open eyes and an open heart – with awareness and compassion – is the process by which we get emotional relief.[4]

Two key words here are 'awareness' and 'compassion'. We are not leaning into the problem in order to fixate on it, or worry it over and over in our mind. Our goal is to acknowledge our stress and to try to see how it arises and what we do when it does. If we really get a handle on how to do this and understand its benefit it will help inspire us when the task of facing our stress feels difficult. This is important for the long-term.

A Formula for Change

A FORMULA FOR CHANGE

Allow yourself to *see your stress clearly*
Learn to 'lean into it'

Once you have seen your stress clearly
use it as an *inspiration for change*

Develop the *wish* to change

Take a step back in order to see your habits clearly
Mindfulness and meditation are crucial here

Become more *self-aware*

Access the mind's natural qualities of peace / clarity / spaciousness
* You are changing your perspective from the ground to the sky *

Examine your habits with *discernment*

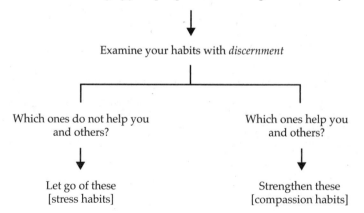

Which ones do not help you and others?	Which ones help you and others?
Let go of these [stress habits]	Strengthen these [compassion habits]

So, the process of using compassion to change how we experience and react to stress is based on learning to understand our habits and letting go of the ones that make things difficult for us. Many of us have numerous habits when faced with stress that are deep-seated – we have been perfecting them for quite some time, after all! Although compassion is natural to us, how we practise and express it is often diluted by our lack of awareness of ourselves and other people, along with a misunderstanding as to how it can help us. It can seem an overwhelming task to learn how to change our attitude – where do we begin? The vital starting point is to develop the *wish to change*. We have seen that one of the most potent qualities of compassion is that it gives us the courage to try something different – something that will enable us to understand how and why we suffer and even develop the capacity to transform it. This is the attitude we need to adopt with relation to our habitual reactions to stress – to take them as an inspiration for change. Let's look at a step-by-step process of reflection that will enable us to do that.

First, we need to *take a step back*. It is hard to see clearly when our mind is caught up in all its habits. Taking a step back allows us some space to see more clearly, which is the basis of self-awareness. One of the most effective ways of creating some space in our minds is through meditation practice. In the next chapter we will look at how to do this is more detail. As we begin to develop self-awareness through meditation it becomes more possible to *access the qualities of our natural mind*, the mind that is not constantly overwhelmed by activity. These qualities include peace, clarity and spaciousness.

Once we have re-engaged with these qualities of mind we are ready to *look at our reactions to stress from the perspective of the sky*, rather than the ground. This means taking a fresh look at what causes us stress and how we experience stress. The key here is to be discerning – to be able *to see clearly which habits help us and which don't*.

After you have reflected on your own habits in this way, you probably have a reasonable idea of which ones may be causing you problems.

Now it is a matter of deciding which one to choose to start working with. You can work with all of them over time, but to give yourself the chance to make a good start it helps to identify just one to begin with. As you do this, you'll be asking a lot of yourself and it is important to be able to feel a sense of accomplishment, to feel that change is happening. So it is a good idea not to begin with your most stubborn habit, as that is likely to need more attention. Instead, choose something that definitely gets in your way but that you feel you can get a handle on reasonably quickly.

An example of how to work with looking at habits in this way

When we go through this process in workshops people often ask for an example of what a habit is in this context. So perhaps it might be useful if I share one of my own that is occupying my attention at the moment. As someone who works for herself I have a lot of freedom to make my own schedule. I enjoy this very much but sometimes find it difficult to balance the routine tasks such as email and travel planning with the more weighty projects such as designing workshops and writing. My tendency is to want to clear the decks of all the mundane stuff and then devote a large chunk of quality time to the projects. Of course, this is hard to do and I constantly find days that were supposed to have been cleared in this way being taken over by unexpected demands. When this happens I experience a build up of tension. If I don't catch this early on it can make me feel overwhelmed. As if that is not bad enough, I then find myself piling on the misery by listing *all* the tasks I need to do in a given period, including doing the ironing and cleaning the windows, until my feeling of being overwhelmed feels really justified! It's a pattern that can end taking a lot of time and energy, as you can imagine.

What I am trying to do instead is to change the basic dynamic that I set up between my routine and my more creative tasks. If I have a clear idea of what I hope to achieve within a certain time then I find there is actually plenty of time to plan the tasks around my energy levels – if I am slow to get started in the mornings I can knock off a batch of emails until things start flowing, and then I can switch to something more substantial. If I get stuck with a workshop design, I take a break and do something less demanding such as arranging flights and travel schedules. Working this way allows me to relax and work in a more organic, less forced way, following my own natural rhythm – which is, of course, much kinder to myself. On the occasions this breaks down, I try to notice if I am piling on the pressure with all my lists. Because I have studied this habit of mine and identified the 'danger spots' it becomes possible to apply remedies along the way. It is always good to have a range of remedies in case one does not work straight off.

Of course each person's habits, their responses, and how they are affected by them will be different – your habits may be overworking, putting yourself down or perhaps letting yourself become more irritable than you want to be. Whatever it is, you will find it easier to work with if you take the time to identify and understand your habit clearly and work out how you are going to try and address it.

Support for Working with Habits

Once we have identified the habits we want to address, then we need a strategy for changing them. We will be looking at how to build up new, compassionate habits to replace the unhelpful habits to do with stress in the next chapters, but here are a few introductory remarks. Wanting to apply compassion to our stress might sound like a tall order, but it is good to remember that learning to work with our habits in this way is just like any other kind of training that we might undertake. If we join a gym and start an exercise programme we know that we will need to work hard over a sustained period of time in order to get results and even then, if we cut back on our routine, the benefits will not stay. It is the same if we decide to learn a new language, or take up a musical instrument – these things require effort and practice and there is a big difference between doing the minimum to get by and really trying to achieve a sufficiently high standard until playing the instrument or speaking the language feels like second nature.

Daniel Goleman, who has written extensively on emotional intelligence, writes:

> [A] new way of thinking, feeling, or acting feels unnatural at first, something like putting on someone else's clothes. At the neural level, a person is forcing the brain to go along a path less-travelled.[5]

In the second sentence Goleman is referring to a relatively new development in neuroscience – the idea of neuroplasticity, the discovery that the brain changes in response to experience. Up until about twenty-five years ago it was thought that once the brain matured it could not change and, except for some deterioration, remained the same until the end of our lives. The discovery of neuroplasticity turns this assumption on its head because it demonstrates that the brain continues to change in response to experience throughout our whole lives. How does this change happen? The actions we take can expand or contract the neural activity in different regions of the brain – we can stimulate activity in quiet areas and calm down overly busy ones. The parts of the brain we use more frequently tend to develop more than the parts we do not use often, so it can be said to provide a map of the kind of life we are living. So, as Goleman points out, what we now know about neuroplasticity underlines what we also know about our ability to change our habits. Realizing that we can 'rewire' our brain makes clear that our endeavour to change is not simply a lofty ambition, but is rooted firmly in the realm of science. The new habit will feel like an effort at first but as we persevere we will be able to rewire our brain to support what we are doing.

Imagine that you live on one side of a forest and your best friend lives on the other side. You visit each other regularly and have worn down a path through the undergrowth between your homes that is easy to find and easy to follow – in fact, you could do the journey with your eyes shut. Now imagine that one day your friend moves to another house on a different side of the forest. Your old path is of no use to you anymore and you need to make a new one by treading down undergrowth and repeating the same journey many times. The journey takes more effort and concentration and does not have the sense of ease of your former route, which continues to look inviting. However, after a few months not only is the new path beginning to look well established, the old path is showing signs of neglect and beginning to grow over. This is the same process that happens with our neural pathways. Gradually over time the new helpful habit will make new neural connections and the connections associated with the old, unhelpful habit will weaken, making it easier to drop.

So, when we have identified our habits through the *formula for change* and are ready to begin to work with them, there are several practical steps we can take to help us.

First of all, as we have seen, it helps if we can be aware of the habits we wish to change so we need to bring them fully into our awareness.

We can therefore try to *lean into* our problems with stress, rather than trying to avoid them.

Then we can understand that external events are connected to what is going on in our minds and that if we wish to work with difficult outer circumstances then we need to work on what is going on inside us – our own minds.

Having decided what we want to change, we need to decide on a new way of responding and then practise it at every opportunity. If we feel confident enough we can ask friends and family to give us feedback on how we are doing.

For example, we may be trying to listen more carefully to what people are saying to us and to interrupt less often. We can ask people to tell us how they think we are getting on.

As we work in this way we can feel confident that gradually new neural pathways are being developed in our brain that will help us to sustain our new, more helpful habits. This is because our brain is plastic and our mind transformable. We are not hardwired into our habits and change is possible.[6]

We will come back to neuroplasticity several times in this book as it is an important scientific discovery that supports the whole idea of being able to change oneself. We started out in this chapter looking at how our mind works and the importance of being able to train it to be more useful for us. Our habits are a result of how we use our mind and how our mind reacts to the events and situations we face. Training the mind requires us to work at several different levels at once, from the level of understanding what our mind is doing, through identifying our habits and applying the techniques set out in this book. It takes time and effort but the good news is that as soon as we begin we can start to experience the difference.

KEY POINTS

- How our mind is determines how we engage in whatever we are doing, but for the most part we rarely realize this and look to factors *outside ourselves* as the causes of our experience.

- Therefore it is important to train our mind so it can be more useful for us.

- There are two different aspects of mind:
  - the busy, distracted aspect of mind.
  - the clear, unobstructed quality of awareness that is the mind's true nature.

- Daniel Kahneman calls these two aspects the *evaluating* mind and the *experiencing* mind.

- We can change our perspective from looking at the clouds from the point of view of the ground below, to looking from the point of view of the sky above.

- We need to develop a wish to change and then follow a step-by-step programme:
  - See stress clearly.
  - Take it as an inspiration to change.
  - Develop the wish to change.
  - Take a step back.
  - Develop self-awareness.
  - Develop discernment.
  - Take a fresh look at our habits from this new perspective.
  - Choose a habit to start working on.

- We can choose how we react to situations.

- We will learn more about our stress if we *lean into* it, rather than trying to avoid it, or distract ourselves from it.

- The new habits we want to establish will be supported by neuroplasticity.

EXERCISES

Exercise 1

Experiment with changing perspective from the ground to the sky.

View thoughts and emotions from the point of view of the open, clear aspect of mind, rather than the busy, crowded aspect.

Try to observe them as if you were watching them on TV.

Make notes in your journal to help you remember these new perspectives and insights.

Exercise 2

Observe how you react to situations.

Try to see when you allow yourself a choice and when you do not.

Make notes in your journal.

Exercise 3

Experiment with *leaning into* your stress, rather than trying to avoid it.

What do you see?

Can you feel how seeing stress clearly can inspire change?

Make notes in your journal.

Exercise 4

Reflect on what you have learnt about neuroplasticity and how this can support you as you start to change old, unhelpful habits.

8 Developing a Peaceful Mind – The Basis of Lasting Happiness

> With the practice of meditation we can develop this ability to more fully love ourselves and to more consistently love others.
>
> *Sharon Salzberg*[1]

Why is Meditation So Important?

In the last chapter we looked at the mind that experiences stress and compassion and we saw that in order to use compassion to reduce our stress we need to work with how our mind is – in fact we need to begin to *train* our mind. Contemplative traditions over the last 2,500 years have found that the most effective way to train our mind is through meditation.

Remember the exercise I asked you to do in the last chapter – to take a moment just to watch your mind? If you tried this exercise the chances are that what you 'saw' was an avalanche of random thoughts, feelings, impressions, memories, projections and emotions. This is completely normal. Perhaps you also noticed how your thoughts tend to rush in unbidden and how your mind is pulled into replaying thoughts and actions from the past, and anticipating what you are going to do in the future. Furthermore, you might have seen that our mind tends to engage in a running mental commentary detailing things we like and things we don't like; things we want and things we don't want – our hopes, fears and worries all endlessly playing themselves out.

This never-ending mental activity means that we spend most of our time on automatic pilot going through tasks and events. Indeed throughout most of our life we are only partially present and aware because so much of our attention is engaged elsewhere. It is this endless and often confused activity of the mind that needs training, because when our mind is chaotic like this it is not being as useful as it could be and, even worse, it can make us feel very stressed. Although, as we saw in the previous chapter, there are two aspects of mind and behind all these thoughts and emotions our essence of mind is naturally peaceful and clear, accessing these qualities often happens only momentarily and in a haphazard manner. This makes it difficult to sustain a compassionate attitude either towards our self, or other people. Meditation is a way of accessing the essence of mind – the clarity and peace that lies hidden behind all the constant activity of our thoughts.

Beginning to Train the Mind Using Mindfulness

Mindlessness: Life on automatic pilot

Have you ever driven home, and as you parked your car realized that you don't remember anything at all about the drive? Or gone around the supermarket and arrived at the checkout with a full trolley but no memory of putting anything in? Just think of all those moments of life we let pass us by. Big deal, you may say, what's so great about going shopping in the supermarket or driving along the motorway? The trouble is that there are large stretches of our lives when we attend to routine matters that may not seem to need us to bring very much of our intelligence to bear – washing dishes, doing the laundry, buying postage stamps . . . the list is a long one. In addition, there are all the times when we do not listen properly to what people are saying to us because we are running through our own mental commentary on the situation. Or the times we say things we do not mean because our emotions are preventing us from seeing a situation clearly. If we add up all this time, we are actually missing a great deal of our life. Remember the research on the wandering mind we looked at (see page 95)? It showed that we are not thinking about what we are doing for 46.9 per cent of the time and that this does not make us happy. We seem to go through large stretches of our lives coasting along, doing what is required of us but without giving full attention to what we are doing or what is happening around us.

If we add to this the idea of the *experiencing* and *evaluating* (judging) *selves* we discussed in the last chapter, we can see that not only are we not present but we try to cover up our periods of distraction by putting together all kinds of thoughts and impressions and then making them into a coherent story. So if I am daydreaming on the bus journey home, caught up in my own thoughts, I will still have a version of the journey in my mind – crowded bus, noisy children or heavy traffic – even though I have not been paying full attention to any of these things and will have missed all kinds of small details. Why do we do this? Largely because we are trying to protect ourselves from the kinds of feelings and experiences that we think we don't want – for example, boredom, fear, worry or indecision. By weaving the moments of our lives into a seemingly unbroken story, we are trying to make ourselves feel safe by distancing ourselves from the reality of the inevitable interruptions that will disturb our lives from time to time. These interruptions are often out of our control, and can vary from minor things like plans that don't turn out the way we hoped, to the more life-changing disruptions of loss and upheaval – all of which have the potential to cause us stress. We forget that such events are part of life and instead try and avoid them. Rather than being simply present in each moment we distract ourselves with all this non-stop mental activity. We are trying to manage our experiences to our satisfaction – in other words, to make us happy and to avoid suffering.

However, as we have seen, doing this requires constant vigilance and is so exhausting that we then need to distract ourselves from all this mental activity so that we can give ourselves a break – so we talk of the need to 'switch off', to 'lose ourselves' in activities that distract us from our struggles. The problem is that we may find that this is not always as easy to do as we had hoped. Think of all the times you were really looking forward to doing something and even spent quite a bit of time imagining how it would be but then, when the occasion came along, you let it slip by while being preoccupied with something else. Have you ever sat down with an interesting book but then spent the first half an hour replaying the day's events in your mind or thinking about your to-do list for the next week? Or had dinner with friends during which you simply talked about work and let the chance to relax and enjoy their company just pass you by? Switching off is even harder to do when we are faced with unpleasant or worrying events. For example, think of the time we spend anticipating a difficult encounter, such as a work meeting or a family get together, going over all the possible scenarios that might take place, stressing ourselves before we even get there.

Mindfulness: Switching off the automatic pilot

Remember the analogy of the sky and the clouds in chapter 7? We saw that although our minds are naturally flexible, spacious and aware, they easily become cluttered by all the activity of our thoughts and emotions. This makes the mind feel more cramped and limited than it actually is. When we switch off our automatic pilot and allow ourselves to pay attention to what is happening for us in the present moment we start to clear away this clutter, to quieten down the incessant noise coming from it. In this way, we begin to calm our mind down, to allow it to settle and discover its own peace and clarity. We can do this because these are the natural qualities of our mind, already there – we simply need to allow ourselves to get in touch with them.

With mindfulness we choose how to position our mind, rather than be pulled along by its ceaseless activity; we learn to pay attention to what we are experiencing in the current moment, and we are able to do this in an open-hearted, non-judgemental manner that has nothing to do with wishing things to be a certain way, but simply accepts what is. With mindfulness comes stability of mind, so that it becomes more reliable. When our attention is focused in this way, our mental resources are fully engaged, which means that we can make better choices with less struggle and effort. At the same time, it becomes easier to respond to events in a compassionate manner, which reduces our stress reactions and makes us less likely to share our stress with others.

Ways to practise mindfulness

So how do we begin? Fortunately we have the most effective support for mindfulness with us all the time – our breath. We can use our breath to anchor our mindfulness at any time and in any place. While we are alive our breath is always there, sending us useful information about how we are and what is happening to us, but we are seldom mindful of it. Learning to tune in with the breath is a way to tune in with our moment-by-moment experience and therefore with ourselves. Here is a very simple exercise we can start with:

Exercise: Learning to pay attention to our breath

Sit comfortably and straighten your back.

Take a few moments to settle and experience the quietness.

Become aware of your breathing.
Notice the rhythm of the breath entering and leaving your body.

Now rest your attention on your breathing.
Notice any changes in its rhythm.

When your mind wanders away notice that your focus is not on the breath, and simply bring it back.

Repeat this each time your attention wanders.

When you first try to do this probably you will find your attention wanders a lot and you will need to keep bringing it back to the breath. Don't be surprised at this. Remember that evolution, and our modern world of constant stimulation, has designed our mind to wander (see chapters 5 and 7). We are just not used to allowing our minds to rest on a specific object, or to remain in the present moment. So it is natural to find it difficult. It helps here if you can learn to 'be curious' about this difficulty – simply observe it. Observe too if thoughts come up like, 'I should be watching my breath! Oh, how can I control stress if I can't even do that!' Just notice these thoughts arising as natural and normal, and bring your attention back to the task at hand (i.e. the breath) until the next 'Oh, what if . . .' and 'Should I be doing . . .' and 'Why can't I . . .' thought arrives – and it will.

The good news is that trying this exercise out helps to create a new habit, and it will become easier over time. Another thing you may find yourself doing is judging how your mindfulness practice is going and keeping up a kind of self-assessment of whether or not you are getting it right. Again, this is completely understandable, but it is best to just notice what is happening and return to the breath, rather than getting into an analysis of your practice. Don't try to stop doing it – because that will make it worse – just notice it, drop it and come back to your breath.

It's helpful to learn to do this sitting down in a room by yourself for sessions of perhaps ten minutes or so, then in time you will feel confident enough to use it in lots of different situations to help you settle in yourself and become more present – for example, while waiting to start a meeting or while queuing up.

Having learnt to steady our attention in this way we can extend our attention to different points – the body, physical sensations, our thoughts and how our senses experience the world around us.[2] Below is a more elaborate mindfulness exercise you can try using these additional steps.

Exercise: Extending mindfulness[3]

Spend a few moments settling down by doing the simple breathing exercise above and then add one or more of the additional steps below, depending on how much time you have. It works best to go from one step to another rather than jumping around.

Body and sensations

Allow your attention to extend to include your body.

Notice what you're sitting on.

Be aware of your hands at rest.

Notice the feeling of your body at rest.

Slowly scan your body from the top of your head to the tips of your toes noticing any changes in your attention as it travels down your body. Take time to do this slowly and patiently, allowing yourself to notice each part of your body in turn.

Be aware of all the sensations you experience in your body.

Return to the breath.

Thoughts

Allow your attention to extend to include your thoughts.

Simply notice the thoughts coming and going in your mind.

Don't dwell on them.

Don't judge them.

Just let them come and go.

Return to the breath.

Experiencing the world

Allow your attention to extend to include the information coming to you through your senses.

Notice the sounds coming into your ears but don't follow after them.

Perhaps you can hear traffic outside in the street, or children playing. Just notice the noise but do not get into a commentary about it: 'there's too much traffic on my street, why don't those children's parents take them indoors . . .'

Just hear the noise and drop the rest.

Now continue with your other senses in the same way.

Notice what your eyes are seeing but don't get lost in it.

Notice all the sensations of touch on the surface of your body.

Notice the scents surrounding you.

Notice the taste in your mouth at this moment.

Let your attention rest lightly, without analysis or opinion.

Return to the breath.

When trying out each of these steps there are a few things to note:

- Notice the occasions when you label sensations, thoughts or experiences as something you want, or you don't want, or you are indifferent to. Keep in mind that judgemental thoughts about liking or disliking will be stimulating parts of your brain that might not be helpful when trying to work with stress. It's not so much whether we experience something as likeable or dislikeable – we are bound to do that – it's more that we start *thinking* about how and why we dislike it, and how we can stop it, rather than just being with it and noticing the feeling of dislike.

- Notice when your mind drifts off into memories, or starts projecting into the future.

- Notice the times when your mind starts to dwell on something that is worrying you – and this is likely to happen if you are feeling stressed, as we saw when we discussed the loops that our mind gets caught up in.

Each of these patterns represents a common way in which we get pulled away from the present moment, and all of them can make us feel stressed. It's often when things are not going the way we want them to that we feel stressed – we don't want to feel that twinge of backache that keeps bothering us; we do not want to keep worrying about our weight and we hate it when we are running late. Of course, if you have a pain in your back it could be a good idea to get it checked out in case there is damage or you need some kind of treatment. Mindfulness is not about doing *nothing*, rather with mindfulness we just *notice* the back pain in the first instance, rather than allowing our mind to run away with itself and get into all kinds of stories as to why we have the pain. Like Sister Helena, the 102-year-old nun whom we met in chapter 5, we are just accepting what is coming to us in the present moment. We are not trying to protect ourselves, or avoid leaning into the sharp edges of situations, allowing ourselves to feel any discomfort that is there. Worrying about the row we had last night with our teenage son, or dreading the family reunion for an important birthday that is taking place next weekend, will not help us with the problem. Instead, endlessly going over and over events will cause us stress. So, again, we can just notice that we are thinking of the row or the party and then return to mindfulness. When we dwell on something that is worrying us – our job, a friend in difficulty or money troubles – we are causing ourselves more stress and yet not addressing the issue. Again, we can simply notice the worry and return to mindfulness. Of course, we will need to give these matters our attention but by being mindful we can choose when to do so and how we want to go about it, rather than having our preoccupation spill out over everything we are doing.

So, each of these ways of not being present can be addressed by learning to return our attention to the object of the mindfulness practice, for example the breath. This attention should be relaxed, light and friendly – not criticizing, just noticing. Try not to be impatient with yourself if you find yourself falling into any of these old judgemental habits. Our mind has been used to wandering for a long time and so we will need to keep practising in order to change old habits – this is why it is referred to as mindfulness *practice*. Every time we notice that we are not present and come back to paying attention we are strengthening our new habit of being mindful.

It is a good idea to practise mindfulness exercises regularly, sitting in a chair in a quiet space, in order to get used to them and make them feel natural, but it is equally important to integrate them into your everyday activities as much as possible. Being mindful when carrying out routine activities can be a good support for your practice – such as mindful walking, mindful eating, mindful drinking and so on. Using the activities you perform over and over again helps train us in mindfulness. In this way our mind becomes more capable of extending mindfulness to more complex experiences – it's easier to be mindful of, say, a mechanical activity like walking than it is to be mindful of one's thoughts. Try out this exercise when you next have a cup of coffee.

Exercise: A mindful cup of coffee

Instead of drinking the coffee at the same time as doing something else – reading, working, talking or watching TV – just allow yourself to take the time to simply drink the coffee.

Sit comfortably and then pick up the cup.

Notice the shape and texture of the cup and feel the warmth of the coffee.

Look at the coffee.

Notice the colour, the bubbles of foam, and the steam rising from the liquid.

Smell the coffee.

Breathe in the aroma.

As you take your first sip notice the changes in how you hold the cup, how the liquid flows in the cup and how it feels against your lips.

Let the coffee stay on your tongue for a moment and savour the taste and then slowly swallow it and feel it going down your throat.

The chances are you will be amazed at how rich the experience of having an ordinary cup of coffee has become! This experience is always available to us but we miss it by not paying attention.

Recently in a workshop I held for managers in the UK, people were sharing experiences of practising mindfulness between sessions. One busy manager shared how he had continued his daily habit of taking a short morning walk before starting off for work, but now he was trying to take his walk mindfully and be fully present, rather than thinking about the work ahead of him for the day. He realized that now that he was trying to practise mindfulness he could hear the birds singing – they had been singing all along but he had not noticed. He said it made him realize how much he had been missing. This illustrates an important effect of mindfulness – it enables us to move from just 'doing' all the time to include 'being'. So much of the time we are so focused on getting things done and accomplishing tasks that we rarely stop to think about how we are while we are doing them. The manager in question was accustomed to 'doing' his walk and never gave a thought to how he was 'being' while he did it. When he walked mindfully he was able to relax and 'be' the person walking. Then he was able to appreciate the experience fully. When he reached his office he felt refreshed and ready for the day, instead of already weighed down by all the worries he had tried to deal with on the walk in to work.

STOP MOMENTS

As well as using our routine activities to remember mindfulness, it helps to try and punctuate our day with moments when we stop, notice we are on automatic pilot and apply mindfulness. We could call these STOP moments because they interrupt our habit of *mindlessness*, stop our distraction from the present and enable us to pay attention. In the exercises at the end of this chapter you will find a list of suggestions of when you could use STOP moments. The more often you do so, the more present you can become. Even stopping mindlessness for a few seconds helps us establish a new habit of mindfulness and each time you do it you are giving yourself a short break from feeling stressed.

Applying mindfulness practice

Let's think of a stressful scenario in which we could apply what we have learnt about mindfulness. Perhaps your ten-year-old daughter comes down with a nasty case of flu and has to go to bed. Both you and your partner work full-time, but one of you will need to stay at home and take care of her. Your partner has an important series of meetings coming up and cannot take time off, so it falls to you. Your boss is not happy about you having to take time off but is slightly appeased when you tell him you'll take work home. So, there you are at home with a sick child and a load of paperwork – not to mention shopping, cleaning, cooking and so on. You feel a bit overwhelmed. Your habit could be to charge into all the things that need to be done, while worrying about how you will cope with it all and trying to make plans to keep everything ticking over.

Let's see how you could try something different.

Exercise: Applying mindfulness to a life situation

Step 1: Take care of priorities

The priority is to see your daughter is settled comfortably. You can already try to be mindful of how you talk to her, stroke her and move around her bedroom. You want her to feel that you are there for her, rather than worried about coping with everything else you need to attend to. You can use her as the object of your mindfulness.

Step 2: Take some time for yourself

Once your daughter is settled you could take ten minutes to do the Extending Mindfulness Exercise on page 149.

Use the time to check in with yourself with mindfulness and notice how you are feeling – in other words take a moment for yourself. The irony is that we usually think we don't have time to do something like this because we have to 'get on' with things. In fact, taking these ten minutes could be the investment that helps you do what you need to do without getting stressed and overtired.

Step 3: Mindfully work through your tasks

Having done the Extending Mindfulness Exercise and taken stock of how you are feeling, hopefully you feel in better shape to get started on all the things that need taking care of. As you work through the list try to come back to what you are doing in each moment (rather than letting your mind range over the next few days and keep asking what will happen about this and that, how this or that will get done). Just be mindful of each task as it comes and pay attention to that. Gently bring your mind back from anticipating problems that have not happened.

Step 4: Apply STOP moments from time to time

As you work through what needs to be done use lots of STOP moments (see above and end of chapter) to bring you back to mindfulness and interrupt any possible spiral of worry.

Getting To Know Yourself through Meditation

In my experience, for people new to these techniques, practising mindfulness offers a simple method for gathering and locating the mind in the present, and therefore of interrupting our internal commentary. When people have had time to appreciate the power of mindfulness, they are ready to move on to meditation, which trains the mind to be not only mindful, but also *aware* and *spacious*.

Because mindfulness is about focus, if it is practised with too much effort or intensity we can lose perspective and our attention can become too

narrow and over-concentrated – that's where spaciousness and awareness come in. Think of a footballer expertly handling the ball, his attention
focused mindfully on how he strikes the ball but lacking an awareness
of the whole pitch and the pattern of the game, so that when there is a
chance to make a skilful pass to a teammate at a crucial moment, he does
not see it and misses the opportunity. An illustration of how mindfulness and awareness work together that I like very much is what happens
when you carry a full cup of coffee across a room.[4] You need mindfulness
to pay attention to the surface of the coffee and to make sure it does not
spill over, but you also need to be aware of the room you are passing
through in order to take care not to bump into anything, or trip up which
would also cause the coffee to spill. The mindfulness is focused attention
and the awareness is a more all-inclusive attention that sees the whole
picture. Meditation includes mindfulness, but also incorporates unobstructed awareness, so that the mind is exquisitely balanced between
being focused – seeing the coffee in the cup – and being aware of the
context of the object of focus – the room as you walk across it. The basis
of this balance is relaxation. The mind relaxes into its natural state of
clarity and spaciousness, and allows meditation to happen.

Meditation is a way of getting to know yourself and then to make friends
with yourself as you are. We could say it is a way of coming home to
ourselves because we are learning to become familiar with what goes on
in our minds and the nature of our experience. This helps us to become
more familiar with our emotional triggers, and what causes us to feel
stressed. As well as becoming more aware of ourselves, we also become
more aware of other people and what is happening around us. This
enables us to choose whether or not we want to act, as well as *how* we
want to act, instead of just responding in our habitual way. Stress is often
difficult to handle because we cannot predict when it will happen, and
this can leave us feeling helpless and not in control. Because meditation
enables us to see both ourselves and our environment more clearly, it
becomes more possible for us to see things as they actually are, and to
recognize that everything is interconnected and changing. As this understanding grows, we can see that stress and the suffering it can cause us

is simply part of life and that it is inevitable that there will be times in our lives when we will feel stressed. We come to accept the suffering caused by stress and become less destabilized when it happens – in a way we learn to *expect* stress to be unpredictable. Because we are learning to work with our minds and train them to be more useful we have more natural control over our reactions to events. Things will still happen to us that we have no control over – we cannot stop the strike at the airport that spoils our holiday, nor can we prevent the cost of petrol increasing, but we can learn to notice our reactions and then begin to make choices about what to do about them. As we become more familiar with meditation, it becomes a little easier to react from a place of calm and stability rather than giving a knee-jerk response. This can help to break the cycle of feeling unable to cope, or helpless in the face of difficulties. It cuts through the cycle of stress. So meditation can go directly to the root of the psychological habits that can make stress worse.

What meditation is not

Although meditation has been practised in Asian cultures for hundreds of years it is still relatively new to the West and as it finds its place in our culture all kinds of ideas have arisen as to what it is that are not necessarily true or helpful. Here are some things that meditation is *not*:

A religion

Although it is possible to practise meditation as part of a religion or spiritual path, it is also of great benefit to people who simply wish to use it to help themselves in their lives and to understand their minds better.

Something for people with special skills

You don't need to be an especially quiet or contemplative person to learn meditation. It is useful for everyone. You do not need any special skills in order to start.

A way of blocking out thoughts

People will often say to me that they just cannot block their thoughts while meditating. Hopefully this has already been explained sufficiently but it's worth repeating one more time – meditation is neither forcing, nor indulging thoughts but simply allowing them to come and go without commentary, neither pushing them away, nor chasing after them, just letting them rise and fade.

A way of emptying the mind

This is slightly different from the blocking thoughts. When people ask me about meditating in workshops they seem to expect it to be about relinquishing control of the mind and allowing it to go into a blank, passive state – like being in a neutral gear, perhaps. Again, this is incorrect. Meditation is all about uncovering and working with the mind's natural dynamism and power, not about dumbing the mind down, or numbing it.

Going into a dream, or zoning out

Sometimes people will say that they already know how to relax the mind and when I ask how they do it, they describe how they may drive home from work and simply allow their mind to switch off from all the worries of the day and go into a pleasant dreamy state without any focus. Occasionally people have described this state as 'my time' – time they feel is truly theirs alone. Again, this is not meditation but a kind of day-dreaming – a way of being on automatic pilot. It may have a short-term relaxing effect but it does not help to train the mind.

Exercise: How to meditate

This method of meditation is the one I was taught myself and have practised for over thirty years. It is an old friend now but one that continues to inspire and surprise – meditation is always fresh, immediate and unpredictable. In this method *the posture is important* – creating the right posture in the body helps the mind to naturally assume the correct mental posture. If you can, it is good to sit cross-legged on a cushion on the floor. You will need to experiment with cushion sizes and shapes to arrive at the best means of support. If the floor doesn't appeal, then it is also fine to meditate sitting in a chair.

Once you are in position, follow these instructions:

Rest your hands lightly on your knees, or fold them in your lap.

Keep your spine straight but not rigid.

Relax your shoulders while aiming to keep them flat, so that the chest is open.

Keep your eyes open and the gaze soft. Angle your gaze at about 45 per cent – neither looking straight ahead, or down at the floor, but halfway in between.

If you feel sleepy, lift the gaze.

If you feel stirred up, lower the gaze.

Breathe mainly through the mouth, with the lips slightly apart.

Rest your attention lightly on the out-breath.

Whenever your attention wanders, simply notice it has wandered and return to mindfulness of the breath.

There are one or two points here that people often ask about – why do we keep our eyes open and why do we breathe through the mouth, rather than the nose? On a practical level, if our eyes are open we are less likely to fall asleep which is very easy to do when we first start to meditate. With our eyes open it is less likely that we withdraw and sink into some kind of detached dreamy state. Meditation is about being at ease with ourselves and with the world – this is demonstrated by keeping the eyes open. If it helps to begin a session with closing the eyes for a few moments then that is fine, just open them as soon as you feel settled. As for the breath – breathing mostly through the mouth helps calm the mind, and slows down the stream of thoughts. Because it feels unfamiliar to breathe through the mouth, you may notice that your lips get dry or it feels uncomfortable. That's no problem – just take a moment to moisten your lips, swallow and then continue. Once your posture is established, the next step is to simply rest your attention lightly on the out-breath. When you breathe in, just breathe normally. Sometimes it is recommended to count the breaths – every time you exhale, count one. At first your attention will quite quickly wander: when it does just bring it back and start counting again.

Exercise: Meditation using a candle

People who suffer from asthma may like to try using an object instead of the breath.

Rest your hands lightly on your knees, or fold them in your lap.

Keep your back straight but not rigid.

Relax your shoulders while aiming to keep them flat, so that the chest is open.

Rest your gaze lightly on the candle flame.
(There's no need to get involved in the details of colour, shape and so on.)

Keep your focus relaxed with just enough attention to hold your awareness of the candle.

When your mind drifts away, just bring it back.

You could also use a flower, a crystal, or an inspiring photo.

Remember, there is no race here, no big goal. We are just taking time to relax and enjoy being quietly with our own mind. In fact, most of our attention should be concerned with maintaining this attitude of *spaciousness and ease* – neither trying too hard and getting tight, nor zoning out and becoming too loose. *Mindfulness* comes in keeping our attention on the breath, and in meditation it is supported by an *awareness* that sees when we have lost our mindfulness and gently reminds us to bring our attention back.

As we have seen, these three elements: mindfulness, awareness and spaciousness, work together to hold the meditation. If we remember the metaphor of the sky and the clouds from Chapter 7 – our mind is naturally uncluttered, peaceful and spacious like a clear blue sky but it is also has clarity, awareness, and a natural intelligence as represented by the sun shining unobstructed. So in meditation we are uncovering the mind's natural qualities by allowing it to rest and its activity to calm down and settle. When we are able to do this we realize that *in this actual moment of meditation* we are not so stressed, and even if the feeling of stress returns after the meditation session, we may be able to see it a bit differently. To begin with, meditation gives us a possibility of interrupting our stress and giving us a respite from it. If we continue to work with our meditation it can help us to develop a different perspective on our stress, which will help to dilute its impact. Let's take a look at working with thoughts and emotions during meditation in order to help us see how this can work.

Thoughts and emotions during meditation

Staying with the analogy of the clouds and the sky, we saw that just as the sky is always limitless and spacious even when obscured by clouds, the essence of our mind is spacious, aware and unaffected by the thoughts and emotions that pass through it. The more we can leave our mind alone and not stir it up the more useful it can be for us. It is our thoughts and emotions that cause us stress – the activity of our mind, not the mind itself. So if we can begin to understand our thoughts and emotions more clearly and work with them more effectively we will be working directly to reduce our stress. You remember that with mindfulness practice the idea is that in order to pay attention to what we are doing we need to notice the thoughts that are distracting us. With meditation we begin to work with the thoughts themselves and to see them for what they are – passing movements of our mind that come and go just like the clouds crossing the sky, or the debris that gets stirred up in a lake during a storm. The trouble is that our usual habit as soon as a thought comes in our mind is to take it as real and worry about it, turning it into something bigger and more substantial than it really is, adding to it with layer upon layer of additional thoughts. So, to begin with we might find it quite hard to see them as passing and transient, but if we can manage it even for a few seconds it will make a big difference. With meditation we are changing our habit of looking at the clouds from the perspective of the ground to looking at them from the perspective of the sky. In this way, instead of them seeming to bear down on us and obscuring our vision, we can see them as simply passing by, without affecting the sky. Clouds do not change the sky, they simply cover it over – the sky does not become the clouds. In just the same way, thoughts and emotions do not alter our mind, they just obscure its natural spaciousness and awareness – we do not *become* our thoughts and emotions. We do not need to block anything, or manipulate anything.

It is a matter of learning to distinguish between our mind and its contents – to be able to see our thoughts and emotions as mental events that come and go. This enables us to be aware of what we are thinking as well as the stories we create about our thoughts. It does not mean that we stop having thoughts – not at all, we need to be able to apply our intelligence – rather that we can choose whether or not we want to act on them, because we can see them in perspective. We do not have to feel bad about some thoughts and good about others. We do not have to beat ourselves up about thoughts we feel embarrassed by. We can simply be forgiving towards ourselves. This will help to undermine our stress reactions at their very root.

I have a friend who is highly intelligent and quite intellectual. He tried meditation in the first place because he got completely fed up with trying to cope with all the activity going on in his mind. I always remember him describing to me how tiring his mind was for him – how his endless stream of thoughts could seem quite a burden at times – and how meditation has made a considerable difference to how he sees and interacts with these thoughts. He said that when he first started meditating he noticed for the first time that in fact his thoughts were not continuous at all. Between each thought was a space – maybe only a very small space but enough to give the impression of the thought surrounded by space rather than by more and more thoughts. This gave him a sense of tremendous relief. Now he has been meditating for many years and is able to experience the space more strongly than the thought and view the thought as a passing experience within the space of his mind. This is the spacious quality in meditation, along with mindfulness and awareness that we mentioned earlier. This is learning to view our thoughts from the perspective of the sky, rather than from the perspective of the ground.

Exercise: Seeing thoughts from the perspective of the sky

You can do this exercise either sitting by a window where you can see the sky, or even outside if you can find a quiet place.

Sit comfortably and straighten your back.

Spend a few moments watching your breath.

Look at the sky for a few moments and watch the clouds.

Ask yourself if the clouds are good or bad. (If you are hoping for a sunny day for an outing perhaps the clouds seem to be a nuisance, whereas if you are hoping for some rain for the garden perhaps they seem like a good idea.)

Think about how other people might view the clouds depending on their own likes and dislikes.

Notice how these labels have no effect on the clouds.

Notice how the clouds move and change and, whatever you do, you cannot make them stay in one place.

Now spend a few moments watching your thoughts as they come and go in your mind.

Try not to follow one thought for too long, just allow your thoughts to come and go.

Notice how quickly you label your thoughts as good, bad, pleasant, unpleasant.

Try to realize that when you label them this way you are seeing them as solid and real, like trying to hold a cloud in one place in the sky.

Look again at the sky and notice how although the clouds move and change, the space around them – the sky – does not change at all.

Now try to apply this to your thoughts as they come and go in your mind.

Notice that the space around the thoughts does not change, only the thoughts.

Try to let your mind rest in this feeling of spaciousness for a few moments.

The process of looking at our emotions is similar. Because our minds are calmed down during meditation we have more possibility to recognize emotions as they arise before they grab us and we start to react to them. If we can recognize our emotions as they start to form in our minds, then we can try to accept them without judgement. This gives us a chance to investigate each emotion and understand where it has come from. In order to do that, we need to be able to separate the emotion from its object. For example, if I am frustrated by an email that I receive and then snap at a colleague who just happens to be nearby, the emotion that I am feeling clearly has nothing to do with my poor colleague! Our tendency, however, is often to justify our reaction by apportioning blame. So in this case I may feel justified in letting off steam at my colleague who did nothing wrong, because I am frustrated by my email. In fact, my reaction – apportioning blame to someone who is blameless – could become a potential source of conflict and stress. It could lead to an argument with my colleague when in fact the frustration is nothing to do with them. When our minds are calmed down by meditation it is much easier to see what is really happening and take responsibility for our reactions. In the final instance it is important not to *identify* with the emotion. Just because you feel frustration, or irritation, it does not mean that is who you are. Just because you feel stressed it is not *who you are*.

Making meditation part of your life

Although meditation is relatively easy to learn, most of us are not familiar with it. Many of the ideas and techniques we have been discussing may be new to you and will take some time to get used to. It is possible to feel quite self-conscious at the beginning and to spend a meditation session waiting for something to happen. Meditation is so simple it can be almost a surprise. However, we can have such unrealistic expectations and be looking for such big experiences and instant results that we miss the quiet simplicity of the experience. It is not unusual in a group meditation session for someone who is new to it to become overwhelmed by giggles, or to be unable to stop fidgeting. At the other end of the scale, some people find themselves falling fast asleep. All these things are absolutely fine – they are just part of the process of getting used to meditation. The main thing is not to judge yourself or your meditation. There is no such thing as a bad meditation.

In fact, sometimes when we begin to meditate it can seem as if our minds have got even busier and that our thoughts and emotions are out of control. In Buddhist instructions on meditation this process has been likened to a waterfall rushing down a steep gorge, and marks the beginning of us becoming aware of how our minds are. In fact, it is not that they have got busier – it's just that with meditation we can start to notice all that activity. Sometimes people find this depressing, but it shouldn't be: it is an important step to see directly how busy the mind is. Gradually, with practice, the stream of thoughts will slow down and will begin to feel more like a great river meandering through a valley. When the mind learns to settle it becomes like a great ocean, with the waves gently ruffling the surface of the water but not disturbing its depths in any way. So we can see that there is no good or bad practice; no getting it right or wrong but simply getting used to observing the movements of our minds.

The best way to get used to meditation is by actually doing it. As soon as we can make it a daily habit the easier it will be to become accustomed to it. Let's look at some practical points that will help us to do this.

When should I meditate?

People often find it helps to get the day off to a good start if they do a session of meditation in the morning but it is really up to you. There are no hard and fast rules. The best thing is to look at your schedule and see where it is easiest to make changes to include meditation.

How long should I meditate for?

Again, there are no rules – except to say the more you can do the more helpful you will find it! If you are a beginner it might be a good idea to build up slowly over a period of a few weeks. Perhaps start with a session of sitting meditation for five minutes every day. After two weeks you could try increasing it to ten minutes and then fifteen, and so on. It is better to start small and build up, rather than planning to sit for an hour every day and feeling disappointed when you cannot keep it up. When your sessions do get longer you could always do half the session in the morning and the other half in the evening. That enables you to do more meditation without having to plan a really long session.

Where should I meditate?

The answer here is, wherever you can! Sometimes people like to have a special place that is their meditation spot. This is nice, but will depend on the size of your home and who you share it with. Beware of making a meditation space that is just so special you never actually use it. I always remember two friends of mine showing me round their new apartment and proudly opening the door to their meditation room. When I commented on how pristine it looked they said it was because they never used it in case they got it dirty!

Are there any special props that I need?

It is helpful not to wear tight clothing – or for women, a short skirt – just because you are likely to find it uncomfortable. Other than that it is up to you. You need a good cushion, or a straight-backed chair. Some people like to wrap themselves in a shawl to keep warm. You might want to set your mobile phone to time how long you want your session to be but you could also use an egg timer. Sometimes people like to ring a bell, or singing bowl, to start their session. Generally speaking, try to keep it simple and flexible.

What do I do when I don't feel like doing my session?

When this happens – and it will happen – the best thing is to try to do it anyway because the more often you manage to do your session the more you are establishing a habit. We don't leave out cleaning our teeth whatever happens. It helps to try to think of meditation as just another part of our routine. Of course, you should not force yourself if you really cannot face it – we need to have some humour as we try to fit meditation into our schedules. I know of someone who promised himself to meditate six days out of every seven and give himself a day off every week. By giving himself this 'holiday' each week he was able to maintain a much more regular practice routine than if he had forced himself to do it every day.

PAUSES

Just as with the mindfulness practice we had STOP moments, with meditation we can insert lots of PAUSES during our day. Think of these as very short meditation sessions – perhaps just one or two moments long – that act as breathing spaces in the day. It may sound strange but one of my favourite times for a PAUSE is when I need to go to the lavatory. It is something that we all need to do several times in a day and we can do it behind a locked door, where no one can disturb us. Just take an extra moment to straighten your back and watch your breath for a minute or so.

Nicki, a social worker, has this to say about using this particular strategy:

> During a very intense team meeting I excused myself and went to the loo to do some meditation practice to calm myself down as I could feel myself getting really stressed, my tension was rising and I could see that the meeting wasn't going anywhere . . . it was stuck. This took me away from the situation and I could return fresher and less stressed. The meeting didn't get any better but at least I was in a better position to handle the outcome.

Having pauses like this during the day will increase the benefits of your daily session on the cushion or chair. In the exercises at the end of this chapter you will find a list of different situations when you can make a PAUSE in your day.

Here is Nicki again describing how she uses these PAUSE moments:

> After difficult situations with a family I spend some time sitting in my car for a few moments watching my breath. This enables me to gather my resources so I can be fully available for the next family I see. However, this is only really effective when I have spent some more time focused on meditation in the morning and so have a base to build upon.

The Benefits of a Stable Mind

Sogyal Rinpoche, Tibetan Buddhist teacher and author of the spiritual classic, *The Tibetan Book of Living and Dying* describes meditation as

> The true practice of peace, the true practice of nonaggression and nonviolence, and the real and greatest disarmament.[5]

As we learn to meditate we learn to become more of a friend to ourselves, and to be more at home with ourselves. We find ourselves more in tune with life as it is with its continual change, the inevitability of stress and suffering and how we are all dependent on and connected to each other. In Buddhist instructions on meditation, the untamed mind is likened to a wild elephant, rampaging, bellowing and stamping all around. An elephant has tremendous power and strength, but if it is not channelled well it can cause damage to itself, to others and to its surroundings. As we have seen, it is the same with the mind. If we allow our thoughts and emotions to pull us this way and that, then we have as little self-control as the elephant. We use an enormous amount of effort in keeping up an endless score of how well, or badly, we think we are doing, and how the world and everyone in it is treating us – what we like, and what we don't like; what we hope for and what we fear. It is chaotic, reactive and damaging, and as we have seen, a means by which we put ourselves under stress. Just as the wild elephant slowly calms down with patient care and discipline, so the mind is calmed and settled through meditation. As the mind becomes more stable and we can discern more clearly how our thoughts and emotions arise, we can begin the process of unravelling the way we use our mind that causes us stress. In time, we can disarm the ways in which our reactions to stress cause us harm and begin to find peace with ourselves and with our world. This does not mean that suddenly everything will start to go our way – all of our personal sharp edges and uncomfortable places are still there, the difficulties we need to deal with remain, but with this kind of stability of mind we can allow ourselves to become open to what needs addressing, rather than distracting ourselves from it. We will start to feel a certain confidence that we will not be so easily thrown off – we won't be dismayed by our own behaviour, nor that of others. This confidence enables us to be accepting of everything as it happens without needing to protect ourselves, and so it has the capacity to transform our reactions to stress.

Inner peace is the heart of the attitude of contentment that was discussed in chapter 5. So, with contentment as our basis we can learn to use our discernment in weighing up which actions will bring us lasting happiness and which will lead to suffering. In this way we can identify our habits. Meditation is the key to the whole compassionate attitude that we are exploring in this book and an important element in developing lasting happiness. It doesn't miraculously remove all our problems or stress but by strengthening the mind it gives us a new perspective to understand them and a sustainable means to work with the challenges they bring.

In the last chapter we looked at a 'Formula for Change'. Let's look at the part meditation plays in that formula. In beginning to train ourselves in reducing our stress, it is clear that to begin with we need to *want* to change. Meditation gives us a glimpse of what our mind can be like if we are able to train it properly, and so reinforces our wish to change our perspective and how our mind reacts to stress. Because we are learning to see our thoughts and emotions for what they are, we are no longer so likely to just react out of habit but rather to take a step back in order to see what is going on with us. Meditation helps us to develop self-awareness by accessing the peace, clarity and spaciousness of our mind and to change our perspective from the ground to the sky. With this fresh perspective we are able to examine our habits with more clarity and kindness instead of self-criticism. We can therefore work out which habits cause us more harm than good and which are helpful. This enables us to see where we want to begin with our process of change and how we want to go about doing it.

Scientific Research into the Effects of Mindfulness and Meditation

Contemplative traditions such as Buddhism have recognized the crucial importance of meditation for more than 2,000 years, and now current neuroscientific research is providing scientific endorsement of this point of view. In November 2004 the first of a series of papers describing the impact of long-term meditation on the brain was published in the prestigious scientific journal *Proceedings of the National Academy of Sciences.*[6] It was the first time meditation had been described in scientific terminology.

Among its authors were Richard Davidson, his colleague Antoine Lutz and Matthieu Ricard. We have mentioned Davidson and Lutz already when we described the partnership between the Dalai Lama and Western science in the Introduction. Matthieu Ricard is a Westerner who has been a Buddhist monk for many years and who has acted as a guinea pig for research into the effects of meditation on the brain. Previously, meditation had been considered to be something beyond objective study, and something that could not be measured, but Davidson and his team have been able to translate meditation experiences into the language of high-frequency gamma rays and brain coordination. To do this they have used two powerful tools for measuring brain function:

- The fMRI: functional magnetic resonance imaging – this measures brain function, rather than structure, by measuring the blood flow connected with emotional changes in the brain. Local blood flow is related to the amount of activity between neurons. It has only been possible to measure this with fMRI since about 1996 and it has greatly aided the neuroplasticity research.

- EEG: electroencephalogram, or brain electrical activity – this is a way of showing the electrical activity caused by nerve cells firing. It is useful for picking up particular brain signals but can only give a rough approximation of where it arises, whereas the fMRI can pinpoint the exact location.

Davidson has worked on establishing an index for the brain's set points for moods. Through the use of fMRI, he found that when people experience difficult emotions such as depression, fear or anxiety there is more activity in the amygdala and the right pre-frontal cortex of the brain, an area connected with hyper-vigilance of the kind a person experiencing stress may engage in. When people experience enthusiasm, inspiration and positivity, these areas are quiet, but the left pre-frontal cortex is activated. In fact, gauging the activity of the pre-frontal cortexes proved to be a quick way to measure a person's mood. Of the people Davidson tested the majority were in a middle range, experiencing both good and bad emotions, and so activity alternated between the pre-frontal lobes.

People who would be described as clinically depressed came out as highly active in the right pre-frontal cortex, whereas people who are content and happy with their lives to a high degree showed higher activity on the left side. The highly experienced meditation practitioners – many of them Tibetan Buddhist monks with thousands of hours of meditation experience – who came to Davidson's lab for testing all fitted decisively into this latter group. The kind of refined coordination of neurons demonstrated by the monks had been associated with mental activities such as focus, memory and learning in previous studies. Their brains also showed the kind of intense gamma wave activity connected to heightened awareness. This research confirms that the brain can be trained to an extent science had not realized before.

What can we take from this? It is unlikely that many of us will ever manage to achieve ten thousand hours of meditation, so does this mean that our brain is not trainable in the same way as those people Davidson tested? The answer is that everyone's brain can be trained in just this way. Whenever we begin the training, change is immediately put in motion. Davidson began his research with what he calls the Olympic athletes of meditation – monks like Matthieu Ricard who had done thousands of hours of practice – because with them the results are clear and easier to detect, but he was also interested in widening the field.

In order to look at the effects of meditation on beginners, Davidson took part in a research project with staff at a cutting edge bio-technology company in Madison, USA, who were reporting stress at work. For three hours a week over a period of two months one group of staff was given a course in meditation practice, while a control group was not. Testing before the meditation course started showed that all participants' brain activity tipped more towards the right – the area of the brain that registers anxiety and worry – but by the end of the course all the participants showed a significant shift to left-pre-frontal cortex activity. People described themselves as having more energy and experiencing less pressure and stress. As a subsidiary study participants were given a flu shot. The immune system of those who had received meditation training caused an increase of antibodies in the blood by 20 per cent. A comparable study was carried out with a pilot group of schoolteachers in 2002–3 with similar findings.[7]

Since this research began, the number of studies of the effects of meditation on the brain and on health generally have grown significantly. The work of Jon Kabat-Zinn has been instrumental in bringing mindfulness meditation into the mainstream of medicine through his mindfulness-based stress reduction programme. He is professor of medicine emeritus at the University of Massachusetts Medical School, where he founded the Stress Reduction Clinic in 1979. The clinic and its research have shown that it is possible to achieve long-lasting improvements in both physical and psychological symptoms, as well as major positive changes in health attitudes and behaviours, such as the management of physical pain. So impressive are the results that the MBSR (Mindfulness-Based Stress Reduction) model has now been adopted in more than 200 medical institutions throughout the world. It was initially developed to treat people with chronic pain and stress-related disorders, but research has continued with studies involving its effects on women with breast cancer and men with prostate cancer; with prison inmates and prison staff, and in various corporate settings. A study conducted with patients suffering from the skin disease known as psoriasis showed that when they were given a mindfulness meditation exercise to do while receiving phototherapy treatment, they healed four times faster than people not taking part in the exercise.[8]

Research into the effects of meditation practice on the brain, on health and on wellbeing are in their early stages and there is much more work to be done, but the signs are compelling and give encouragement to the experience that any meditator can vouch for – that meditation helps in one's life. Davidson's work demonstrates that the trained mind, or brain, is physically different from the untrained one.[9] Any meditator can begin to experience that a trained mind is more workable, more stable, more equipped to deal with the inevitable challenges, joys and sufferings that life brings than an untrained one. The more the mind is trained, the deeper that experience.

Meditation is currently being used in a variety of institutions, such as schools, hospitals and prisons. It is even finding its way into the corporate world with companies such as Apple, Google, Starbucks, Walt Disney and IBM using it as part of their support programmes for staff.

Applying meditation practice

Let's imagine the following scenario – you enjoy visiting your husband's family and get on well with his parents and his brother. However, you find his brother's wife intimidating. She has a high-powered job as a human rights lawyer, and is quite bookish and political. She's also very attractive. You trained as a primary school teacher and now work part-time in a local school so you can be home for your children when they get back from school. Juggling work and the family means you often feel like you have not enough time for yourself and certainly do not have the means to spend a lot of money on your appearance. Your sister-in-law decided not to have a family in order to pursue her career and is always immaculately turned out. She is always polite and friendly to you but you suffer from feelings of inadequacy around her, and feel frumpy and out of touch. You even worry you are letting your husband down. You get either tongue-tied or over-talkative from nerves. You find the whole thing quite stressful and feel you dislike your sister-in-law.

How can meditation help with this? In the first place, the experience of meditation will help assuage the feeling of running to catch up. By spending some quiet time each day simply watching your breath and training your mind you will help create space and ease in your day – however busy it is. This provides a more reliable basis for dealing with challenging circumstances. Secondly, it will provide a space to look at your feelings of 'not being good enough' and allow you to see them for what they are – just fears that have no real basis and just rise and fall in your mind. You have a chance to notice they are only there when you think of your sister-in-law. They are not there when you are working in the school, caring for your children or being with your husband. You may even remember a time, perhaps from your own schooldays, when one of the older girls put you down for not wearing the right kind of shoes and not being cool, and realize that this old hurt is triggered by your sister-in-law but actually has nothing to do with her. You are able to create a distance between the thoughts and feelings you have when you see her from how things actually are. As you do this you may even feel a slight sense of amusement at the games your mind has been playing, but instead of chiding yourself for being so silly, you acknowledge what has been going on and resolve to let it go and enjoy the family visits more in the future. With meditation the whole situation has more ease, more space and an increased capacity for healing and reducing stress.

KEY POINTS

- Meditation is important because it is an effective way of training the mind, which will help us to develop compassion and reduce our stress levels.

- The mind as it is now it like a wild elephant – powerful but out of control. We need to calm it down in order to harness its natural potential.

- Mindfulness practice will help us to switch off the automatic pilot on our mind and enable us to be more present to our activity. This will release our energy and resources and help directly with stress.

- Meditation is a way of coming to know yourself and to make friends with yourself.

- Meditation adds relaxation and awareness to the practice of mindfulness to provide a complete way of working with everything that comes up in the mind – all the thoughts and emotions that take up so much of our attention.

- The point is not to block our thoughts and emotions but to see them like clouds crossing the sky – they come and go and make no lasting impression.

- Meditation enables us to be more in tune with life as it actually is, with its continual change, the inevitability of stress and suffering and interconnectedness.

- Current scientific research is endorsing the experience of meditators by showing that it has a positive effect on our health and wellbeing.

EXERCISES

Exercise: Switching off the autopilot

Choose a routine activity that you perform every day and use it as a focus of mindfulness.

Begin by connecting with your breath, then as you enter into the activity become mindful of each step.

Check each of your senses – what can you hear, see, feel, smell or taste?

Note any changes as they happen.

Notice when you lose your mindfulness and your mind wanders off – simply bring it back to what you are doing, with a feeling of kindness towards yourself.

Exercise: Cutting the commentary

The next time you are in a difficult situation – an uncomfortable visit to in-laws, a difficult meeting with a work colleague – try to stay with what is actually happening, rather than engaging in your own silent running commentary.

Begin by connecting with your breath as you enter the situation.

Notice your inner monologue of hope and fear, like and dislike.

Drop it and come back to the breath.

Do this again and again.

During the conversation, whenever you catch yourself sliding into your commentary, just let it go and come back to the breath.

Exercise: Cloakroom meditation

Everyone needs to go to the loo several times a day – why not make your visit a couple of moments longer and take a meditation break?

Just stay in the cubicle and take a while to watch your breath and then carry on as usual.

STOP moments

In the shower.

Washing up.

Vacuuming.

Cleaning your teeth.

Chopping vegetables.

Ironing.

PAUSE opportunities

When you have to stop at a red light in traffic.

Entering a supermarket.

Standing in a queue.

Waiting for the kettle to boil.

Standing at the photocopy machine.

Waiting for your computer to boot up.

Meditation slogans

Remember the breath.

Let it go.

Come back to the present.

The brain is trainable and responds to experience.

There are further meditation exercises in the Appendix on page 319.

9 Identifying our Unhelpful Habits

> Most people are afraid of suffering, but suffering is
> a kind of mud to help the lotus flower grow. There
> cannot be a lotus flower without the mud.
>
> *Thich Nhat Hanh*

We have looked at how the mind works and how, through mindfulness and meditation, we can train it to be more effective for us. This provides the basis for beginning to become aware of and work with our habits. We can make a start by turning our attention to our unhelpful habits – the ones we need to change in order to reduce our stress. In chapter 6 we looked at some basic causes of our suffering, such as our tendency to live as if we were independent, permanent and unchanging even though all the evidence of life shows us that this is not how things are. The effort we put into trying to feel secure and avoiding what makes us feel uncomfortable limits our view of life, causing us to develop a range of unhelpful habits. It is these habits that determine how we cope with and respond to stress. As we have already discussed, taking the time to become familiar with our habits is an important first step but, as we have discussed, our tendency is rather to try and *avoid* suffering. Accepting that stress is a symptom of suffering can help us to try and find out more about why we get stressed and how we behave when we are feeling it – in other words, stress can have something to tell us about ourselves. This puts us in a more effective position to apply new, helpful habits such as compassionate mind techniques. We will start to explore how to do that in the next chapter.

Layers of Stress

When we get up each morning it is likely that we are dealing with several layers of potential stress – stress that may stay as a distant murmur on our personal radar, or land decisively in our field of vision demanding a response. Understanding how these layers operate can help us to see more clearly what is a potential stressor for us, when stress occurs, the times when we are especially vulnerable to it and how we react to it. Some of the outer layers may remain at low levels of worry, but taken together they can add up to a kind of sludge of potential stress that we carry around with us, which is probably already taxing our resources. Often we do not even notice this continual, low-level activity and can be surprised when we boil over at a relatively small provocation.

The outer layer

The layer the most removed from us personally is an outer one made up of lots of potential stressors to do with conditions in society. Maybe you need to fly when there has been a recent plane crash or terrorist threat; perhaps the economic news is weighing heavily on your mind; or you are feeling sad because of a recent hurricane or flood that has featured heavily in the news. The news provides an on-going display of painful events that may not impact on us directly but, nevertheless, affect us as human beings and colour our outlook.

Then there is the tone of the culture in which we live and our relation to the trends of the moment. Perhaps we have experienced a recent change in government that we do not agree with and are constantly troubled by policies that seem shortsighted to us. Maybe we worry about the rise of religious fundamentalism, or the slow, seemingly unstoppable progression of global warming.

An example of this cultural stress is the growth of consumerism as an answer to our problems which invades so much of our lives. I remember as a child watching television with my parents that advertising breaks were carefully timed every twenty minutes or so and were heralded by an announcement that adverts were coming and then a second announcement when we returned to the programme. My father used to joke that it was just time to make a cup of tea. Nowadays I notice that the breaks come much more frequently and with no warning – you can be absorbed in a programme, only to have a number of different images flashed across the screen that jolt the senses and take a moment to register as adverts. Shopping seems to have become a leisure activity in its own right, with a shocking impact on the level of personal debt people are willing to sustain. In fact, 'retail therapy' is even seen by some people as a means of relieving stress.

In his book *The Age of Absurdity*, Michael Foley writes:

> Shopping is no longer so much about the gratification of desire as the thrill of the desire itself, which must be constantly renewed.[1]

Oliver James takes this further in his study of what he calls the Affluenza Virus:

> A set of values which increase our vulnerability to emotional distress. It entails placing a high value on acquiring money and possessions, looking good in the eyes of others and wanting to be famous.
>
> . . . the Affluenza Virus increases your susceptibility to the commonest emotional distresses: depression, anxiety, substance abuse and personality disorder.[2]

He sees the Affluenza Virus as a product of what he calls 'selfish capitalism', a system geared towards profit at all costs that he believes has affected almost all aspects of modern life.

Each of us will be sensitive to different possible stressors in our cultural surroundings. We have just explored a few here in a general way but it is worth taking some time to think about how and when your own buttons get pushed, because you will almost certainly find that those are the places that get rubbed repeatedly, making you vulnerable in a way that can undermine you at the most unexpected times.

Layers of stress to do with our own world

Closer to home are the layers of potential stress that have to do with our own environment – our neighbourhood, family and friends. I have an example of my own that illustrates this kind of stress. My partner and I live in a very attractive area of Amsterdam. Previously the old dock-land area, it is skilfully planned in order to maximize access to the water with lots of trees specially planted. We pay quite high charges for street cleaning, rubbish and recycling collection but the service we receive is excellent. Unfortunately, however, not everyone keeps to the simple rules of placing household waste into the large bins provided, and putting out oversize items on Thursday evenings for collection on Friday. Time after time we see small children stagger to the bins with large plastic sacks that they are not strong enough to lift into the bins and so leave them beside the bins to pile up. Often, just after all the large items have been removed on a Friday morning, someone will discard perhaps an old cupboard or chair and leave it by the bins, knowing it will be several days before any-one will collect it and in the meantime it will be kicked around the street. Even though it happens on a regular basis, it unfortunately never fails to irritate me. I can easily find myself holding forth on how antisocial people can be though, of course, no one hears except my poor partner! It does me no good at all and just leaves me feeling stirred up, but it is so hard to just accept that this is the way things are. Unless I catch myself it can act as an uncomfortable irritant, a minor source of stress.

Events in our extended family life, or the lives of our friends can occupy our minds in a similar way – we can find ourselves fruitlessly question-ing why a certain member of the family cannot make a relationship work, or why our friend is having trouble at work once more. We can find our-selves going over the same ground again and again, worrying about a problem without reaching any solution – it's those mental loops again. It has not yet become a full-blown stressor but it has the potential for wearing us down and reducing our resilience against stress when it does occur. The more of these kind of worries we dwell on the more seriously we wear ourselves out.

Immediate stress

For each of us, the most active layer of stress is what is happening for us directly in the course of each day, but this can take many different forms. For many of us work is a major source of stress as we find ourselves trying to cope with situations that seem beyond our control. A friend of mine is a Family Resource Worker, which means she is assigned to families whose children are experiencing difficulties in school. She has to deal with all kinds of human suffering – including child abuse, truancy, under-age pregnancy, alcoholism, and domestic violence. Her caseload, and that of all members of her team, is enormous, and her power to actually bring any solution to the families' problems is limited. As a responsible and caring person this is a source of tremendous worry to her. She told me of a recent dream in which she became aware of a crowd of people gathered around the entrance to a multi-storey car park, shaped a bit like a giant filing cabinet. As she approached to see what the commotion was all about she became aware of an awful stench coming out from the car park and a cloud of bluebottles rising up from the ground. She threaded her way through the crowd to see that they were all gathered around the decomposing bodies of one of the families that had been assigned to her and that she had not had the time to visit yet. The dramatic image in her dream sends a clear message of overload, and yet she does not have the luxury of changing her work conditions. She is thrown back on her own strategies for coping and has no choice but to examine her habits in relation to stress.

You may be struggling to communicate with your teenage son, or you may be caring for a parent who has dementia. Your partner may be suffering from ill health, or your neighbours might be noisy and antisocial. Many people live with continual, low-grade pain and discomfort such as arthritis, or back injuries. At a workshop that I gave recently two of the participants had just been made redundant, and another had had six migraines in three months due to the stress she was experiencing at work.

It is rare to find anyone who is not coping with one or more sources of stress in their daily life, and this is not taking into account the random, unexpected events that can happen to us such as bereavement, sickness or loss of a relationship. These are the things we always hope we will not have to face and spend quite a bit of time quietly dreading at the back of our minds. Strangely, when they actually happen they tend to draw on reserves of courage and strength we hardly knew we had and we get through them somehow – we are stronger and more resilient than we think.

On top of this, there is the constant wear and tear of everyday life. Perhaps you are familiar with Charles M. Schulz's cartoon character Charlie Brown? For me, one of the most poignant descriptions of leaving behind the security of childhood and becoming an adult is when Charlie Brown becomes aware that he is now too old to fall asleep in the back of the car on the way home from a family outing and have his parents carry him indoors and put him to bed. He realizes that if he falls asleep he'll need to wake up and sort himself out when the family gets home, and it is his younger brother who gets carried in to bed. It sums up for me the moment when it all comes down to you: however many people you have who care about you, it is basically up to you to take care of yourself.

Some Psychological Factors Affecting Stress

Predictability

Research shows that when stress is unpredicted its impact tends to be worse than when we are expecting it. Likewise, when we are experiencing stress, if we have an idea of how long we are going to have to deal with it we find it easier to cope than if we have little or no idea when it is going to end. This was demonstrated when London was bombed during the Second World War. Londoners knew to expect bombing every night for a protracted period of time, whereas the suburbs were hit more sporadically. Research on people suffering from ulcers showed that more people in the suburbs suffered from ulcers than in the much more severely hit areas of London. Furthermore, the increase in ulcers only lasted for three months. By the end of that period of time people

in the suburbs expected sporadic attacks and so they were less unpredictable.[3] A more current example could be the difference between the
stress of going for an interview for a new job and that of worrying about
the safety of our current job in an unsettled economic climate. However
stressful the job interview is, we know when and where it will happen
and how long it will take. The current economic difficulties are beyond
our control and no one can tell when they will end.

If we understand that stress of all kinds is an inevitable part of life, then
it is possible to have a different take on the whole idea of predictability.
Without being pessimistic, or anticipating difficulties which may not
even happen, we can learn to become familiar with the different layers of
stress that each of us deal with on a daily basis, so that we are prepared to
cope with them. Too often stressful events can seem as if they have fallen
from the sky and just landed on us and then it can be hard to get things
in perspective. If we can learn to expect and, most importantly, to *accept*
that there will be stress in our lives, then rather than fighting this idea,
we will find it easier to deal with stress when it does come our way.

Control

When we believe that we are in control we tend to experience less stress
than when we feel that we have none. Air travel is safer than driving and
yet because when we fly we are not in control of the plane, more people
are afraid of flying than are afraid of driving. Even things we enjoy doing
lose their attraction if we are told we *have* to do them, because we are no
longer exercising control over whether or not we wish to take part. Raising
teenagers can be a stressful time when children that we thought we knew
and understood seem to turn into partial strangers, often with different
agendas from our own. Our family may no longer feel within our control.
This can also be a major factor in workplace stress, where workers feel
that they have little control over what happens to them in their jobs.

> [At work, people may see] little variation in how to do their tasks,
> but they still have other kinds of choices in terms of their attitudes,

how they interact with their co-workers, whether they utilize certain inner qualities or spiritual strengths to change their attitudes
at work.[4]

The quote above, which comes from *The Art of Happiness at Work,* is referring to work life but in fact holds true for all aspects of our lives. We can
have control over and change how we react to the stress that life throws
our way by understanding and working with how our mind is. Rather
than fighting the stress, trying to get rid of it completely or wishing it
wasn't happening, we've seen that instead we can work with how our
mind is and thereby reduce the negative impact that stress can have on
our lives. This is the take-home message of this book.

Learned helplessness

Learned helplessness is a condition that was discovered by accident by
psychologists Martin Seligman (who we came across when we talked
about Positive Psychology in chapter 5) and Steven F. Maier. It is a state
that we can get into when we have been subjected to repeated, unpredictable and uncontrollable stress, and it is characterized by a sense of giving
up on being able to manage a particular aspect of your life. For example,
if you are told often enough as a child that you cannot sing, it is going to
be hard for you to find the confidence to try out your voice later on, and
much more likely that you will agree with the verdict and try to restrict
your singing to the privacy of the shower. During my years of teaching I
met many children who had been treated as second-rate learners for much
of their school life and were subsequently failing. Fortunately in most
cases this was reversible once their self-confidence was boosted. Sadly,
though, all too often the degree of stress that someone has been subjected
to can lead them always to expect the worst outcome from whatever they
attempt. With their perception clouded by their past experience they lack
the clarity to see when things are actually going quite well for them.

This is something that I see from time to time in training sessions that I
am engaged in for people at work. Highly stressed people can become

so battered by their experience that they become almost deaf and blind to any support that is offered to them, and seem to be almost afraid to believe that change is possible. Indeed, many of us feel this way from time to time. Maybe we're going through a particularly stressful time at work, or are looking after someone who has been ill for a while. It is easy to lose sight of the fact that things won't necessarily stay the same forever.

The best way to approach this feeling of being battered and slightly helpless is to spend time identifying what *is* working well and use that as a starting point for building our courage. If we can do that it becomes easier to identify the particular stressors that are causing us the most worry. It is important to pick out individual threads from the general sense of helplessness and then work out what to do about each one. For example, things might be tough at work but perhaps the shared worry has brought you closer to a work colleague and the strengthened relationship provides support. Maybe you realize you have isolated yourself too much and need to work on building closer relationships. This gives you an attainable goal in a challenging situation and helps you feel a sense of control. Be prepared for it to be a slow process, but the good news is that as soon as you make even a small start things begin to feel different.

Survival Mechanisms to Deal with Stress

When we looked at how our body reacts to stress in chapter 2 we saw that these reactions were designed to help us to escape from hostile circumstances and to survive danger. We also saw that in modern times most of our stress is not caused by life-threatening situations at all. For example, we are capable of raising our blood pressure by recalling an argument we had several years ago, anticipating how a difficult boss will respond to our request for an early holiday, or leaping to the defence of a friend who's being criticized. Given that our potential stressors have become so varied and numerous it is not surprising that we then find ourselves trying to protect ourselves from the results of our own stress.

Unfortunately many of the ways we try to do this not only do not help us manage the stress in a more effective way; they can actually make things worse.

We may try to comfort ourselves by having an extra glass of wine with a friend, or by taking up smoking again when we've just managed to kick the habit. Treating ourselves to a chocolate bar or cream cake can seem like a good idea to help us relax but if we do this several times in a week we're going to gain a few extra pounds. Distraction from the cause of our stress can seem like a good way of giving ourselves a break from a problem, but we often find that it's still there when we emerge from the movies, the nightclub, the restaurant – or wake up in front of the TV. Perhaps an even more damaging way of dealing with stress is to shut ourselves off and not allow anyone to help. We might think that by doing this we are at least not spreading our stress around, but in fact we are also depriving ourselves of one of the most effective support mechanisms – talking problems through with people who care for us. As we have seen, no one wants to feel they are not in control, and stress can undermine our sense that we are in charge of our lives. If we respond by pushing down our emotions, and denying our needs in order to give ourselves the feeling we *are* in control and we *are* coping, then we will end up feeling more isolated and increasing the pressure we are under. When we establish boundaries to keep people away, and set limits in order to feel secure, we are making it harder to access our inner resources to nourish ourselves in a compassionate and healthy way. It is as if we close an inner door in our heart that in fact shuts us off both from our own capacity for caring and self-nurture, as well as any feeling of empathy for other people. We may be trying to cope but it is a short-term strategy that will not help us to understand and look after ourselves over time.

I recently delivered a workshop to a group of people working in the third sector[5] in the UK. One of the people attending was the CEO of an organization experiencing cuts and redundancies – let's call her Lynn. Lynn had come along to the workshop, as she wanted to find a way of managing her working life differently. Her stress level was beginning to affect her health and she was concerned as to where she was heading. She was an intelligent, articulate woman, obviously dedicated to her job, but she came across as someone under siege. Although she was drawn to the idea of developing mindfulness and empathy skills, she had great difficulty in applying them to her own situation. Each time we came to talk about it she would present her case as being especially challenging, or herself as being less able to apply the techniques we were learning than the rest of the group. After a while I saw that she was quite skilled in deflecting the very help that she was seeking and thereby maintaining the circumstances she claimed she wanted to change. We discussed how to integrate a short session of meditation at the beginning of the working day and I asked her to describe her early morning to the group. Lynn shared that she woke up to the news on her radio, and then turned on the TV so she could watch the news while she dressed and ate breakfast. She did not allow herself one moment of quietness from the moment she woke up until she went to bed at night. We talked through how she could change her alarm call to music and keep the news off while she got ready for work. Somewhere between dressing and eating breakfast she would try five minutes of sitting meditation. Her breakthrough moment came with a very simple mindfulness exercise, similar to the one presented in chapter 8 on page 147, which meant that for a few moments she just stopped and watched her breath. The ease of this almost shocked her and enabled her to see how effective silence and attention can be in cutting through habits of stress – in her case, the habit of having noise and activity going on all the time.

Up until the point where she had a direct experience of the power of mindfulness techniques, Lynn demonstrated how easy it can be to justify unhelpful coping patterns to ourselves based on a misperception of our capacity to change. Even when we feel like our back is against the wall and our health is threatened, we can still find ourselves clinging to the way we always do things and believing it's the only option available. So for each of us it is not only important to recognize where we are vulnerable to stress and what is likely to cause it, but also the coping styles we bring to bear in trying to manage our stress.

In order to examine this more closely we will look into specific habits we can assume with regard to stress.

Habits that Increase our Stress

We have seen that the ways in which we try to cope with the insecurities of life can mean that we are limiting our view of ourselves and the world we live in. Although our intention is to try and maintain a feeling of security – and to be happy – the events life repeatedly puts in our way demonstrates that this limited view does not serves us very well – in fact, it causes us suffering and stress. Let's consider some of the habits that we can develop that increase our stress.

The habit of not paying attention in the present moment

We already talked about this in the last chapter when we looked into mindfulness. This is one of the most common causes of stress. Our tendency to dwell on things that have already happened and try to plan and anticipate things that have not yet happened means that we are often unable to see what is actually going on right at this very moment. Jon Kabat-Zinn, whom we already met in chapter 8, is engaged in bringing mindfulness into the mainstream of medicine and society. Here he expresses the impact of not paying attention:

> If we sum up all the missed moments, inattention can actually consume our whole life and colour virtually everything we do and every choice we make or fail to make.[6]

This inattention means that when it comes to stress, we do not notice it building up until it is right on top of us. We miss the clues that could help us defuse things at an earlier stage. When we don't take the time to notice and pay attention to our stress triggers we lose our chance to choose how we are going to react, and instead carry on with our usual habits or responses.

The habit of hoping for what we want and fearing what we don't want

Animals tend to respond to the world as they experience it, but as we have already seen, we humans are much more complicated because we are able to respond to things that exist only in our imaginations. As Professor Paul Gilbert writes:

> We humans can respond to the world we have created in our heads.[7]

Part of what we do when we are *not* paying attention to what is happening in the present moment is to speculate as to how we would like things to turn out. When we plan a holiday we imagine all kinds of fun activities – sightseeing, swimming, sunbathing and so on. We are hoping for a pleasurable trip and if anything goes wrong, such as flight delays, bad weather or a disappointing hotel, we feel life is rather unfair. I have a close friend who reviews each day in terms of 'nice' and 'nasty' things that happen to her. She is an intelligent person, holding down a major job and yet she judges the success of her day according to the balance between the two totals. When we prepare a meal for our family we want them to appreciate it and praise our cooking and we are disappointed if someone criticizes the food. As we put together a presentation for work we visualize our boss being pleased with us, rather than blaming us for not having been sufficiently thorough. We want our colleagues to like and respect us, rather than avoiding having to work with us. In all our endeavours we want to gain some advantage and benefit for ourselves. We certainly want to avoid losing out, or suffering any reversal of our fortunes.

There's nothing wrong in principle with wanting things to turn out well. It is part of our human make-up to strive to improve our lives and to increase our wellbeing. We know that everyone wants to be happy and avoid unhappiness. The problem here is the way we grasp so strongly on to our hope that things will go well and at the same time try to shut out the possibility that they may not go exactly as we would wish. Right there we are setting up a range of circumstances that can become possible stressors for us. Instead of accepting the natural movement of life – the ebb and flow of situations and events, the inevitability of some disappointment and loss – we try to impose our wish for happiness as if the harder we focus the more chance we have of success. Deep down we know that life just does not work like that, indeed experience shows us this repeatedly, and yet we continue to hope that this time things will be different.

Our emotional habits

Our emotions can be powerful weapons, and many of our reactions to stress are expressed through our emotions. Think about your own reactions to stress – when you're under a lot of stress, how do you feel? Short-tempered? Anxious? On edge? Upset? Frustrated? Downhearted? The following metaphor is a great way of visualizing what happens to our emotions when we get stressed: imagine a freshwater lake on a sunny day – the water is calm and so clear that you can see the stones and plants on the bottom of the lake. Then a storm comes and the water is whipped up and disturbed, so grey and muddy that you cannot see anything – until the storm passes and everything becomes calm and clear again. Our mind is like the water of the lake – in itself it is clear and calm but when it is full of emotion it takes on the colour and intensity of the emotion itself. Emotions come and go, they are not who we are, but strong emotion changes our perception, and prevents us from seeing things clearly. This is particularly true of destructive emotions – the kind that undermine our peace from within, such as anger, worry and frustration. Love and forgiveness, on the other hand, are expressions of our intelligence and enhance our peace of mind. When we are feeling hurt or angry it is hard to imagine ourselves without the hurt or the anger, and yet these feelings always pass in time. So when we find ourselves in the grip of a strong emotion it helps to remember that while that particular feeling occupies our mind, we will not see things clearly and can easily make wrong decisions about how to act. Instead of allowing these strong emotions to overwhelm us, it will help to restrain our feelings as much as possible, rather than acting them out, and give them time to settle and pass over.

It may be hard to realize when emotions are surging up in us but it is possible to spot destructive negative emotions just as they start to bubble up to the surface. If we are distracted and our minds are confused we won't be able to do much about it, but if we have some experience of meditation we will be more aware of what is happening. This allows us to be able to notice the emotion and decide how we want to react. This is a wonderful opportunity to catch our emotional reaction before it causes us discomfort, or hurts someone else. We will look into this more when we look at self-compassion in chapter 11. We are not talking about suppressing our emotions here – that never works and usually means they explode at another time in an even less helpful form. It is more a question of understanding our emotional habits, seeing what is going on with us in any given moment and realizing that a destructive emotion is going to end up making our stress worse and therefore making us unhappy. We may enjoy letting off steam by snapping at our partner, or gossiping about a work colleague, but if we think about how we feel afterwards, we can usually see that we don't tend feel so good about ourselves when we are angry or when we gossip. If we remember the Golden Rule – *Treat others as you would wish to be treated yourself* – then we realize we don't like it when people are angry with us and we would hate to find ourselves the subject of office gossip. The key word here is discernment – we are trying to learn to discern which of our emotions will contribute to our wellbeing and the wellbeing of those around us, and which will detract from both. We will explore this further in this chapter and the next one.

The habit of addiction to stress

As I mentioned before, my professional training was as a schoolteacher. Although I have not taught for many years, I enjoyed my time in the classroom very much. Most of my teaching career was in inner London schools with tough kids who had lots of energy and faced lots of challenges. It was certainly a potentially stressful environment but it was exhilarating too with a great deal of interesting, innovative and creative work. One of the reasons I eventually stopped teaching was not the pressure from the children but the culture of stress among the staff. It got to the point where if you were enjoying your work and not complaining about it all the time, it was thought that somehow you were not taking things seriously enough and missing just what a tough time everyone was having. I met some wonderful people who were teaching but sadly most of them subscribed to the 'them and us' attitude – 'them' being the government, the parents and the head teacher. If you did not join in this siege mentality, laced with a heavy dose of cynicism, then it was hard not to be seen as eccentric.

I sometimes come across a similar attitude in my workshops – people who are suffering from various sources of stress related to their work and their attitude to it but who feel safer clinging to the way they have always done things, rather than risk trying something new. It's a case of better the devil you know – in this case sticking with stress. It may be eating up their energy, undermining their private life and leeching the joy from their work, and yet it is familiar and they feel they are just about able to manage it. This addiction can be quite a subtle process, affecting people who have high levels of responsibility and commitment to their work but who take that sense of responsibility to extremes and place themselves in the role of a saviour for the situation – indispensable, always available and ready to pick up the pieces.

In chapter 2, we looked at how the repeated activation of the stress response can have all kinds of negative consequences. The habit of addiction to stress can be one result of living in a constant state of what the author Rick Hanson calls 'simmer'[8] – an ongoing low-level stress response. Because of the impact this has on the amygdala and hippocampus this can mean that our tendencies to be anxious, or even depressed, are increased. The higher levels of adrenaline coursing through our body keep us on a permanent state of high alert, which can be very hard to switch off. This is one reason why stress can become so endemic in certain situations.

Evolutionary habits

If we think back to our predecessors living on the savannah all those thousands of years ago, it is not hard to see that it would have been negative experiences that taught them the rules for survival rather than the positive ones. For example, failing to understand that it is better to run away from a sabre-toothed tiger, rather than to try to stroke it, could have resulted in instant death – so the fight-or-flight response was developed. Whereas, if our ancestors had a positive experience, like finding something new to eat, but did not have time to investigate it right then it could always be sampled the next day – our brain didn't need to learn to respond immediately to the positive.

Because of the advantages of being more alert to bad things happening to us than to positive things, our brain is more geared to keeping an eye out for the negative and, in fact, this has become a habitual response – in other words, a habit, and part of our threat and protection system. Our brain is constantly on the look-out for threats because that is how it needed to be in order to protect us from attack in the past, and the brain carries on doing it today even when it is no longer so necessary. Although this has some advantages, the downside is that it can leave us with a continual low-grade feeling of unspecified anxiety – the experience of 'simmer' that we just mentioned – which we cannot quite find a focus for. Similarly, our brain detects negative information more quickly than positive information and tends to remember it for a much longer time. We cannot do a lot about this in the short term but we can learn to be aware of these tendencies and learn to be ready to balance them out, rather than simply react to them. Over time we can learn to begin to override them with more helpful habits.

The Stress Response and the Stories we Create

If I feel that what is going on around me is demanding more of me than I feel I have the resources to cope with, then I am experiencing stress. How we *respond* to stress will determine how it affects us – not everyone reacts in the same way. We all know people who are thrown into a tailspin if they break a nail, and others who experience constant challenges with the minimum of fuss. Recently, a work colleague was sharing with me the difficulty his parents were experiencing with some new neighbours who were turning out to be very noisy. He described how he had gone round to see his parents and his mother was talking on and on about the noise and its effect on her. He said he suddenly realized that at that particular moment the neighbours were being completely quiet, and yet his mother continued to fill all the space with her anxiety about the situation. This story demonstrated for me how much we add to our stress by the way we react to it.

My colleague's mother was certainly in an unpleasant situation, but she added to her suffering by talking about it all the time. How many of us find ourselves doing this? We end up talking about the potential cause of stress, often to the extent that we make ourselves feel more stressed. I need to fly quite a bit for my work and one of my stress triggers is going through the security check. I always want to get through quickly and settle down to do some work in an airport café before my flight. Inevitably I find myself in the slowest moving line, with people taking ages to unpack their bags, take off their shoes, repack their bags and move through. If I am not paying attention I can find myself getting quite irritated by the people ahead of me as well as the over-zealous security guards. When I catch myself, I feel awful for harbouring resentment towards someone innocently wanting to get on their way, just as I do. So, when I get stressed in this situation, I am adding at least two more layers of stress on to myself – firstly, my feelings of irritation and secondly, by my feeling bad about feeling irritation. Fortunately when I am working I am usually travelling alone, or else there could well be a fourth layer when I share my feelings with my companion!

My airport story is an example of how something fairly minor can cause us stress and we can make it worse by the way we react to it. Exactly the same process applies to more serious sources of stress. Perhaps you know of a friend or relative who, on being made redundant, decided to make the career change they had always wanted to make but had been afraid to do so. Another person faced with the same situation might slip into depression and feel like a failure. A major health scare can leave us with tremendous fear for the future, or it may leave us feeling determined to use our time really well. Divorce certainly marks the end of an important phase in our lives, but it does not have to signal the end to any hopes of happiness. The stories we tell ourselves about the situations we find ourselves in can help us to either cope in a healthy, long-term way, or they can undermine our confidence and sense of wellbeing. If we are aware of what our stress triggers are, and the habits we have for dealing with them, it will provide us with considerable support in cutting down on the extra layers of stress our reactions can create. We will look at this in more detail in Part 3. For now, here is an exercise which will help you look at how you react to stress and identify any habits you fall into.

Exercise: Reflecting on how you react to stress

Sit for a few moments and watch your breath.

Remember an occasion recently when you were feeling stressed. Take time to remember the situation clearly.

Now take time to identify:

What happened.

What your thoughts were about what happened.

What your feelings were about what happened.

How would you describe your reaction to the stressful event?

Have you responded to stressful situations in this way before?

Can you identify any habits you fell into here?

Take responsibility for your thoughts and feelings at the time but don't judge them.

Now consider these questions as you remember this incident:

Did you take time to calm down with mindfulness or meditation?

Were you able to separate your feelings from your behaviour?

Can you identify any additional layers of stress that you added to the situation?

Did you spread your stress to others by how you behaved?

Did you behave in a way that you yourself would like to be treated?

On reflection, is there anything you would like to have done differently?

Sit again.

Make some notes in your journal about what you discovered about how you respond to stress.

Stress Pollution

In chapter 4 we looked at how the discovery of mirror neurons has extended our understanding of how we communicate and showed how connected to each other (interdependent) we are. Mirror neurons are cells in the brain that fire when an individual performs an action, as well as when he/she observes a similar action performed by someone else. When this connection is helping to spread compassion it promotes a sharing of healthy feelings, but when it works in terms of stress it adds to an already tense atmosphere. We can transmit our feelings of stress in a myriad of ways – through our body language, our mood, through the words we choose to express ourselves with and by how accessible we are to other people. Some people cope with stress by sharing their feelings with everyone around them, not always realizing the impact it has on those who have to listen.

At the other end of the scale, it is easy to pick up on the stress of people we work or live with and to become affected by it. A bad tempered boss will cause a ripple of unease to spread through a whole office, even reaching people who do not come into direct contact with them. In Japan there is a phenomenon known as *karoshi* – which means 'death from overwork'. There are support groups devoted to supporting the widows of men who have died from it. Here is an extreme example of a culture of working hard spilling over into one of intolerable stress. We can see how the poor people who fall victim to *karoshi* are not just highly stressed in themselves, but operating in a culture where everyone's stress is allowed to infect others.

We call this 'stress pollution' and it happens when we are not paying attention to the present moment and have become focused on our own feelings and reactions to things. When it takes hold of an environment it can seem self-perpetuating, limiting the chances for that environment to change. It can happen in small ways almost before we realize it, which is where paying attention comes in. When discussing this during a workshop I was giving, one of the participants, Margaret, had an example close to home that she shared with the group. She has to travel quite a bit for work. Both she and her husband have a well-balanced view of this and enjoy the time they spend apart engaged in separate projects. They communicate frequently by Skype and text messaging when they are apart, and look forward to being reunited when the trip is over. Whenever he can, Margaret's husband picks her up from the airport on her return and has supper ready at home. Margaret described her feelings of often being tired after the trip, longing for the supportive environment of her home, and looking forward to exchanging news and stories with her husband. She says by the time she arrives home she can find herself feeling quite vulnerable as she makes the shift in mood from the work trip to her quieter home rhythm. This can make her oversensitive to anything that does not go smoothly. For example, if she finds that her husband has not kept their apartment as tidy as she likes it she can find herself getting irritable over a few unwashed lunch dishes or some unwatered houseplants. Quite rightly, her husband may feel he is doing all he can to ensure a pleasant homecoming and that she is being unappreciative. She laughed as she described how they have both tried to work with this dynamic where her stress from her work trip and journey can spill over and spoil a happily anticipated homecoming. She said the trick was to recognize her own patterns of behaviour before they took hold and to pay attention to her reactions while she is feeling very tired. If she does not notice in time her husband finds a way of gently pointing it out to her.

It is not hard to see that without this kind of awareness, stress pollution can spread through a family, or workplace, with corrosive results. Naturally there are times when it is important to talk about things that are bothering us, and to discuss our stress, but it is better to do that when we are feeling calm and able to have a productive discussion. Stress pollution starts with a person allowing their stress to spill over in an uncontrolled way, which is difficult for them and for the people around them.

KEY POINTS

- We have already begun to put some tools in place to help us work with stress.

- Most people try to manage several different layers of stress of different intensity at the same time, the most challenging being the immediate stress of each day.

- Psychological factors affecting stress:
  - Predictability: understanding stress is part of life.
  - Control: we have control over how we react in any given situation.
  - Learned helplessness: a result of too much stress.

- Unlike animals, humans can feel stress about events that happened long ago, events that may never happen or events that just exist in their imagination.

- Unhelpful strategies:
  - Distracting ourselves from the pain of stress.
  - Shutting ourselves off from support.

- Becoming rigid about being in control.
- Putting up limits and boundaries.

- It is important to recognize where we are vulnerable to stress and the way in which we try and cope with it.

- It is very helpful to become familiar with what our own habits are when faced with stress, so we can spot them when they become active and try and change them into something more helpful. Typical habits are:

  - Not paying attention.
  - Getting caught up in hope and fear.
  - Emotional habits.
  - Becoming addicted to stress.
  - Evolutionary habits.

- We cannot avoid stress in our lives but we do have a choice in how we react to it. Cutting down the negative stories we tell ourselves about the situations we are working with will help us to be more effective in managing our stress.

- When we are not paying attention we can spread our stress around in an unhelpful way as well as picking up the fallout from other people's.

EXERCISES

Exercise 1

In your notebook draw a mind map that describes the *different layers of stress* you feel yourself to be experiencing. Distinguish between simmering stress and acute stress.

Exercise 2

What is your *strongest habit that leads to stress*?

Exercise 3

Identify your *triggers for stress* – the things that can easily result in a stressful reaction for you.

Exercise 4

List your *negative coping styles* (unhelpful strategies).

Which is the one you would most like to change?

Exercise 5

Try to notice when you *spread your feelings of stress* to other people.

How can you take care of yourself without affecting others with your stress?

10 Adopting Beneficial Habits

> Compassion automatically invites you to relate with people because you no longer regard people as a drain on your energy.
>
> *Chogyam Trungpa*

Basic Principles

In this second section of this book we are trying to become aware of our habits, gathering as much understanding of them as we can, and deciding what we want to do about them. So far, we have examined the habits that may increase our stress – the unhelpful habits we need to learn to let go of. Generally these are habits that we have acquired to try and make sense of what is happening around us and to us – something that is not always easy to do. In fact, as we have seen, many of the habits we use when faced with stress are exhausting. They tend to make the problem worse and actually increase our stress levels.

Among the beneficial habits we can learn to help us reduce our stress are habits to do with developing compassion for ourselves and for other people. The instinct for compassion, as we have seen in chapter 3, comes from a very different place than our stress responses. The potential for compassion exists in all of us as part of our human make-up – it does not have to be contrived or forced. Habits based in compassion have the potential to nourish us as well as other people – we can start to be less harsh with ourselves and develop kindness instead of anger in our dealings with other people. The challenge is to learn to understand what compassionate habits are, how we can develop them, and to put them into practice so that they become our default way of responding to stress, rather than our habitual less helpful reactions.

Stress tends to reduce our possibilities for action. It is as if our room to manoeuvre is shut down. When we pitch our strength against a perceived threat we tend to see the possibilities for action as more limited than they actually are. Because compassion is about appreciating things as they really are, it creates possibilities and opens up space for movement – there is nothing to struggle against, so we are able to relax and look at the situation calmly. This enables us to engage with the two psychologies of compassion as described by Professor Paul Gilbert and covered in chapter 3. You will remember that the first psychology is *the ability to engage with and stay with suffering* – the wish that all people could be free from suffering; and the second psychology is *the willingness to help bring this about*. So, compassion could be said to open an inner door in our heart, whereas stress closes it.

Chapter 3 introduced the importance of understanding interdependence in relation to compassion, whereas in chapter 6 we considered how being unaware of interdependence leads to stress. Interdependence is a way of describing the interconnectedness of life and the interrelationship between people. Here is what Martin Luther King had to say about interdependence:

> It really boils down to this: that all life is interrelated. We are all caught in an inescapable network of mutuality, tied together into a single garment of destiny. Whatever affects one directly, affects all indirectly. We are made to live together because of the interrelated structure of reality. Before you finish eating breakfast in the morning, you've depended on more than half the world. This is the way our universe is structured, this is its interrelated quality. We aren't going to have peace on Earth until we recognize the basic fact of the interrelated structure of all reality.[1]

If you find this a lot to take in then it can help to just start by spending some time thinking about what King is saying about your breakfast. Maybe you have cereal, toast, fruit and coffee or tea, or perhaps you go for something more elaborate? Whatever your breakfast choices, think of just one item – your cereal perhaps – and ask yourself who helped get it from the field where it grew into your bowl. There are the farmers who grew the grain, the people who picked it, the packers and transport people but there are also their families and the people who made the clothes they were wearing as they worked. Then there are the people who brought it by plane or truck to the distribution centre and through several steps into the local supermarket – so by now we can include all the people who built the plane, or truck, and the supermarket, the designers of the packets and the advertising agencies who convinced you to buy this kind of cereal – and their families too. Even then we are not covering everyone. If we start again with the milk that goes with it, or the bowl itself, we include more huge groups of people who have been involved in your breakfast as you sit in your kitchen at home. This is how interdependence works – we can see that it has an impact on all aspects of our lives.

Training our mind to bring this understanding of the inter-relatedness of all aspects of life into the forefront of our thinking is an essential and helpful habit to acquire in terms of developing compassion. It helps us to develop awareness of other people and to realize how much we all depend on each other.

Another way in which we misperceive the world we live in and so cause ourselves stress is by clinging to the idea that things are permanent and continuous, in other words, things are here to stay and will carry on as they always have. In fact everything is changing all the time. The quote below from Yongey Mingyur Rinpoche sums up this idea brilliantly:

> Very simply put, everything in our experience is always changing. The world around us, our bodies, our thoughts and feelings – even our thoughts *about* our thoughts and feelings – are in constant flux, a progressive and ceaseless interplay of causes and conditions that create certain effects, which *themselves* become the causes and conditions that give rise to still other effects.[2]

There are aspects of this that are easy to understand but others may be more challenging. It is not so hard to accept that everything is changing and moving all the time – although we often choose to ignore it. It is harder to see how one thing leads to another – if I grab the last carton of milk on the supermarket shelf, it could mean that you need to go and buy some milk in the late-night shop on the corner because you need milk to make a sauce for the dinner party you are hosting. While buying the milk some teenage boys rush into the shop and steal your purse. All the resulting upset means you are late home to prepare the meal for your friends. You're a bit shaky and the cooking does not go well, so you end up needing to get a takeaway and spending more than you intended. We can see in this way that one small incident is in fact part of a much bigger web of events and they are all connected.

A few months back I visited a town in Holland where we used to have family. My partner and I remembered a café we visited a few times and looked forward to having our favourite dish for lunch, but when we reached the place the café was closed and boarded up. So was the one across the road – in fact the whole street had gone downhill a bit and it was hard to remember what it was that we had enjoyed about it. The changes that had happened made it a different place from the one we remembered and spoilt our pleasure in revisiting it. It is annoying when your local supermarket stops stocking the brand of shampoo that you always buy, or your neighbours move away and are replaced by ones you don't find as easy to get along with. These are the more obvious changes that happen in our lives, but there are more subtle kinds of change also happening all the time, which are harder to notice. Do you know the surprise you feel when you see the children of friends or family that you have not seen for a while, and are taken aback by how much the children have grown? We rarely apply the same passing of time to ourselves and reflect how we too have changed as we have grown older. Consider the changes in our body as blood is pumped around our system and we digest our latest meal. Our body is constantly getting rid of old cells and replacing them with new ones. Of course, it is not just in our body that molecules, atoms and subatomic particles shift and change – the wood of my desk where I am writing is undergoing the same process, as is my computer and the very room I am sitting in. Think about the thoughts and feelings that course through the mind – none of them last for very long before they are replaced by the next wave and yet we bundle the whole lot together and refer to it as 'me'. This 'me' is not the same as it was yesterday, let alone five, ten, fifteen years ago, and yet we treat it as if it is.

Exercise: Reflection on the changes in your body

Sit comfortably with your back straight and breathe naturally through your nose.

As you do so pay attention to the changes in your body as you breathe:

The movement in your lungs.

The rise and fall of the muscles in your belly.

If your mind wanders away, don't worry, just come back to awareness of your breathing and the changes in your body.

Stop after about a minute.

Review what you noticed.

Perhaps you were aware of the breath flowing in and out of your nostrils, or your thoughts and sensations as you sat. All this is fine – we are just taking time to observe the constant small changes that happen all the time in our body.[3]

Learning to be aware of the state of flux we live in, to recognize that everything is changing, is another beneficial habit to adopt in terms of understanding compassion. It helps us to realize that nothing lasts forever and encourages us to appreciate the good things in our lives while we have them, while understanding that the difficult things will also pass.

Although these habits are a natural expression of our human nature, they are not easy to establish and it requires sustained effort over a period of time to replace less helpful habits with new ones. Think how hard it is to establish helpful habits such as losing weight, exercising, or giving up smoking. In relinquishing our ingrained habits of stress, we will need to overcome our conditioning.

Evolution has provided us with survival strategies that enable the human race to survive but are not always in tune with the bigger picture. For example, our brain has been programmed to separate the world into what belongs to 'me' and what belongs to the 'other'. Our ancestors needed to learn to do this in order to protect their tribe and keep out of the way of other tribes. However, as we have seen, everything is inter-related and interdependent, so it not possible to make such neat distinctions. We see an example of this when a big oil company develops oil fields without paying sufficient attention to the needs of the country they are working in – the oil belongs to the country of origin but is accessed through the machinery of a global company, which is then responsible for environmental issues. In a case like this it can be hard for the global company to take all the necessary factors of interdependence into consideration, which can have negative results.

Our brain has been programmed to maintain stability in order to keep things in balance and provide the right environment for bringing up children. But in fact, everything keeps changing and stability is only ever temporary. The way we have evolved as a species makes us approach opportunities and avoid perceived threats in order to protect ourselves and escape from situations that threaten our survival. However, life shows us that not all opportunities turn out to be beneficial, and not all threats can be avoided.

Our ancestors learnt quickly that banding together in tribes increased their chances of survival and so it was a natural progression to want to care for and nurture other members of the tribe. This is still the prevalent attitude in most societies today – showing kindness and compassion to our family and friends is relatively easy, but reaching out further than that small circle is much harder. When we do manage to do so often we find that we have preferences for the kind of people we find it easy to show compassion for – it is often easier to have compassion for poor people than it is for rich ones, and the victims of crime and misfortune tend to receive more compassion than the perpetrators. So if we are interested in learning to develop our compassionate minds we will need to move beyond this social and cultural conditioning that favours people we know and like. Biased compassion of this sort is limited because it does not include people outside our circle. It means that we are evaluating the object of our compassion to judge whether or not they are worthy recipients. Once they disappoint us, or annoy us in some way it becomes much harder to continue to be compassionate. In a similar way, if our compassion for others is driven by the hope of getting something in return, or the desire to get a good name for ourselves, then it is also limited because it has more to do with our own interests than the interests of the other person.

The best way to address this is to bring to mind over and over again that, just like us, everyone wishes to be happy and to avoid pain and suffering. Thinking in this way extends the circle of compassion beyond our immediate family and friends and moves beyond any preference for one group or another because it touches on a universal human truth. If we take it a step further and remember that in spite of this aspiration, everyone encounters pain and suffering as an inevitable part of life, then we touch a deep tenderness in ourselves, which is like a seed for compassion.

Compassionate Reasoning

Let's take some time to consider what we mean by a seed of compassion. Each of us has experience of situations that touch us deeply and the corresponding feeling of openness, warmth and softness that can arise

– looking after someone when they ill, or seeing the love of a mother for her child, could affect us in this way. This is like the first spark of compassion in our hearts, but along with this there often comes a feeling of sadness. I remember that when the shootings happened in Mumbai in November 2008 among those killed were a father and his daughter who had travelled from the US for a meditation retreat in India. The whole incident touched me deeply as the stories of people's ordeals came out, but this story seemed very close to home, and brought a deeper layer of sadness, as I reflected on how easily that could have been two people close to me. As this thought came to mind, it was closely followed by the realization that, of course, these two people were close to all kinds of other people who would be in great pain.

Feelings like this can leave us feeling vulnerable and exposed. Perhaps we are afraid of showing such feelings and prefer to keep them hidden and ourselves well defended. Compassion requires the cultivation of a daring heart – one that is capable of cherishing itself, other people and life itself. Developing this kind of daring is another important habit of compassion.

Along with developing this courage, however, it is also necessary to have some sense of acceptance – acceptance that suffering is part of life but also acceptance for yourself as you are. Compassion is not about being perfect, nor is it about being able to be perfectly compassionate. In order to show compassion for others we need to draw on all our own experience of suffering, fear and making mistakes. Remember how we talked about learning to *lean into* our suffering so that we can fully understand it and engage with it as a means to awaken compassionate feelings for ourselves and others? Without knowing our own suffering, how can our feelings for other people who are in pain and afraid be genuine? In choosing to develop our compassionate mind we are also choosing to change our own unhelpful habits. This is one reason why developing a compassionate mind is so effective in helping to reduce stress. In order for it to work we need to pay attention to all our habits to do with stress, to recognize that we hold them in common with many other people. This makes us realize that as we work with our own habits our understanding of others' deepens. As that happens we become more able to address our own stress. Compassion is not pity, it is not about condescension – nor is it a relationship between the healer and those to be healed. It is simply a question of starting with what we have, attempting to learn from our mistakes and pain and then relating our struggle to the struggles that every other human faces.

It is all too easy to judge ourselves continuously as getting things 'right' or 'wrong'. As we develop compassion we try instead to just stay alert and open to our experience, without judgement, and to then extend this same attitude to others. Try this exercise when you are watching the news and see if you can apply what we have been talking about.

Exercise: Watching the news

Try to watch the news a few times over the coming week.

Just sit down and watch it without engaging in any other tasks at the same time.

Notice any feelings of warmth, openness and softness that you feel in response to some of the news items.

Notice any feelings of revulsion or pain that you feel in response to other news items.

Notice any feelings of vulnerability that arise in you, along with the wish to protect yourself from unpleasant news.

Can you relate any of the news items to your own experience?

Try to view all of your reactions – both positive and negative – as part of the process of working to develop compassionate habits and remember it is not about you being perfect.

The logic of compassion

As we work to develop compassion we will engage in emotions such as love, patience, tolerance and forgiveness. All of these qualities will help us to develop lasting happiness and so bring benefit to ourselves as we try to benefit others. Here is another clue as to how compassion can help with stress – as we cultivate compassion we are also cultivating the very qualities that will support us in dealing with our own stress. For example, recent research[4] has indicated that as we practise showing compassion to others, we open ourselves up to receiving support ourselves. Social support – the support of friends, family and so on – is an effective means of developing resilience to stress. Developing compassion can be likened to practising non-violence, because it is not possible to truly refrain from being harsh to others if we continue to punish ourselves. By showing compassion to others we inevitably learn how to show compassion for ourselves. We can learn to recognize ourselves in other people and be willing to take on the challenge of compassion. As social beings we are more at ease when we acknowledge our connection with other people and try to act in accordance with it. This is such an amazing aspect of compassion – that helping others helps us too.

Research on the impact of volunteering brings home this point very convincingly. In the book that he co-wrote with Peggy Payne, *The Healing Power of Doing Good*,[5] Allan Luks gives a fascinating account of the beneficial effects of helping others. He conducted a survey of 3,300 volunteers in more than 20 organizations in the USA that covered a wide range of volunteer activity. This was the first study to analyse the experience of helping and to demonstrate that a certain kind of helping could lead to measurably better health for the helpers themselves. Since then his findings have been confirmed by other studies.

The majority of volunteers reported experiencing what Luks has termed 'a helper's high' – an immediate physical feel-good sensation, along with feelings of warmth and euphoria. This feeling is a sign of a decrease in stress in the body. After this initial reaction comes a second, longer-lasting phase, characterized by a sense of calmness, along with increased feelings of self-worth and relaxation. Eight out of ten volunteers described how this sense of wellbeing could reoccur whenever they *remembered* helping out. Ninety-five per cent of helpers reported improvements in their health ranging from a reduction in the effects of stress, less awareness and experience of pain, and improvements in immune system functioning. It seems that these health benefits were more likely to occur in helpers who volunteered on a weekly basis rather than, say, once a year. Another factor that improved volunteers' health was personal contact with the people being helped, as was the importance of helping people who were not family or friends.

These findings are in keeping with what we learnt about compassion in chapter 3. When we focus too fixedly on our own concerns then we can lose perspective and see our problems as overwhelming. Connecting with the suffering of others helps us to see our own situation differently, and helps us to develop our natural capacity for empathy. When we place ourselves in the service of other people we open ourselves up to considering their problems as being as worthy of attention as our own. If we can help them, then we feel useful and our sense of self-worth increases. The social contact that volunteering provides is also nourishing in itself and provides us with support in return.

Luks includes this quote from physician David Sobel and psychologist Robert Ornstein:

> The greatest surprise of human evolution may be that the highest form of selfishness is selflessness.[6]

As we learnt earlier, compassion starts with where we are right now. We do not have to wait to become more capable of compassion than we are *at this moment*. All that we need in order to practise compassion right now lies in our current experience and capacity to work with our unhelpful habits. Recognizing that helping others actually helps ourselves gives us a wider range of tools to start to address these habits. It is a helpful motivator to put in the work that is needed to truly develop compassion. As we understand more about compassion, we can learn to extend the natural concern we have for our own wellbeing to include the wellbeing of others.

Habits Based on Compassion as Antidotes to the Habits that Increase our Stress

In chapter 9 we talked about a number of habits that play a large part in the extent to which we are affected by stress. Now that we have explored some compassionate habits it's useful to look at how these work in relation to stress. To begin with, let's look specifically at two habits that have a particularly big impact:

−   The habit of not paying attention.

−   The habit of hoping for what we want and fearing what we don't want.

The more specific habits we mentioned in chapter 7 will be picked up in Part 3.

Habit 1: Not paying attention

As we have already discussed, we all tend to spend a considerable amount of time thinking about the past or the future, and subsequently miss a lot of what's happening in the present moment. This is a shame, because if we think about it carefully we realize that the present moment is all that we have to work with. The past has gone and the future is uncertain

– however much attention we give to it we cannot change that. Thich Nhat Hanh, meditation teacher and Nobel Prize nominee, often speaks about each of us having an appointment with life – an appointment that is right now. If we are not present then we miss it. Our tendency to spend the present moment with all these thoughts about the past and the future tends to tire us out and means we are rarely bringing our full attention to bear on what is right in front of us. Even more serious is our habit of filling in the gaps in our attention in order to reassure ourselves that we are in touch with what is going on. This is why we can all have such different memories of the same event – each of us will have filled in the gaps in our attention with details from our own experience of the situation.

So as we have seen, we behave as if we are independent units that just carry on with our own concerns when, in fact, we are part of a deeply interdependent world – one that is constantly moving and changing. As we train ourselves to adopt a compassionate mind, we are becoming more aware of the interconnectedness of all aspects of life, as well as seeing that it is in perpetual motion. This helps us to pay attention to how things actually *are*, rather than as we would *like them to be*. Learning to pay attention is the basis of awareness – self-awareness in the first instance and then awareness of others. It is in itself an act of compassion for ourselves and other people because it reduces the extent to which we misperceive our life, and so decreases how stressed we feel.

Habit 2: The habit of hoping for what we want and fearing what we don't want

Many of us put so much effort into trying to organize our lives to fit with the expectations that we have developed as we have grown up and that are now part of our worldview. As a means of trying to fulfil our wish for happiness, there is nothing wrong with this approach *if* we can combine it with the understanding that things do not always work out as we wish – if we learn to be more accepting of what life throws at us. Unfortunately this is something that many of us do not do and so we end up experiencing the repeated stress of trying harder, planning more carefully and still facing disappointment.

Compassion for ourselves begins when we notice this cycle and realize that instead of enabling us to achieve our goals it is making us stressed and exhausted. If we can see our own suffering clearly then it becomes a springboard for being able to see the suffering of others and to want to do something about it. Compassion for other people begins when we see that just as we are caught in this cycle of stress, so are most other people. This touches us so deeply that we want to do something about it. Reflecting in this way reduces our focus on our own stress and so helps us to approach it in a more useful way. Training in compassion reduces the intensity of one's own problems because it helps us to see that our problems are not unique, or a special punishment for us, but are simply part of the inevitable ups and downs of life.

Research Findings on Compassion

I mentioned the Dalai Lama's collaboration with Western science and the work of the Mind and Life Institute in the Introduction. The field of neuroscience – the study of the nervous system – has proved to be an especially fertile area for exploration and exchange between Buddhist scholars and Western scientists. We have already mentioned the important role of neuroplasticity – the discovery that the brain changes in response to experience – in this collaboration. One of the earliest studies into neuroplasticity was carried out on violinists whose brains were found to devote more space to the region that controls the digits of the hand that they use to manipulate the strings of the violin. Other studies have suggested that even simply thinking in a certain way can lead to changes in the brain.

Sharon Begley, science columnist for the *Wall Street Journal* writes:

> Something as seemingly insubstantial as a thought has the ability to act back on the very stuff of the brain, altering neuronal

connections in a way that can lead to recovery from mental illness and perhaps to a greater capacity for empathy and compassion.[7]

The discovery that our habits are not hardwired into our brain – that new connections between neurons can be formed, old ones fall away and even completely new neurons develop – gives an interesting scientific perspective on the Buddhist view of the importance of training the mind. Buddhist training emphasizes the need to train the mind in order to become free from suffering and to be able to help other people become free from suffering. Neuroplasticity demonstrates that by training our minds we can change our brain and support new, helpful habits.

Sharon Begley continues:

> Because the science is so new, the limits of neuroplasticity are largely unmapped. But there is no question that the emerging science of neuroplasticity has the potential to bring radical changes, to both individuals and the world, raising the possibility that we could train ourselves to be kinder, more compassionate, less defensive, less self-centred, less aggressive, less warlike.[8]

In terms of the impact for training in compassion, we have already discussed Richard Davidson's work with highly experienced meditators. Here are some findings from Davidson's studies on meditations on compassion that are very relevant to the areas of stress and compassion (we will be learning some of these meditations in the last section of the book):

- During compassion meditations, the brain regions that deal with what is self and what is the other became quieter as if the meditators' focus had shifted to include other people.

- The experienced meditators displayed increased activity in the brain regions connected to empathy and maternal love.

- When the experienced meditators were meditating on compassion the part of the brain to do with planned movement showed an increase in activity – it showed a readiness to go and act to help others immediately.

- While the meditators were generating feelings of compassion, activity in the left prefrontal cortex (the site of activity that indicates happiness) swamped activity in the right prefrontal (associated with negative moods).[9]

- The rate of gamma wave activity in the brain is associated with perception, problem-solving and consciousness. The experienced meditators showed a higher rate of gamma activity than had ever been recorded before. Even more impressive was that the gamma activity continued to be higher than usual even when the experienced meditators were not meditating. This shows that meditating on compassion leaves an imprint on the brain that lasts beyond the actual meditation session.

From this we can see that meditating on compassion can change the way the brain function: changes that are beneficial for us. [10]

Davidson comments:

> As a neuroscientist, I have to believe that engaging in compassion meditation every day for an hour each day would change your brain in important ways ... The message I take home from my own work is that I have a choice in how I react, that who I am depends on the choices I make, and that who I am is therefore my responsibility.[11]

What does this mean for us in terms of using compassion to change how we experience stress? In simple terms it means that everything is malleable – nothing is fixed. The habits that lead to stress and deal with stress are not hardwired into our brain but can be replaced with more healthy ones, such as habits based on compassion. By applying ourselves we can unlearn old habits and learn new ones that will help change the way our brain functions. The bonus is that changing the way our brain functions will actually support these new habits further. As we have seen, through practising compassion, activity in the parts of our brain associated with depression and anxiety is reduced while activity in the parts of the brain to do with happiness and wellbeing is increased. Developing a compassionate mind enables us to create the conditions for a greater sense of wellbeing that will help us as we work to reduce our stress.

KEY POINTS

- Stress tends to reduce our possibilities for action, whereas compassion creates space and room for movement. Compassion could be said to open an inner door in our heart, whereas stress closes it.

- Training our mind to really understand the inter-relatedness of all aspects of life is an essential and helpful habit to acquire in terms of developing compassion.

- Learning to be aware and to recognize that everything is changing and nothing stays the same is another good habit to adopt in terms of understanding compassion.

- In order to work with compassion we will need to overcome conditioning from our evolutionary history and our social circumstances. We can do this by remembering that everyone is looking for happiness.

- Compassion requires the cultivation of a daring heart – one that is capable of cherishing itself, other people and life itself.

- Compassion is not about being perfect, nor is it about being able to be perfectly compassionate. In order to show compassion for others we need to draw on all our own experience of suffering, fear and making mistakes.

- Helping others will also help us. ·

- Training in compassion reduces the intensity of one's own problems because it allows us to see that our problems are not unique but part of the inevitable ups and downs of life.

- The idea of neuroplasticity – the idea that the brain changes in response to experience – underpins the idea that we can change our habits for the better and so reduce our stress levels.

EXERCISES

Exercise 1

As you get dressed in the mornings take a moment to reflect on which countries the items of your clothing have come from and all the people involved in making them.

Exercise 2

Consider taking up a volunteer activity, ideally one that you can do on a regular basis (for example, once a week or once a month).

Exercise 3

In chapter 9 one of the exercises was designed to help you to identify your strongest negative habit with regard to stress. Look at it again and see if you can apply anything you have read in this chapter about compassionate habits that could work as an antidote.

How could developing a compassionate mind help with this stress habit?

There are further exercises on compassion in the Appendix on page 322.

Conclusion to Part 2

We have covered a lot of important ground in these four chapters. You may find you want to go over them again from time to time to become really familiar with the ideas being expressed. We have seen that changing how we react to stress is possible; in fact the very make-up of our brain supports us to be able to change. However, as we know, even though we can change how we work with stress for the better, it is not easy to change our habits. We need to *want* to change them and the best way to develop this wish is by realizing how our current habits are causing us suffering and that we would be better off without them. Not only that, but there are a whole of range of alternative strategies that we could use that would actually help us – the habits based in compassion. Once we understand this it becomes easier to develop the determination to take on our habits; to let go of the harmful ones and replace them with helpful ones.

PART 3

Making Change Happen

Having spent time understanding our starting points for both stress and compassion in Part 1, and looking at how our habits work, and what we can do about them in Part 2, we can now turn our attention to compassion as a skilful way of changing our experience of stress. In Part 3 we will take a detailed look at how to increase this compassion until it encompasses ourselves, other people and the widest possible perspective by exploring compassion for ourselves, compassion for other people and compassion with a big perspective. With each chapter the scope of the compassion we are talking about increases and we can explore how understanding and appreciating this can provide us with a rich set of resources to bring to reducing our stress.

11 Compassion for Oneself – Peeling Away the Layers of the Heart

> Compassion isn't some kind of self-improvement project or ideal that we're trying to live up to. Having compassion starts and ends with having compassion for all those unwanted parts of ourselves, all those imperfections that we don't even want to look at.
>
> *Pema Chodron*

Meditation is an effective way of taking care of oneself and establishing lasting happiness. It can be considered to be the basis for self-compassion because it enables us to connect with our sense of inner wholeness and deep wellbeing, and from that perspective develop a sense of acceptance of ourselves and of our world. We are more able to see things as they actually are rather than clouded by our thoughts and emotions. Because in meditation we are not defending anything, it is easier to connect with our own soft spot, our capacity for love and kindness. This soft spot is the source for compassion for ourselves and for others. Practising meditation is a way of giving ourselves the best quality attention. As we noticed already, it helps to spend some time doing a session of meditation in the morning to set up the day. This is what Sylvia shared in a feedback session at the end of a recent training:

> I find that my inner resources are established during my more formal practice time, which I have in the morning. If I don't manage to find time to do this fully – the snapshots of mindfulness and compassion I inject during the day have less impact in helping me. For me my morning practice is the most important as it sets the environment for the rest of the day.

Having established the basics of meditation in chapter 8, we are ready to look into how to develop self-compassion. We have seen that compassion can be defined as the wish that everyone could be free of suffering and being willing to help bring that about. When we look at self-compassion we apply this definition to ourselves – we wish to be free of suffering and we are willing to take action to bring this about. In chapter 9 we looked at learning to understand our suffering, so we can do something about it and in chapter 10 we looked at learning compassionate habits to help with this. Let's see how we can apply this.

Why Having Compassion for Ourselves is Important

Some of the work that I do is with people who work in the caring professions. I often notice that such people have a highly developed sense of care and concern for their clients but are routinely hard on themselves – and often on their work colleagues too. This dynamic is usually evident when we explore compassion fatigue. When you are not used to working with yourself compassionately then there is more effort involved in showing compassion for others, along with a sense that your compassion is a finite resource that can become depleted and even exhausted. We may be able to respond to the suffering and pain we see in others but often when faced with our own we are more likely to tell ourselves not to indulge and to buck up our ideas. We can tell ourselves off about how we look, the way we do our job, the kind of parent we are, our level of competence in the world – this list is endless. One friend of mine often says she feels as if she is carrying her mother around on her shoulder, and she is engaged, all the time, in a running commentary of all the ways my friend should be doing better. The climate of individual achievement and the importance of success that is part of our society fuel this tendency in us. We are brought up to feel that anything is possible but, as life unfolds, if we feel we are not making it all happen as we wish then we worry that we have let ourselves down.

We have seen in earlier chapters that our brain has been designed to pay attention to negative stuff as a way of ensuring our survival, and so self-criticism can play a useful role for us. However, we need to temper it with kindness and wisdom and not allow it to be a habit-based response formed from the patterns of behaviour laid down in our childhood. Just as any attack from outside triggers the threat and self-protection system in the brain, so does any attack from *within our own mind*. Each time we criticize ourselves we are stimulating the same threat and self-protection system and triggering the same stress responses that are triggered when we are threatened by other people, and which lead us to feeling anxious and upset. Because we do not see that these are just random thoughts that come up in the moment, and may have more to do with things that have happened to us in the past rather than what is actually going on *right now*, we tend to ruminate on our imagined shortcomings, going over them again and again. If we do this often enough it will have the effect of making us feel frustrated and disappointed in ourselves and, sadly, even contemptuous at times.

We can be successfully holding down a demanding job while raising a family and running a home and yet the whole time we are showing an image of perfection that we feel we are not living up to. Each time a deadline approaches we fear we will not meet it. If the children get sick or do badly on a test we may feel that we're failing them. We are convinced the house should look cleaner, smarter, better. We know that we could look younger, thinner, more interesting. We talk about ourselves to ourselves in a much harsher way than we would talk to anyone else. In fact, if we were to say out loud to someone else the things we say to ourselves we would probably be deeply shocked. We push ourselves harder than we would push any work colleague, child or friend, and yet we still do not feel we are doing as well as we should. This can be because we carry memories from our childhood of being punished for getting things wrong with our parents or teachers, and this can leave us with a fear of being rejected in our adult life. This makes us try even harder to fit in and be good enough. It's really only when *someone else* tells us we are doing well, or praises something we've done, that for a moment we feel some ease. Then the next thing happens and our self-criticism starts up again. It's as if we do not believe in our own accomplishments unless another person confirms them for us.

This tendency can be seen as a misinterpretation of our wish to find happiness and avoid suffering – that we can only really be happy if things are just as we want them to be and everything is ticking over according to plan. If we experience pain and stress then we are letting in the possibility of unhappiness, which is not what we set out to achieve. We saw in chapter 6 that as long as we have this attitude of believing we can hold stress away from us by effort and will power, we will certainly suffer. It is only by recognizing that stress and suffering are an inevitable part of life that we will find the strength to deal with them from a basis of self-compassion. Let's look at the following story from Simon, who is a manager of a medium-sized organization:

> I sometimes find myself getting locked into a bit of a self-destructive emotional cycle. Interestingly it can be triggered by a strength that I have – the ability to see quite clearly what is lacking, like a skill or information, in a complicated or difficult situation. Unfortunately this strength can manifest in a way that quickly shows where I myself lack skills or experience, because I can get quite judgemental and frustrated. The skill turns from being helpful to something that undermines my confidence when I realize I am no longer communicating my point well to my colleagues. It is quite easy to get locked into this negative pattern – especially as our work culture seems to encourage focusing on what's wrong or not going well. While I think I'm a pretty mindful person, I can become fixated, clamped on to this habit or pattern. It can be quite painful to be mindful of a destructive habit – so then I try to remember the spacious aspect of mindfulness practice and inject a compassionate attitude which makes it all the more workable.

Because of Simon's familiarity with mindfulness and meditation practice he is able to see clearly what he is doing and identify the different strands of his patterns of behaviour – both the helpful and unhelpful ones. Remember we talked about the three elements of meditation – mindfulness, awareness and relaxed spaciousness? By applying the third quality – relaxed spaciousness – Simon is able to defuse some of the negative habits he tends to fall into, before they overwhelm both him and the situation. Injecting a compassionate attitude enables him to see what he is doing without feeling bad about it – noticing his tendency without judgement, and so showing kindness to himself. He does not pretend the habit is not there, or blame someone else for it; neither does he beat himself up about it. In this way, the potentially stressful situation provides an opportunity to explore a habit that could cause him problems and learn to change it.

Instead of trying to be perfect, we need to learn to show ourselves kindness and learn to love ourselves.[1]

The notions of actively being kind to ourselves and loving ourselves can seem like quite new ideas. If I close my eyes and try to imagine having a conversation with my parents – both of whom passed away some years ago – about trying to learn to love myself, my mind cannot quite make the leap to picture how the conversation would go. Both responsible, hardworking, decent people, they simply did not look at life in that way, and they did not think about themselves from that point of view. They would have felt it was taking your eye off the ball to worry about whether or not you were kind to yourself, and would have considered it self-indulgent. Perhaps this is a concern many of us feel – that if we let go of our constant inner critic we somehow let ourselves off the hook and it will all be downhill after that. The idea of loving ourselves can seem like going soft on ourselves and rather airy-fairy. We need to understand that by looking at ourselves in this way we are *not* being indulgent but in fact we are recognizing and harnessing our inner potential. In turn this will help us work with the difficulties life throws up from time to time and be of more use to other people. Learning to be self-compassionate represents a deep change in our attitude and way of being. It takes time and work. I have noticed in working with people who are beginning this process that they can misunderstand this and think that buying oneself an ice cream at the end of a tough day, or allowing oneself to spend a day in bed with a good book, is being self-compassionate. There is nothing wrong with doing either of these things, and as part of a process of learning to care for ourselves differently they may have a place, but on their own they are not self-compassion.

Looking Again at this 'Self' we are Showing Compassion For

In chapter 6 we looked at this 'self' that we live with and our habit of treating it as more solid and permanent than it actually is. We have discussed the interconnectedness of life several times so far in the book and talked about it as an element of our basic wholeness and wellness. Generally it is so much easier to see how this all works in terms of other people and external situations. It is harder to look at the 'self' in the same way because it seems too close and even threatening to consider that we are not simply one self-sufficient, continuous thing. However, if I can change my habit of seeing myself as simply going on forever, and instead accept that this 'self' is also an interconnected, evolving entity, then change is possible. The idea is to learn to see ourselves as a work in progress that can develop according to the influences and circumstances we meet in our lives.

If you think back to when we looked at happiness in chapter 5, one of the ideas we discussed was what Daniel Kahneman sees as the two selves we work with: the *experiencing self*, which lives in the moment and relates with experience directly, and the *evaluating self* which is responsible for making our life into a continuous story. It is this evaluating self that tries to keep checks on everything. So we talk about 'I', 'me' and 'mine' as we attempt to divide the world up in a way we can feel safe with. Once we know what 'mine' is then we can identify what is 'yours' and solidify things even further. As soon as we label things in this way then we want to protect what we see as ours and hold on to it. Think about queuing up for tickets for a new movie – once you have your place in the line, it becomes 'yours' and you are prepared to defend it. When your friend comes to join you, you are happy to let them in, but if someone else pushes in front of you, you feel annoyed and object. On any other day the place you are standing in is just a part of the cinema and it would never occur to you to try to 'own' it but once our self-interest is involved we try to protect our position. This gives us the illusion of being in control and being able to manage – to be able to maintain our happiness and avoid any pain and suffering. When something unpleasant happens to this 'I' we are unhappy and when something nice happens it makes us feel good. We tend to grasp at what feels good and feel aversion to what we don't like, but because it is impossible to always enjoy the good stuff and never have to deal with the bad, this is a tremendous source of stress. We are trying to swim against the tide of how life is and cause ourselves distress in the process.

Meditation helps us to see our 'self' more realistically. As we become more able to see the movement of our thoughts and emotions we can see the stories that we create about our lives. We can allow ourselves to be in each moment without judgement and without wishing things were one way or another. Meditation helps to peel away the layers that obscure our natural kindness, revealing a rich resource with which we can face life's difficulties. Becoming an adult does not mean that we have developed a mould for our self that we then need to maintain, but rather that we can learn to know all the different aspects of our self and how they interact. At certain times in our lives some aspects of ourselves will be more important than others and then when circumstances alter this will change. When I was teaching in school I was very confident about this 'self' that taught children. At the time it was not possible to see that this part of myself would grow and mature into a coach and trainer for adults. During the years that I described myself as a 'Londoner' there was no suggestion that in time I would come to see myself as an 'Amsterdammer'. When we can think back over our lives in this way we can glimpse the many facets and interconnections that have brought us to the place where we are now, and see that in our current situation lie all the seeds and possibilities of the future. Seeing ourselves in this way empowers an attitude of self-compassion because it takes us out of the constraints of perfection, of success and failure, and simply allows us to see ourselves responding as best we can to whatever comes our way. In this way we can develop a resilience to life's difficulties that is a firm basis from which to cope with stress.

Becoming a Friend to Ourselves

So practising compassion for ourselves includes both cutting through the stories that limit us and bring us down as well as building on our natural capacity for wholeness that we described in chapter 3. Meditation helps us to access the spaciousness, clarity and calmness of our minds and reminds us of our potential. The analogy of the sky and the clouds (see page 129) that we keep returning to helps us to see this clearly. Each time we remember our potential to do this and try to act from that basis we are showing compassion for ourselves. This gives us the courage to stop trying to avoid pain and instead to turn towards the difficulties that come our way. We can do this because with self-compassion we can see these difficulties as opportunities to learn and to grow, rather than as evidence of our shortcomings. It is a more beneficial and lasting way of fulfilling our innate wish for happiness than the simple seeking of pleasure.

In his study of self-compassion[2] Christopher Germer relates the fight-or-flight stress response to how we react when we feel under threat in the following way:

- When we are faced with a so-called threat which comes from our own mind – our inner mental and emotional functioning – rather than an outside stressor, the 'fight' response can become self-criticism

- The 'flight' response becomes self-isolation

- And the 'freeze' response leads to us getting caught up in our own thoughts to the extent that we are not able to act.

Let's look at how this might work in practice. Let's imagine that you have been made redundant and are out of work. The job was one you enjoyed very much and knew you were good at. You did not foresee the situation that would lead to you losing your job. In your initial reaction to the shock you feel angry and frustrated with yourself for not having read the signs correctly and tried to do something about them. You beat yourself up for having been gullible and stupid but in spite of this you push yourself to start looking for a new job, because naturally money is a factor and the bills still need to be paid. Your first couple of applications are unsuccessful and your sense of failure deepens. You are worried about the future and how you are going to manage to pay the bills. It becomes harder to talk about the situation with friends and you start to cut yourself off from the social support that is essential to help you through this. Because you are seeing fewer people you have more time to dwell on all the worries, anxieties and stories that are churning around in your mind. You forget that up until a couple of months ago you were holding down a good job successfully and happily, and you fear that you will never find work that you value again.

Now, let's try and look at the same scenario from the standpoint of using self-compassion and being a good friend to yourself. To begin with, it is important to acknowledge to yourself the shock you have had in being made redundant, and to give yourself permission to feel the pain of your loss. Although our instinct will be to try and put it all right as soon as we can, we need time to replenish our resources and take stock. We need time to gather our strength. If there is any way you can financially afford it, try to allow yourself an interim period before you start looking for a new job in which you give yourself some quality care – take some exercise, do some of the things you never have time for when you are working, do a little extra meditation. Gradually, as you feel up to it, you could spend some time updating your CV and reminding yourself of the skills you have. The idea is to try and create a feeling of space and support for yourself as you start to look for work, rather than feeling like a failure that needs to cover up the embarrassment as fast as you can. When self-criticism arises, just try to look at it in a detached way and check if there is anything for you to learn from the situation and take forward with you. Instead of isolating yourself, remember that you are not the only person ever to be made redundant and this is part of life that affects many people. You might even ring others in similar circumstances and check how they are doing. Talking through what happened can help to reduce your own worries and may even open up new possibilities. If you can work with these first two stages (the self-criticism Germer suggests can indicate the fight response and the self-isolation of the flight response) in this way the chances are that you will avoid the third stage of becoming locked in your own fears and feeling frozen. Perhaps if you wake up in the night and lie awake for a while these worries may come, but then you can try and apply some mindfulness practice and simply transfer your attention to your breath until your thoughts settle. None of this will make the problem go away, but by being a good friend to our self we can use our resources to meet a stressful and painful period of our life with a higher degree of resilience and so reduce the stress we experience.

Kristin Neff, an associate professor in human development at the University of Texas, is a pioneer in the field of self-compassion. She identifies three core components in self-compassion:[3]

- Self-kindness: being gentle and understanding with ourselves.

- Recognizing our common humanity: feeling connected to others rather than isolated by our suffering and pain.

- Mindfulness: holding our experience with a balanced perspective, neither exaggerating our experience, nor avoiding it.

If we look again at the scenario we just went through, we can see that *self-kindness* acts as an antidote to the *fight* response of self-criticism; *recognizing our common humanity* is an antidote to the *flight* response of self-isolation and *mindfulness* is an antidote to *freezing*, trapped in our fears. We looked at the function of the hormone oxytocin in chapter 4 when we looked at the biological basis of compassion. Neff states that research shows that self-compassion can actually stimulate production of the hormone in our own bodies, helping to soothe and comfort us.[4]

Exercise: Working with stress and anxiety

This is a useful exercise in which we use our underlying, fundamental wholeness to support us in difficult times. For the purposes of the exercise we will divide ourselves into two parts – for simplicity we call them 'A' and 'B' here but you could apply whichever labels work for you:

A – is the aspect of you that is well, relaxed, compassionate, self-aware, a true friend to you, always responsive and never-judging.

B – is the aspect of you that feels stressed, frustrated, overwhelmed and misunderstood.

This exercise focuses on the breath and there is a different activity for the in-breath and the out-breath. On the in-breath the A aspect takes away all the difficulties the B aspect is experiencing, and on the out-breath gives healing and nourishment. This enables B to relax and find some relief.

As you breathe in, consider that A opens their heart completely and warmly and compassionately accepts and embraces all of the stress and frustration that B is experiencing.

Touched by this, B can relax and open their heart, so that their pain and suffering melts away.

As you breathe out, consider that A sends out to B all their understanding, healing, comfort, love and confidence.

Continue the exercise for several moments and then sit in meditation.

Let's apply this exercise to the scenario in which you just lost your job. We could imagine that at last you have a job interview coming up – it's for a job that you know you could do well and have a good chance of getting, but your recent experience since losing your job has left your confidence at a low ebb and you are feeling very nervous and insecure. This would be a good exercise to do to help you prepare for the interview. The A aspect of yourself would be the one that knows it can do this job and is well-qualified for it, whereas the B aspect is the one whose confidence has been undermined by recent events. The idea is that as you do the exercise, the A aspect does not change so much but the B aspect finds comfort and healing, and the stress and anxiety you have been feeling is eased. You may need to do it several times but that is fine. Once you have become familiar with it, then on the way to the interview you could do an informal version of just paying attention to your breathing and imagining your nerves settling.

Some Practical Ways of Showing Kindness to Ourselves

A common way in which a lack of compassion for ourselves can manifest is how hard we drive ourselves. We tend to make greater demands on ourselves than on anyone else and feel guilty and frustrated when we cannot keep up these unrealistic expectations. In order to help us break this unhelpful habit it is useful to pay attention to some practical steps we can take to guard against treating ourselves so unkindly. Putting them into practice, even in a small way, will help us to build resilience in ourselves, which will help us when we work with any difficulties we might face. The happiness research we looked at in chapter 5 has shown that there are certain activities that can be counted on to increase our happiness. We can take a look at four of them here:

- Taking exercise

- Making changes in our routine

- Connecting with friends

- Expressing gratitude.

Taking exercise

We all know that taking exercise is good for us but few of us find the time to do much about it. So what we are talking about here is not making yet another resolution to join our local gym and get really fit, but simply to build time for exercise into our routine. In modern society it is very easy to find that we do not move very much at all, with most of our exercise consisting of short walks to and from the car, train or bus. It is a pity to wait until we are overweight or over-stressed to take the time to fit in some exercise as part of a programme of caring for ourselves. We can begin in a small way by looking at where we could find some opportunities to exercise within our existing schedule. Perhaps we could walk to work a few times a week, or even get a bicycle to go about on. Instead of having lunch at our desk we could go for a walk. A home trainer that enables us to fit in an exercise routine while the dinner is cooking can work very well. Maybe you used to play tennis or badminton and gave it up because of lack of time. You may enjoy playing a game with friends after work, or with other parents from your children's school. The truth is that exercise helps us to feel better about ourselves – it helps to reduce anxiety and increases production of mood-enhancing hormones. Exercise also stimulates the production of dopamine, which is associated with pleasure, happiness, motivation and interest. When we do things we like, dopamine is released. However, from our teenage years onwards our brain's capacity to produce dopamine decreases – it's a case of 'use it or lose it'.

Research has shown that low dopamine levels can be associated with various diseases – for example, one of the characteristics of Parkinson's disease is low dopamine production. So increasing dopamine production by generating pleasant experiences in our lives could be beneficial for us. Neuroscientific research shows that stress can impair the brain's ability to create new neurons, whereas exercise can promote the growth of neurons.[5] We feel better about ourselves when we take control of our body and our health, instead of just fretting about it and wishing we were a few pounds lighter.

Making changes in our routine

We can be so busy just keeping up with all that we have to do that we may suddenly find our lives have settled into a predictable routine that has lost some its freshness and excitement. If we pay attention to this and instead of feeling trapped by routine, decide to make some changes, then we can reconnect with the moment-by-moment quality of life and feel refreshed. We can do this by looking at our routines and reviewing which of them are necessary and helpful, and which are simply habits that we can change or cut out altogether. It can start with very small things – do you put out your clothes for the next day the night before, or do you wait to see how you feel in the morning and what you would like to wear? Do you always eat the same things for breakfast? Then you could tackle bigger things such as what you usually do at the weekend and where you normally go on holiday. Trying something completely different introduces us to new impressions and experiences that can inspire us. Sometimes our routines are just ways of trying to over-organize our lives and are not really necessary. We can get much more satisfaction from responding to how life is in the present moment.

Connecting with friends

We have discussed the evolutionary basis of social support several times so far in this book. We need and benefit from loving relationships with other people. All the happiness research agrees that the happiest people are those with the most supportive social networks. People seek relationships in order to be happy and happy people attract relationships. Sadly, our relationships beyond our close family circle can suffer from our tendency to drive ourselves too hard and we can often feel we have not enough time to include meeting with friends. Changing this attitude provides us with a way of coping with stress, as it provides us with people who care for us and are willing to offer us support – whether it is *practical*, such as babysitting our children if we need to go to the doctor; *emotional*, such as when you talk over a problem with a friend and benefit from their advice, or *informational*, such as giving us advice on which new computer to buy.[6] We tend to think that our friendships will take care of themselves and we can pick them up when we have time. We drive ourselves so hard that we think the 'fun' things can wait. All too often we allow so little time for seeing friends that we drift apart and lose touch. Making time for a morning coffee, an after-work drink, an occasional meal together is a good investment in our wellbeing. We could start by taking out our diaries and looking at the month ahead and seeing where we can fit in at least one social event each week with a friend.

Expressing gratitude

Appreciating what you have in your life and expressing gratitude for it helps us to move from being a glass is half-empty kind of person, to a glass is half-full kind of person – with all the accompanying benefits to our wellbeing. I recently talked to a man who had been a senior buyer for a large Irish retailer for almost thirty years. He was made redundant when the Irish economy crashed in 2008 and, at the time we met, was working as part of the airport assistance team in Dublin airport. He could have felt bitter about his change in status but in the half hour we spent together all he talked about was his gratitude for having work in an economy in which so many people are unemployed and his pleasure and satisfaction in having such a worthwhile and interesting job. He was a great example of someone who was capable of working through stressful situations by choosing to focus on the aspects of the situation that were beneficial for him, rather than the aspects that were disappointing and difficult. We can learn to do this by taking the time to notice the things in our lives that are working well and savouring them, rather than shrugging them off and focusing on the things that may not be going so well. Incidentally, research is showing that this helps to reduce our tendencies to adaptation and comparison, two of the ways in which we undermine our happiness that we looked at in chapter 5. If we are grateful for what we have, it keeps it fresh and we are less likely to take it for granted (adaptation) and if we are happy and contented with what we have we have no need to compare it to what others have (comparison).

Adopting a Compassionate Attitude Towards our Emotions

We started to look in chapter 9 at how our emotions work as part of our exploration of the habits that cause us stress. We mentioned how important it is to develop discernment in order to see which of our emotional reactions can be of benefit to us and other people and which are more likely to hinder us or cause harm. We saw that as meditation helps our mind to calm down, it becomes easier to take advantage of the space this opens up. This makes it easier to apply this discernment and so choose how we wish to react emotionally to situations. It is easy to give emotions a bad press and blame them for getting us into trouble but emotions are a natural part of our human make-up and necessary to help us survive. For example, if we did not experience feelings of desire and longing at some level we would not feel motivated to get up in the morning and do all the things necessary for our survival. Anger can help us to avoid situations that threaten our safety and even an emotion like pride can give us the energy and inspiration we need to explore and create. It's not the emotions themselves that cause the problem but *our reaction to them* that can sometimes be excessive – we just need to watch ourselves quietly cursing the driver who nips ahead of us into a coveted parking space, or the people in the long queue ahead of us in the post office, to realize we can get our emotional reactions out of all proportion. As part of our exploration of self-compassion we will look at some exercises to help us work with our emotions.

Again the analogy of the sky and the clouds, or the lake disturbed by a storm can provide us with strong visual images of how our mind is not just our thoughts and emotions – that our natural mind is spacious, calm and clear and that our thoughts and emotions are simply events in our mind that come and go. Because our thoughts and emotions are not the nature of our mind itself there is a mental and emotional environment that exists prior to every action of mind where we are free to respond to what is going on and not simply subject to the habits we have developed. The more self-awareness we have, developed through meditation and compassion training, the more freedom we have to choose how we react to situations. If we can apply this to observing our emotions it will help us build knowledge of how to work with them. We have seen that the positive emotions, such as kindness and love, will enhance our peace of mind while the negative emotions, such as anger and irritation, can destroy our peace of mind – so it is these 'destructive' emotions that we need to choose to avoid. Just as it helps to identify our triggers for stress, it is also helpful to understand ourselves well enough to know what are the kind of things that can trigger our destructive emotions. For me tiredness is a trigger to get irritable, or defensive, so it is important for me to recognize this and either stop and rest before I get to that stage or, if that is not possible, to be particularly vigilant of my emotional reactions in order to avoid being irritable while I complete what needs to be done. Another personal trigger is when someone I care for is criticized or not cared for in some way – I can suddenly turn into a mother tiger and cause all kinds of complications by interfering in an unhelpful way! People with very strong opinions who insist on trying to convince you of them really challenge my compassion and so it is important for me to be extra patient and alert to my reactions when I am with such people.

If we look closely at the times when we experience a destructive emotion we can see that the event can be divided into three stages:

- A *preparatory stage* which takes place when our peace of mind is under threat.

- The *actual event* which takes place when our peace of mind has been disturbed and we react.

- The *concluding event,* or the *consequence,* after we have acted from the place of a disturbed mind and things may need to be put right.

So if we take an emotional event such as getting angry, the *preparatory stage* would be when we feel anger rising in our minds but we are not yet angry. The *actual event* would be when we express our anger, with all that goes with it, and the *concluding event* would be when we set about trying to sort out what happened and to apologize and heal where necessary.

We will look at an exercise that we can use to work with each stage of an emotional event to try and stop it escalating to the next stage.

Exercise: Don't go there – recognizing what will undo your composure

This exercise emphasizes the point that we have a choice when dealing with our emotions. It is good for working with the first stage of emotion: the preparatory stage. It is an effective way of avoiding responding to our emotional triggers by simply not giving them attention. One word of caution though – *this exercise is not about avoiding difficult emotions but rather choosing how you wish to react to them.* It is a way of cutting the loops that our mind can get into when we go over and over a problem. So, this is not about avoidance; we are not trying to avoid things because we are too frightened to deal with them, but instead choosing to focus the mind on what is helpful. It is similar to the way that we avoid high-fat foods – not because we are frightened of them, but because we know they are bad for us.

Take the time to identify a specific source of frustration:

It could be at work, for example a coffee machine that never works properly and always irritates you.

It could be in your neighbourhood, for example the noise made by teenagers hanging out late at night.

It could be in your family, for example your husband's habit of placing a new roll of lavatory paper on top of the old, empty one instead of replacing it.

Reflect on it for a moment or two, to fix it in the mind.

Decide not to engage with it further – feel really determined about this.

Whenever you are faced with the thought pattern, or circumstances that upset you and cause you stress, say to yourself 'I'm not going there!'

This can be used in so many ways. I have a friend who prevents herself from getting into gossiping by saying, 'Well, we don't need to go there,' whenever the conversation verges on being catty about someone. Years ago I held a series of workshops for some barristers based in London. They worked in beautiful offices with lovely gardens. One of the older barristers found the noise of a fountain beneath his window very distracting and annoying. He had written letters of complaint demanding that it be turned off but all to no avail. He asked me what to do and I suggested this exercise and it worked! He allowed himself to hear the water but dropped the feeling of irritation that usually accompanied it. You can also use it to tackle a personal habit that brings you down but you keep repeating, such as a tendency to blame yourself when anything goes wrong, or constantly worrying about being on time for appointments. This exercise does not transform the emotion, but it buys us some time while we choose how we wish to react.

Exercise: Using the breath – for when our sense of calm is disturbed

This is the exercise to use for the second stage – the actual event. The emotion has taken hold and our sense of calm is disturbed but we can still try and not let things go too far. The exercise is very simple: we try and catch the emotion on our breath and do some deep breathing to try and help ourselves calm down. As we breathe deeply we imagine the emotion settling, and dissolving in the area of the belly. It's like a more elaborate way of counting to ten when we feel frustrated. Let's imagine that you tried to 'not go there' when your husband didn't change the lavatory paper, but you're tired and already irritated that he came home late from work and left you with all the evening chores. As he comes in, you immediately begin to share your annoyance and settle on the lavatory paper as a way of demonstrating your point that he is not pulling his weight around the house. Your emotion is disturbing your sense of calm and leads you to build one negative impression upon another. Suddenly, mid-flow, you remember that he told you he would be late home and you forgot. Not only that, he has suggested going out over the weekend to spend some quality time together. You realize that you have got carried away by your anger and are being unfair. You want to catch your emotion before it does any more damage.

Say to yourself, 'I am angry,' and then focus on breathing deeply into your belly.

Imagine that you can catch the anger on your breath and as you breathe deeply it settles and loses its intensity.

As it settles say to yourself, 'anger dissolving, anger dissolving . . .' Keep doing it until you feel you have established your calm again and the danger is past.

If the anger flares up again, just repeat the exercise.

The breath has a great capacity to calm and transform emotion and as it is always with us we can use it to good effect.

Exercise: Putting things right – for when you've lost it

This last exercise is for the third stage when everything has gone wrong and we have made an emotional mess. Perhaps we have got completely wound up and upset ourselves, or we have acted harshly towards others and caused them pain. The aim of this exercise is to help you to process what happened, put right what needs to be put right and move on with-out holding on to negative feelings. It enables us to forgive ourselves for behaving in a way we regret and to do all we can to learn from the experience. The exercise uses the breath in the same way as the one we had earlier in this chapter for working with our stress and anxiety.

Imagine vividly a situation where you have acted badly, one about which you feel guilty – it's hard to even think about it.

Then, *as you breathe in*, accept total responsibility for your actions in that particular situation, without in any way trying to justify your behaviour. Acknowledge exactly what you have done wrong, and in your mind wholeheartedly ask the other people involved for forgiveness.

Now, *as you breathe out*, send out reconciliation, forgiveness, healing and understanding.

So you breathe in regret, and breathe out the undoing of harm; you breathe in responsibility, breathe out healing, forgiveness and reconciliation.

We can cause ourselves a lot of unnecessary stress and waste a lot of time feeling bad about messy emotional situations. With this exercise we have a means to deal with all the difficult aspects that we would rather not face. When we do this we are using compassion and kindness for ourselves to heal our pain and suffering, and, at the same time, enabling ourselves to put things right with the other people involved.

So in this chapter we have seen that with meditation and a clearer understanding of how we view our 'self' as a basis we can learn to be a good friend to ourselves. We need to learn this because we do not always know how to be kind to ourselves in the best way. As we understand more about the importance of self-compassion we can create a more reliable and sustainable way of dealing with life's challenges and reducing our stress. We can begin in practical ways by looking at how to stop driving ourselves so hard and by making time to engage in activities that will help us to be happier. We can also work in a more creative way with our emotions.

KEY POINTS

- Meditation practice is the basis of self-compassion.

- Self-compassion is important because we can cause ourselves a lot of stress by being very hard on ourselves and beating ourselves up about any mistakes we may make.

- This 'self' that we live with is an interconnected, evolving entity capable of change at all times and also of trying to respond in the best way possible to life's challenges.

- Becoming a true friend to ourselves means cutting through the stories that limit us and bring us down and building on our natural capacity for wholeness.

- Stress from within our own mind can mean that the fight-or-flight response manifests as self-criticism, self-isolation and getting caught in our own thoughts and feelings.

- Self-compassion includes self-kindness, recognizing our common humanity and practising mindfulness.

- While we are working on developing the deeper aspects of self-compassion we can begin by driving ourselves less hard and making time for activities that enhance our wellbeing.

- Working with our emotions will help reduce our stress levels by helping us to feel more in control.

- An emotional episode can be divided into three stages: the preparatory stage, the actual event and the consequences. There is something we can do at each stage.

EXERCISES

It is a particularly good idea to record your experience of doing these exercises in a notebook. That way you can chart your changing habits and ways of seeing things as you put these techniques into practice. It will help you to see how much you are changing.

Exercise 1

Reflect on the ways in which you are hard on yourself.

After reading this chapter, what do you see differently?

Exercise 2

Think back over your life and try and identify as many of your 'selves' as you can – you might think of your childhood self, your single self, your self living somewhere else . . .

The idea is to see how many different 'selves' you have already been in your life.

Exercise 3

Try to recognize when you are going into the three stages of the fight-or-flight response as described on page 238 – self-criticism, self-isolation and freezing – and see if you can apply self-kindness, recognizing common humanity and mindfulness as antidotes.

Exercise 4

Over the next month make a realistic plan to:

Take exercise.

Make changes in your routine.

Connect with friends.

Express gratitude.

Note down the results.

Exercise 5: Identifying your early warning signs of stress

In the exercise sections of chapters 1 and 2 we started to look at becoming aware of our reactions to stress. Now we have come much further in our work on reducing stress, try to identify your specific stress alerts. Use the following questions to help you:

At what times do I experience a high level of frustration over relatively small events?

What do I know about the effect this is having on my body?

How does it feel in my body?

What do I do about it?

What new strategies have I learnt in this book to deal with it?

Exercise 6: Identifying your emotional triggers

In the same way, think carefully about what are the triggers for your destructive emotions.

Note them down.

There are further exercises on compassion in the Appendix on page 322.

12 Compassion for Others – Removing Our Armour

> Compassion doesn't mean feeling sorry for people.
> It doesn't mean pity. It means putting yourself in the
> position of the other, learning about the other.
>
> *Karen Armstrong*[1]

When you think about it, engaging in compassion for others is the most effective way of ensuring a peaceful and stable world. If each of us took as our guiding principle that whatever action we take to benefit ourselves should also benefit others we would have no need of police forces, armies or defence systems. Although this no doubt sounds idealistic, we can begin to work towards such a transformation right now by paying attention to how we relate to other people and benefiting from the effect this will have on all our lives. We have said that compassion is having the wish that everyone becomes free of suffering, along with the willingness to help bring that about. So, compassion is based on our ability to identify with other people, as well as our willingness to help them in any way we can. When we are working with compassion for ourselves we learn to accept ourselves as we are and try to offer ourselves kindness and understanding. It works in the same way when we engage in compassion for other people. Compassion is not dependent on whether or not people are shaping up to our expectations or standards, but is a response to their suffering without judgement. It is not an easy process. It requires courage and daring as it goes against much of the way we have been conditioned and means we need to learn some new ways of relating to other people.

This is why the subtitle of this chapter is *removing our armour*. As we learn to develop compassion for other people we will find that we need to undo many of the protective mechanisms we hold on to – such as fighting our corner or automatically putting our own point of view first. We do this in the mistaken belief that these strategies will help us and keep us safe. Defending and protecting ourselves takes a lot of effort and because it is impossible to do it effectively all the time, the effort we put into trying can become a source of stress. If we can replace this constant effort to defend ourselves with a sense of trust in our own fundamental wellness and capacity for thinking of others, then we have a more reliable basis from which to tackle stress because we are not forcing anything.

A few years ago I gave a two-day training session on compassion fatigue and burnout for palliative care nurses in Majorca. They were wonderful people, dedicated to their work and deeply caring. They dealt with human suffering and pain on a daily basis and had stories to tell that were heartbreaking to hear. However, they claimed that they coped with the obvious stresses of their jobs by making a separation between their work and the rest of their lives. One experienced nurse described this as like changing the chip in her mobile phone – one chip connected her phone at work, and the other connected her phone at home. She did not want the two to connect to each other because she did not want to take her concern for her patients home with her. She felt that would undermine her recovery period at home, intrude on her peace of mind and interfere with her family life. For her, compassion meant making a definite separation between what she needed and the needs of others. What struck me was that she was setting herself up for compassion fatigue by seeing her compassion as a finite commodity, and her peace of mind as something that needed defending. As we will explore in this chapter, compassion shows us that we are stronger, happier and more able to work with our stress when we remove these limitations from our attitude and our actions.

In chapter 3 we looked at how the development of compassion is a gradual process incorporating the following stages:

- Trying not to cause harm.

- Melting the ice in your heart.

- Seeing other people as just like you.

- Putting yourself in the other person's shoes.

- Seeing others as more important than yourself.

In the last chapter we looked at not causing harm to ourselves by beating ourselves up and being harshly critical. We also went into detail about the importance of caring for oneself and showing kindness to oneself, and so melting the ice in our hearts. In this chapter we will revisit both these stages in the light of compassion for other people, as well as going through the third stage.

How will Developing Compassion for Other People Help Me Reduce My Levels of Stress?

There may be some people who think that our quest to discover how to use compassion to reduce our stress ended with the last chapter on self-compassion, and are at a loss to see how having compassion for other people could help their own stress levels. It is a reasonable point of view. It is not common in our society to connect healing oneself with concern for others – in fact, when we are feeling stressed and over-stretched our tendency can be to turn inwards and focus more attention on our own situation. However, most of the time this does not help us to feel better. Instead it serves to intensify our problems.

The thing is that when we try to engage with compassion we are connecting with a part of our deepest nature – our fundamental wholeness and wellbeing. Automatically we tap into the richest and most effective parts of our self – so, as we work with others we are working with ourselves at the same time. We have a natural capacity for compassion; it is part of who we are. As we learn to express this, it is as if an inner door in our heart opens and we can communicate more directly and effectively. Stress, on the other hand, can have the effect of closing this inner door as we seek to defeat any threat to our wellbeing, and we tighten up as we try to do so.

We have seen that compassion involves using constructive emotions such as love, kindness, patience, tolerance and forgiveness. Constructive emotions, unlike destructive ones, enhance our peace of mind and contribute to the development of lasting happiness. So, by being compassionate we are engaging with behaviour that is *beneficial* to our wellbeing – by being willing to be available to others we are automatically taking care of ourselves and behaving in ways that will reduce our own stress responses. If your boss at work stresses you out because she seems to be a bully who doesn't appreciate your efforts you could well feel resentful, frustrated and even angry. All these emotions disturb your peace of mind and make you feel wretched. Say you decide to turn this around by trying to practise patience instead of frustration and resentment, and by going out of your way to be friendly and cooperative instead of angry. When you do this you are engaging with compassion for her and benefiting yourself in the process. By replacing painful emotions with compassionate ones you can reduce your stress and feel more satisfaction with how you are handling the situation. You have taken matters into your own hands, rather than simply reacting in a defensive way. Furthermore, we can see this as a process of inner disarmament – the disarming of our destructive emotions – which in turn helps to disarm the outer situation we find ourselves in. It is like the practice of non-violence and it comes about by trying not to cause harm and instead showing compassion towards others.

Another clue as to how compassion for other people can help us with our own difficulties lies in the point we made in the previous chapter about making the connection between our own difficulties and the difficulties of others. This allows us to recognize these difficulties as part of the human experience. We explored the suffering we're trying to avoid in chapter 6. When we show compassion we are acting in accordance with our understanding of the deep interconnectedness between ourselves and other people and the knowledge that we all experience stress, suffering and pain at various times in our lives. This helps to reduce the intensity of our own feelings of stress and to see things from a wider perspective. If we think again of the fictitious boss who seems like a bully, it helps to spare a thought for how her life is and why she may behave as she does. The chances are that she is just trying her best to do her job well and perhaps feels pressurized and anxious. Maybe you appear threatening to her and so she over-reacts, so if you show more friendliness it will help soothe her fears. A compassionate attitude creates the space for this kind of reflection and gives us a choice as to how we wish to behave.

This lessening in intensity of our stress levels by practising compassion to others is borne out by scientific research. We have already seen that the part of the brain called the amygdala is activated in response to a perceived threat, but research is now showing that the extent of this activity is modified when we can transform destructive emotions into constructive ones and engage in compassion. A similar reaction has been detected in the case of the hormone cortisol, which is released during the fight-or-flight response. Cortisol has a natural daily cycle of production – peaking in the early morning with the sunrise and tapering off after sunset – which dictates when our body should be active and when it is time to rest. Anyone who has experienced jetlag will know how it feels when this cycle is disrupted. In people who are good at transforming destructive emotions, the natural low level of the hormone in the evening is especially low. This also indicates that they will be more effective in reducing stress – it suggests that if we can work with our own negativity we can contribute to keeping our cortisol levels down. There is an area towards the front of the brain called the ventromedial pre-frontal cortex, which is involved in emotion regulation and decision-making. Not surprisingly, people with higher activity in this area of the brain also have a lower level of cortisol in the evening.[2]

All the evidence shows that practising compassion is good for us. By connecting us with our inner source of wellbeing it enables us to heal ourselves while being open to the feelings of others. Contrary to the popular belief that compassion is demanding for us and may cause us to deplete our resources, it is an opportunity to work with ourselves effectively from a sustainable basis. This is worth remembering when it seems hard to be compassionate – which it certainly does sometimes. We have seen that the development of compassion is a gradual process that starts from our current position and then goes step-by-step as we feel ready to take on more. If we feel inspired to practise compassion in the first place because it is good for us, that is called being 'wisely selfish'. A lot of the time we are just selfish, but when we recognize that compassion will help us in reducing stress that represents a start in the development of compassion that can grow from strength to strength as we experience its benefits.

Not Harming

When we looked at practising compassion for ourselves we focused on how we often use our thoughts and emotions to give ourselves a hard time. For example, we may be fiercely critical of ourselves, we may not give ourselves the benefit of the doubt and we may generally feel bad about ourselves. We saw how these patterns of behaviour cause us harm and how, by being compassionate, we can remove and transform this harm. When we think of compassion for other people the process is the same. Most of us will rarely feel provoked to strike out at someone physically and yet we regularly strike out with our thoughts – for example, when we decide we do not like someone we have just met, or have angry thoughts about an inconsiderate driver. Becoming aware of how often we do this, as well as what causes us to do it, and trying to change this habit is a very effective place to start with compassion for other people.

Quite often we hardly realize that our behaviour can cause harm. Stress will make the tendency more pronounced and cloud our perception of how we react. In a recent workshop the group was discussing this issue and I asked for examples from their recent experience. Claire, a woman in her late forties, shared how she does some volunteer work for a local charity. She is happy to do it, but from time to time the pressure of her other commitments becomes intense and she relies on good management from the team in order to maximize her time and contribution. She told the group that recently in her voluntary work, one of her routine jobs had come up at a time when her line manager was under a lot of pressure from another project and was less efficient than usual. Claire started on the task but halfway through got the feeling that she was duplicating work that had already been done. She asked her line manager for advice by email but got no response, so she investigated further on her own initiative and found that she was right and time was being wasted. Claire confessed that at the time she was feeling quite stressed, as she had a lot on besides this volunteer job, and she felt badly let down by her manager. She said she felt justified in being frustrated and angry with her. She found herself being critical and annoyed, and felt put out and taken for granted. This went on for several days until she received an email from her line manager who shared her regret at what happened. Her line manager also confessed that she herself was finding her voluntary commitment too much but could not find anyone else to take it on. Claire said that hearing how things were just as difficult for her manager as for herself helped her to see she was being judgemental and critical. Once she saw this she was able to drop the issue and immediately felt better. She ended up feeling grateful for the manager's attempt to take the blame for what was happening and so remove the harm from the situation. It enabled her to stop 'harming' her manager with criticism and so reduced her own stressful feelings.

Most of us have numerous such situations cropping up during the average week. With each one we have a choice as to whether we go with our feelings of anxiety and stress and end up thinking negatively about other people, or whether we try to apply a bigger perspective and view them as an inevitable part of the frustration of life, give people the benefit of the doubt and so remove the harm from ourselves and the situation. Taking time to come to terms with our own suffering and pain helps us with this. As we understand the far-reaching effects of suffering more deeply, we want to avoid contributing to other people's pain. This can help us develop the courage not to harm. Being able to disarm our reactions in this way is important because, as we have seen, our responses to stress become stronger and more ingrained the more we use them. This means that the spiral of stress can build from one event to another. Take Claire's story – the pressure she was under made her more reactive to the disappointing behaviour of her line manager and reduced her resilience. If the situation had not been defused by her line manager's email she would have carried that stress forward to her next challenge and been at risk of reacting even more strongly the next time.

Melting the Ice in your Heart

Trying to pay attention to whether or not we are causing harm to ourselves and other people helps us to bring into focus how we are expressing our capacity for compassion. As we learn to do this our perspective opens up and the defensive measures we put in place to protect ourselves begin to seem less useful than we thought. When we try to practise compassion for other people we can start by taking the natural concern we have for ourselves, and extending it to include others. As we learn to treat ourselves with compassion it becomes easier to want to share a similar process with other people. This process can be said to be like melting the ice in our heart that keeps our interests separate from the interests of others. In the Buddhist teachings on compassion there is a set of exercises called The Four Immeasurables, which are designed to help with exactly this process. These exercises have been tried and tested by meditators for more than 2,500 years and are a powerful way of helping us to transform our destructive emotions. We already touched on them briefly in chapter 3 but now we will go through them in more detail and look at how we can use them.

The Four Immeasurables are immeasurable loving kindness, immeasurable compassion, immeasurable joy and immeasurable equanimity (a sense of acceptance of how things are). There is an exercise to do for each one. You will see that some of the exercises follow a formula: they begin with developing the quality for yourself and then extend it to the people you love, the people you are fond of, people you do not have strong feelings for one way or the other and people who you have problems with. After going through the sequence the idea is to try and extend the practice as widely as you can.

As we have seen already, practising compassion is based on working with positive, constructive emotions that broaden our perspective, whereas negative, destructive emotions limit us and keep us focused on ourselves. So these exercises enable us to work on a range of our difficult emotions while at the same time developing compassion for other people. They are a good example of how sharing compassion with other people brings benefit to us as well. Through developing the qualities of these exercises we are learning to replace the unhelpful habits of destructive emotions with helpful habits of loving kindness, compassion, joy and equanimity. We saw this process is part of the Formula for Change presented in chapter 7. *Loving-kindness* overcomes anger and hatred, *compassion* overcomes craving and attachment, *joy* overcomes envy and jealousy and *equanimity* overcomes ignorance, pride and prejudice. The exercises are known as 'immeasurable' because there is no limit in sharing them – the idea is to develop these qualities in order to benefit the greatest possible number of people.

Immeasurable equanimity

> A person is a person because he recognizes others as persons.
>
> *Archbishop Desmond Tutu*

Equanimity is the ability to view other people and the circumstances we find ourselves in without bias – with a sense of acceptance of how things are, rather than according to our likes and dislikes. It is all about taking a fresh look at our tendency to have preference for our loved ones or things we like to do, and to avoid those people and situations that we are indifferent to or do not like. We saw that developing equanimity gives us the opportunity to transform our habits of ignorance, pride and prejudice. We could see this as ignorance of the interconnectedness both of how things are and between us and other people – one of the habits of stress we identified in chapter 9. If we really take this to heart, how can we instantly like some people and feel only dislike for others? Pride comes when we favour our own country, our own friends, the people who agree with us and so on. Prejudice is when we are not willing to listen to the needs of people outside our own circle. With equanimity we recognize ourselves and everybody else as a person worthy of attention and respect. We can learn to face the circumstances of life with more patience and detachment, which allows us to feel more at ease. This brings a corresponding reduction in our stress levels.

Exercise: Developing equanimity

Close your eyes.

Imagine you are sitting on a chair.

On your right side is a good friend.

On your left side is a person who is challenging for you.

Reflect on the following points.

Your friend

Have you always had the affection for this person you have now?

Does this person ever behave in a way that you don't like?

Can you imagine them doing something that would prevent you continuing as friends?

Your challenging person

Have you always experienced this person as challenging?

Does this person ever behave in a way that touches you?

Can you imagine them doing something that would enable you to become friends?

Make notes of what you discover.

This exercise is quite easy to do and helps us to question the assumptions we make about people. Even the people we love can behave in ways we do not like and if we give them a chance, people we think we do not like can surprise us by behaving in a pleasant and friendly way. Also, relationships change, as anyone who has been through a divorce will know. At the very moment that someone agrees to marry another person and is full of love for them, the seeds can be there for the ultimate collapse of the relationship. In the same way, first impressions can be misleading and if someone we thought we did not like shows us kindness then often our attitude towards them will change. Doing this simple exercise can help us to develop a greater awareness of how fluid relationships are and how no one is purely lovable, or purely unlovable. If we can do it with one or two other people, it will help when we look at our prejudices on a wider scale – people who do not share our views, people we see as causing harm and so on. Remembering the sequence that was just mentioned, we could try to develop equanimity for all our family members, then all our friends, then the people at work, then in our community – pushing the limits further and further out as we feel more confident. We don't have to rush it, just go at our own pace.

I am often reminded of my experience with a CEO of a voluntary organization in the UK who attended a long training session I was involved
in delivering. Let's call him Steve. In the early sessions of the training I
found Steve quite exhausting – he had something to say at every stage of
the day, and seemed to have no idea about how much of the group time
he took up. He would talk for ages about his own relationship to what
we were discussing and whenever I managed to include someone else in
the discussion he would come in again and respond to their comments as
well! It took me a few sessions to see that Steve was actually connecting
deeply with the material and was moved and excited to the extent that he
could not stop talking about it. He had no intention of dominating – he
was simply thirsty for information and experience. Once I realized this
it became easier to see how to handle his input because I could do it
from a basis of sympathy rather than irritation. The discipline required
by my role as trainer ensured that Steve never knew I had ever felt any
impatience with him, but in the cut and thrust of ordinary interaction we
do not usually have those safeguards. We need to learn to give people
the benefit of the doubt and allow time for a good rapport to develop,
instead of jumping to a position of like or dislike that we then defend
and solidify. Defending people we like and dealing with people we do
not like can cause us a lot of stress. Equanimity can help us cut through
our stress responses by enabling us to see people from a different, less
threatening perspective.

Immeasurable loving kindness

> Constant kindness can accomplish much. As the sun makes ice
> melt, kindness causes misunderstanding, mistrust, and hostility to
> evaporate.
>
> *Albert Schweitzer*[3]

Loving kindness is about wishing everyone to have happiness and all
the causes of happiness. Remember in chapter 5 when we explored lasting happiness and its power to benefit those who experience it. When

we focus on generating loving kindness for other people this is what we want to share with them. Not surprisingly, loving kindness is the antidote to anger and hatred – it is hard to wish someone lasting happiness and be angry with them at the same time. So here we have an opportunity to transform the habits of anger and hatred, which we have seen tend to cause us unhappiness, and replace them with loving kindness.

In chapter 2 we looked at the relationship between hostility and heart disease. We saw that hostility and anger trigger the threat response in the amygdala, which results in the release of the stress chemicals adrenaline and cortisol. These chemicals contribute to higher blood pressure; raised cholesterol levels and faster blood flow through the arteries. All these conditions are believed to play a role in damaging the arterial inner lining. Once this deterioration has started, cholesterol accumulates at the delicate spot, forming blockages. Furthermore, frequent rises in blood pressure cause the walls of the arteries to thicken. This condition is known as arteriosclerosis and leads to heart disease. To make matters worse, for a person in whom this response is frequently activated the parasympathetic nervous system is weakened. We saw in chapter 2 how this is the system that calms and restores the body once the fight-or-flight response is no longer necessary. If it becomes too weak it cannot provide the stress protection the body needs and so increases vulnerability to heart disease. In addition, research shows that an attitude to life that is very focused on oneself and one's own interests contributes to stress and a greater likelihood of heart disease. People tested who used the terms *I*, *me* and *mine* frequently in their conversation had a greater tendency to anger and high blood pressure.[4]

The good news is that research is also showing that changes in behaviour that result in a reduction of hostility can help to reverse this process of deterioration in the heart.[5] Behaviours such as consideration for others and showing kindness and love featured highly in this process. Generating loving kindness can help us to soften our attitude and disarm our anger and hostility, thereby reducing our stress levels and increasing our sense of wellbeing.

We can see this clearly when we look at the importance of forgiveness. When we hold a grudge against someone because they have caused us pain, not only are we preventing them from making amends but also we are causing harm to ourselves at the same time. Research shows that when we just think of a person, or group that we feel has treated us badly, our body responds with pent-up anger. Our system is flooded with stress hormones, and our blood pressure rises. Each time we feel this way, the same damaging response occurs. Forgiveness reverses this process and lowers our blood pressure, heart rate and levels of stress hormones.[6] In his extraordinary book, *I Shall Not Hate*,[7] Palestinian doctor Izzeldin Abuelaish recounts the story of his determination not to surrender to feelings of hatred after three of his daughters were killed in an Israeli airstrike on the Gaza strip where he lived with his family. He wanted to honour his daughters by transforming the tragedy of their deaths into an opportunity for dialogue and peace, rather than them simply becoming another statistic of anger and revenge. On his release from prison, Nelson Mandela in *Long Walk To Freedom* expressed a similar wish to transform his anger and hatred in order to be free of it and use his experience creatively when he wrote:

> As I walked out the door toward the gate that would lead to my freedom, I knew if I didn't leave my bitterness and hatred behind, I'd still be in prison.

When we are unable to forgive, we deny the person or people who have hurt us the possibility of changing and reconciling with us. We also deny ourselves the benefits of forgiveness and reconciliation. We give up our faith in the future of the relationship and maintain a painful division between friend and enemy. This locks us into a stressful, defensive position that keeps us in a prison of conflicting emotion.

Some years ago a friend of mine suffered a painful and protracted divorce. Her husband had become emotionally unstable and developed an alcohol problem, which meant he often behaved in a way that was frightening for her and her daughters. When the divorce was finally over, my friend had no wish to hear news of her ex-husband – although she did not stop her daughters seeing him if they wished. She remained hurt and angry. Recently her eldest daughter died tragically – an event that shook the whole family. My friend's ex-husband suffered a breakdown and could not attend the funeral. Some time later my friend told me that she was visiting her daughter's grave and her ex-husband turned up and joined her by the graveside. She said that seeing his grief close up softened her own heart and they sat together and talked for the first time in years about their time together, the children they had borne and their affection for each other. My friend said that she felt a huge relief as her anger and resentment ebbed away and she could see her ex-husband as an ordinary man – sad and alone – rather than a monster. It took a terrible tragedy to help her drop her hostility but when she was able to do so it brought her ease in the midst of her grief.

Here is the exercise we can do to help us develop loving kindness.

Exercise: Loving kindness meditation

Settle your mind.

Think of a time when you have felt fully loved by someone, or think of a person that symbolizes love for you, e.g. Mother Teresa, the Dalai Lama, your grandmother, a favourite singer and so on. We can either use the memory of this feeling from the past to spark that feeling in us in the present, or we can use the inspiration of a compassionate figure.

Allow the memory, or inspiration, of this love to nourish you, so that you yourself feel full of love, worthy of love and able to offer love.

Connect with the feeling of gratitude for having known this love and the wish to share it with others, so that they can benefit also.

Say to yourself several times, 'May I be well and happy, may I be well and happy . . .' The key here is not just the words but trying to contact your heartfelt wish for this to happen; put as much kindness and warmth as you can into the words as you say them in your mind so that they are not just words but help to focus your compassion *feelings*.

Now think of someone that you love very much and imagine that the immeasurable love flowing from your own heart enters theirs and fills them with loving kindness.

Say to them, 'May you be well and happy, may you be well and happy . . .'

Now think of a friend that you are fond of and again imagine the immeasurable love flowing from your own heart enters theirs and fills them with loving kindness.

Say to them, 'May you be well and happy, may you be well and happy . . .'

This time, think of someone that you have neutral feelings towards, or to whom you are indifferent and in the same way imagine the immeasurable love flowing from your own heart enters theirs and fills them with loving kindness.

Say to them, 'May you be well and happy, may you be well and happy . . .'

Now, think of someone that you find difficult and in exactly the same way imagine the immeasurable love flowing from your own heart enters theirs and fills them with loving kindness.

Say to them, 'May you be well and happy, may you be well and happy . . .'

Consider that the feelings of love in you continue to grow, so that you can wish happiness and wellbeing to all the people you have already brought to mind.

Try to extend this circle of love more and more . . .

Remember that the sun shines on everyone in the world, whoever they are, whatever they have done – our loving kindness is just like the sun in that it can touch anyone and everyone.

Drop the visualization and sit with this feeling for a few moments.

A key thing to remember when you do this exercise is that the loving kindness you are generating in your heart is *immeasurable*, without limit – it will not get exhausted, or worn out. We start with ourselves so we can get in touch with our natural capacity for love and kindness and really bring it out. Then we can even direct it towards people we find challenging and eventually towards people we have not even met. The phrases, 'May you be happy, may you be well,'can be used to remind yourself of the practice in everyday life situations. I like to repeat them when I am among crowds at an airport, or passing by lots of drivers on a motorway. This is how Matt, a primary school teacher, uses it at work:

> When I'm in tense, stressful situations involving people being very angry and upset I try to cope with it by reciting silently to myself, 'May you be happy, may you be well'. I find when I do this I am more able to listen to their pain and hurt rather than taking it personally. This gives them space to air their issues and enables me to not react but instead to respond to them in a creative way. This approach I found helps de-escalate heightened emotions and therefore we can move forward in resolving the underlying issues.

We can see clearly here how by using the exercise even in a very simple way, Matt is able to defuse difficult interactions at work and at the same time reduce his own stress and increase his effectiveness. He can do this because it feels so much better to give love, rather than anger and resentment – when we are engaged in being kind and loving we are more well in ourselves and experience less stress. This enables us to attract more kindness and affection towards ourselves, so it becomes a mutually beneficial dynamic. We have seen that social support is a big factor in dealing with stress and that a strong friendship network is an important factor in our wellbeing. Having this kind of support nourishes us and reduces our tendency to offload our frustrations on others.

In his book, *The Happiness Hypothesis*,[8] Jonathan Haidt, professor of psychology at the University of Virginia, has coined the term 'elevation' to describe the mutually enhancing beneficial effects of acts of love and kindness. Research has already shown that people who regularly engage in acts of kindness are happier but Haidt claims that the effect goes further – we benefit from witnessing another person perform an act of kindness, or compassion, even if it is not directed at us. When this happens our mood is 'elevated' with hope, inspiration and optimism – and this feeling is contagious, affecting anyone who comes in contact with us.

Immeasurable compassion

> Until he extends his circle of compassion to include all living things, man will not himself find peace.

> *Albert Schweitzer*

You may be surprised to find the word compassion used here, as we have been using it in a larger sense than one specific context. This is because the Buddhist approach to training in compassion goes in stages, as we have already seen. At this stage compassion features as part of the immeasurable exercises, and can be seen as part of the process of removing the ice from our hearts in order to apply compassion in an even wider context. We will look into that in chapter 13.

Here compassion is specifically about wishing that everyone could be free of his or her suffering and pain. As we saw in chapter 6 when we looked at suffering, we are not seeking to deny its existence, nor do we give in to despair when we experience it, but rather we try to learn what it has to show us. Immeasurable compassion is the antidote to craving and attachment – so here we have an opportunity to transform these potential sources of stress and replace them with a helpful habit. When we crave a person, or object or lifestyle we tend to exaggerate its positive side and view it as essential for our happiness. This view is based on self-centredness, a narrow wish to have perfect circumstances for ourselves. Even if we manage to obtain the goal of our craving we rarely find the satisfaction we hoped for because possessing it brings its own problems – we fear that it may be taken away from us; it does not live up to our expectations and we are disappointed in it, or we feel we have to guard it jealously. Generating immeasurable compassion and wishing people to be free from suffering reverses these tendencies. When we looked at the beneficial effects of volunteering in chapter 10, we saw how helping other people with their problems helped the volunteers themselves. Being able to connect with other people and their suffering makes us feel better about ourselves and counterbalances the stress we may incur by simply pursuing our own cravings. It softens our hearts, enabling us to care more deeply and so be less likely to cause harm to others. This attitude is a basis for compassionate action – not only the wish for people to be free from suffering but the willingness to do something about it.

Here is an exercise for developing Immeasurable Compassion.

Exercise: Compassion meditation

Settle your mind.

Allow yourself some time to connect with your own suffering and pain by thinking of a time in your life when you were having a difficult time.

Say to yourself, 'May I be free from suffering and pain, may I be free from suffering and pain . . .'

Think of someone you love who is dealing with suffering and pain.

Say to them, 'May you be free from suffering and pain, may you be free from suffering and pain . . .'

Think of someone close to you who is dealing with suffering or unhappiness – a friend, perhaps, or someone at work.

Say to them, 'May you be free from suffering and pain, may you be free from suffering and pain . . .'

Think of someone that you have neutral feelings towards, or who you are indifferent to and try to create the same wish that they may be free from suffering.

Say to them, 'May you be free from suffering and pain, may you be free from suffering and pain . . .'

Now think of a person that you find challenging and who is dealing with suffering and pain.

Say to them, 'May you be free from suffering and pain, may you be free from suffering and pain . . .'

Try to extend this circle of compassion more and more . . .

Drop the visualization and sit with the feeling for a few moments.

This is an exercise that I often do when I am watching the news. If you are like me you may find the evening news an intense time of the day. It is easy to feel overwhelmed by the plight of some of the people we see on our TV screens. It is then that I find simply wishing that all the people involved in the news stories of the evening be free from suffering and pain at least helps me to feel a connection with what they go through and keeps my heart accessible, rather than becoming hidden behind a protective cover of cynicism.

Immeasurable joy

> Find a place inside where there's joy, and the joy will burn out the pain

Joseph Campbell[9]

The last of the immeasurables is joy, a quality that can easily get overlooked. Not surprisingly, generating joyfulness in the wellbeing of others is the antidote to jealousy – by developing joy in life both for our own situation and for the situation of others we can transform our unhelpful habits of jealousy. Being able to savour what we have in life, to express gratitude for our good fortune and to appreciate the qualities of other people are all factors that can add to a sense of joy. We can find ourselves waiting for a successful outcome for a project we are working on, or looking forward to a holiday, or anticipating a new job – all of this can get in the way of simply connecting with the joy of the present moment. It helps to slow things down and take time to rejoice in a piece of good news we hear, or to enjoy the beauty of our surroundings – or even to appreciate our own good qualities.

When we apply this to our coping strategies with regard to stress it is clear that a person who copes well is someone who experiences the least amount of arousal of the body's response to stress when confronted with emotionally demanding situations. An optimistic, joyful attitude to life in general can act as a buffer against stress arousal because a joyful person does not have the habit of perceiving every potentially stressful situation as a threat – their amygdala has not become hyperactive due to being constantly stimulated. In chapter 9 we looked into the evolutionary pattern of always seeing the negative side of a situation first and allowing its effect to last longer than any positive aspects – joyful people are at an advantage in dealing with this because of their less reactive amygdala. Furthermore, when we have to deal with a difficult situation a joyful attitude can help us count our blessings even in the face of adversity. It enables us to reinterpret stressful situations positively so that we can adjust to them, and move on, learning what we can along the way.

A close friend of mine was diagnosed with cancer a couple of years ago. He immediately had to undergo routine tests to see if the cancer was contained, or if it had spread. When he was told that there was no spreading he said he experienced overwhelming joy, which seemed surprising when he still had all the surgery and treatment ahead of him. He explained that having some good news to rejoice in gave him a lot of energy to face what lay ahead, and to examine his habits of pushing himself too hard which he believed had contributed to his becoming ill.

Below is an exercise that aims to help you develop immeasurable joy. The point here is to focus on feeling delight in every kind of happiness that the people you bring to mind are enjoying. It is a good idea to try to drop our habit of resenting someone else being happy, successful or well off and wishing it was us instead of them.

Exercise: Meditation on joy

Sit quietly and settle your mind.

Bring to mind someone who is prosperous, powerful, intelligent and enjoys good health, with many friends, good circumstances and plenty of comfort and happiness – someone who in your opinion has a life other people would dream of.

Without any feeling of jealousy, or rivalry, wish them even more of all these good things.

Then reflect on how wonderful it would be if everyone could enjoy circumstances like these.

Firstly imagine someone that you love enjoying all these benefits and allow yourself to feel joy for them.

Next do the same for a good friend and allow yourself to feel joy for them.

Now imagine someone you have no special feelings for enjoying all these benefits and allow yourself to feel joy for them.

Finally, imagine someone who is challenging for you enjoying all these benefits and allow yourself to feel joy for them.

Try to extend this circle of joy more and more . . .

Drop the visualization and sit with the feeling for a few moments.

It is hard to feel this kind of joy for other people if we feel that their good fortune in some way encroaches on our territory – that somehow it should be us rather than them. Jealousy is like a combination of craving and hatred – we want good things for ourselves so badly that we feel negative towards anyone else who has them. We can undermine our jealousy by looking more closely at exactly what we are jealous of and by realizing how fragile good fortune at times can be.

Seeing Other People as Just Like You

> If we could read the secret history of our enemies we should find in each man's life sorrow and suffering enough to disarm all hostility.
>
> *Henry Wadsworth Longfellow*

The basis of seeing people as just like you is remembering that everyone wants to be happy and to avoid pain and suffering. We could also add to this the essence of what we covered in chapters 5 and 6 – that although we may wish for happiness, finding lasting happiness is not easy and in the meantime, suffering and pain come along as an inevitable part of the difficulties of life. Just as we experience this in our own lives, so does every other person on the planet – so, in that sense, we can view other people as being 'just like us'. This may seem relatively straightforward when we are dealing with friends and loved ones, but becomes increasingly demanding as we widen the circle to include people we do not see eye-to-eye with and even dislike. Greg, a social worker, tries to use this perspective in spite of the sometimes perplexing behaviour of his work colleagues:

> The approach to my work is the belief that everyone is doing their best given their set of circumstances. Their underlying wish is to

be happy – even if the way they are going about it can be very dysfunctional. This enables me to be more compassionate towards them because they are just like me, just another me.

This is a sensible and pragmatic view – we can see that other people may not behave as we want them to but at the same time we can recognize that their behaviour simply comes from wanting to be happy. We do not need to take it personally. In fact, with a bit effort we can even imagine that our own behaviour can seem odd to other people on occasion and yet we know we are just trying our best!

The exercises of the Four Immeasurables create the basis for this attitude. By helping us connect with the wellspring of love, kindness and compassion within us, our attitude becomes softer and more tolerant. The more we are able to extend that innate feeling and the more people we can embrace within it, the more possible it becomes to see other people as being just like us. Just as we try to include challenging people within the immeasurable exercises, so we can use the perspective of our basic similarity even with people we find difficult. I had a small but interesting reminder of this recently. I have become hooked on a 'reality' singing competition on TV. As is usual with these sorts of programmes my partner and I have our favourite singers and ones we don't like so much. When I watched an episode recently, one man that I had been finding quite irritating was facing going out of the competition. As I watched his face and listened to his interview about how he was feeling, it came to me so strongly that he was not irritating at all – he simply really wanted this to go well for him, just as I would have done if I were in his situation. It reminded me strongly of how easy it is to make a separation between oneself and others and how unhelpful that can be. Even people we may think that we do not like are just like us underneath – sharing the same hopes and fears. As Longfellow says in the quote at the beginning of this section, remembering this can indeed help to disarm our hostility towards them.

The exercise below will help you to see another person as just another 'you'.

Exercise: Seeing another person as just like you

Sit for a few moments and settle your mind.

Consider how everyone wishes to have happiness and to avoid suffering.

Bring to mind someone you know and think about them in this context.

Reflect on how, just like you, they simply wish to be happy.

Reflect on how, just like you, they wish to avoid suffering.

Try to experience them as another 'you'.

Reflect on what effect this has on your perception of them.

Sit again.

Make a note of what you realize.

Empathy

We talked about empathy and imagination in chapter 3 and then in chapter 4 we talked about the recent discovery of what scientists call 'mirror neurons'. We saw that these neurons enable us to understand the meaning of the actions of other people, the intention behind those actions and the emotions they are feeling about them. Our brain is actually built to connect us to other people. This ability to 'feel with' another person is the basis of empathy. It is the impulse that moves us to respond and try to help when we hear a cry of pain, or see someone else in trouble. Empathy can be seen to have three forms:

- Cognitive empathy: *knowing* another person's feelings.

- Emotional empathy: *feeling* what they feel.

- Compassionate empathy: *responding compassionately* to their distress.[10]

Cognitive empathy can help in motivating people to make their best efforts but if it is not combined with feeling what they feel it can be cold and detached. Politicians can read people's feelings and turn them to their own advantage while not really caring about them very much. So cognitive empathy alone is not enough, we need emotional empathy as well. However, here again there can be problems – if we feel what is happening to another person too intensely there is a danger of us becoming emotionally overwhelmed and distressed ourselves. This is why medical practitioners and rescue workers cultivate a positive detachment, so they do not fall apart while trying to help. If we can turn our understanding of another person's feelings and our feeling for them into compassionate action then we are combining all the elements of empathy in a constructive and practical way.

Empathy is a particularly important skill in our technological age when it is theoretically possible to stay in one's apartment and conduct much of one's life online without ever having to actually meet another human being. We need to make the most of our opportunities to connect with other people and recognize our common humanity in order to maintain our wellbeing. Although we may think that compassion for others is all about helping other people, we have seen in this chapter that actually it helps us at the same time. Compassion for other people lifts us out of a preoccupation with our own affairs and at the same times provides us with ways of working with destructive emotions that cause us unhappiness.

KEY POINTS

- Engaging in compassion for others is the most effective way of ensuring a peaceful and stable world.

- It requires courage and daring as it goes against much of our conditioning and means we need to learn some new habits of relating to other people.

- We have seen that compassion involves using constructive emotions such as love, kindness, patience, tolerance and forgiveness, which enhance our peace of mind and contribute to the development of lasting happiness. So, by being compassionate we are engaging with behaviour that is beneficial to our wellbeing and will lessen our stress responses.

- All the evidence shows that practising compassion is good for us. By connecting us with our source of wellbeing it enables us to heal ourselves while being available for others.

- The first step in practising compassion for others is to try and avoid causing harm.

- The next stage is melting the ice in our hearts and here we can use the exercises of the Four Immeasurables:
  - Immeasurable loving kindness, the antidote to anger.
  - Immeasurable compassion, the antidote to craving and attachment.
  - Immeasurable joy, the antidote to jealousy.
  - Immeasurable equanimity, the antidote to ignorance, pride and prejudice.

- The next stage is seeing others as just like you: remembering that everyone wants to be happy and to avoid pain and suffering.

- The basis of this is empathy.

EXERCISES

Exercise 1: Avoiding harm

During the next week, try to observe yourself whenever your mind strays into being unnecessarily critical or judgemental.

Exercise 2: Developing kindness

In the next week try to perform an act of kindness for yourself, for someone you know, and for a stranger.

Exercise 3: Developing compassion

When you watch the news this week try using the slogans from the immeasurable compassion exercise: 'May you be free from suffering and pain . . .'

Note any changes you see in your attitude.

Exercise 4: Developing gratitude and appreciation

Write a letter to someone thanking them for something they have done for you. It could be a relative, or friend, or it could be your local car mechanic who fixed your car for you.

Make a list of people you know who have qualities you really appreciate and value.

Exercise 5: Transforming destructive emotions

Equanimity transforms ignorance, pride and prejudice; loving kindness transforms anger; compassion transforms craving and attachment; joy transforms jealousy. Choose one quality to work on for a day and observe any changes in your attitude.

Exercise 6: Seeing other people as another you

As you go about your day, try to look at people you pass and think of them as being just like you.

There are more exercises on compassion for others in the Appendix on page 328.

13 Compassion with a Big Perspective – Removing our Blindfold

> To serve the world out of [a] dynamic union of wisdom and compassion would be to participate most effectively in the preservation of the planet.
>
> *Sogyal Rinpoche*[1]

As we have seen there are five stages in training the mind in compassion, which are:

- Trying not to cause harm.

- Melting the ice in your heart.

- Seeing other people as just like you.

- Putting yourself in the other person's shoes.

- Seeing others as more important than yourself.

We have already covered the first three and now we can take a look at the final two stages:

- Putting yourself in the other person's shoes.

- Seeing others as more important than yourself.

We will look into these in this chapter as part of our exploration of compassion with a big perspective. Here, we build on the work we have already done on developing compassion for others and try to take it even further by being willing to actually put ourselves in the shoes of another person – to see things from their perspective. That is why we talk here of 'removing our blindfold' – the last barriers to being willing to understand the importance of seeing things from another person's point of view.

Putting Yourself in the Other Person's Shoes

In the earlier stages of developing a compassionate mind we were still using ourselves as a point of reference for our compassion for others. There is nothing wrong with this, but now with putting ourselves in another person's shoes we make a shift and become more willing to take ourselves out of the centre of the picture.

When we are working on the earlier stages it is as if we are walking along in the rain with a big umbrella. We want to stay dry and to enable other people to stay dry too, so we invite them to come under our umbrella. We are in the middle, holding the umbrella and everyone else is crouching underneath as best they can. When we put ourselves in the other person's shoes we hand the umbrella over to someone else and we take our place with everyone else who is crouching underneath for shelter. For most of us this is not something that is easy to do on a daily basis. We have not been brought up to see things from another person's point of view, and society is not set up to support us doing so, so it is understandable if we forget to do it from time to time. The thing is to understand *why it* is a good idea both for other people and as a way of reducing our own stress. Once we are clear about this, we will feel more inspired to experiment with it and to try to make a place for it in our dealings with people.

We heard from Simon, the manager of a medium-sized organization, in chapter 11 when we looked at self-compassion. Here he describes how he tries to put himself in the other person's shoes when he is in a work meeting.

> I often find myself in tense meetings with conflicting problems and pressures. What I notice is that when I hold strongly on to my own point of view, it quickly causes me to tighten up, physically fuelling a sense of frustration. But when I do remind myself to mentally swap places with someone else – even for a couple of seconds – straight away I can feel something release, my awareness

seems to expand and my frustration eases. I definitely hear what is being said more clearly, with more discernment, rather than with a heavy, loaded, judgemental mind. I also find I'm able to present my own point of view with more clarity. However, if I'm honest, I often forget this mental exchange very quickly, especially in a difficult meeting – I quickly feel self-justified in defending a stance. But I've noticed over the long term, having this defensive approach seems to wear on relationships – even if I do win the immediate argument. So I try and remind myself, again and again, to swap places in my mind. I have noticed when I do, the quality of my interactions with other people does improve, compromises become possible and relationships with others develop in a more sustainable way.

Simon is saying several things here. Holding on tightly to his point of view causes him frustration and stress, and reduces his ability to express himself well in a meeting. Whereas if he can mentally change places with another person in the meeting and get a direct impression of how things are looking for that person it enables him to hear their point of view better and express himself more effectively. He acknowledges that he often forgets to do this, but because he experiences the benefits – improved relationships and more cooperative working – he is inspired to keep trying to remember to work in this way.

Below is an exercise you can try which can give you a direct experience of the effectiveness of this kind of compassion. This can be quite a powerful exercise if you take the time to really feel that the other person is sitting there in a chair opposite you. It might be a good idea to try it out a few times before working with someone you find challenging. You could imagine your brother or sister sitting in the other chair and experiment with thinking about how they see you. Then move on to a work colleague and eventually get to your challenging person.

Exercise: Putting yourself in the other's shoes

Arrange two chairs sitting opposite each other.

Start by sitting in 'your' chair.

Sit for a few moments.

Think of someone that you are challenged by.

Invite them to come and sit in the chair opposite to you.

Look at them carefully for several moments.

Think about:

How they want to be happy and they do not want to be unhappy.

How they are a human being with all the same kind of hopes and fears as you have.

Recall what you know about their personal life.

Take time to think about their life in general.

Reflect on what stress they may be suffering.

Sit for a few moments.

Change seats and sit in the 'other person's' chair.

Now imagine that you are the other person looking at you.

What do they see?

How do they experience you?

Have you caused them worry, or pain?

Sit for a few moments.

Go back to your own chair.

Look again at your guest.

Do you see anything differently?

Sit for a few moments.

Silently think to yourself, 'I forgive you any pain or frustration you have caused me.'

Sit again.

It is helpful to give yourself at least fifteen minutes to do this exercise. You need plenty of time to really look at your chosen person and reflect about them in the first section. It will then be easier to make the shift to looking at yourself through their eyes. Allow yourself time to take in the information you receive about yourself when you see yourself from another person's point of view. It could give you some important clues as to how you come across in all your relationships – with friends, work colleagues and casual acquaintances. It is hard to accept that we may behave in ways that other people would not like but it is useful information for us. Seeing how we can be misunderstood will help us avoid similar situations in the future. Being able to get a sense of how other people may see us is a very effective way of putting ourselves in another person's shoes. It can help to avert all kinds of miscommunication and potential conflict.

On a recent return flight to Amsterdam from the UK I had an opportunity to observe a situation where putting yourself in the other
person's shoes might have helped. As the refreshment trolley came
around, I overheard a fellow-passenger giving a flight attendant a
really hard time. It was hard to catch the full story from where I was
sitting but it involved the passenger asking for hot water in a plastic,
see-through cup. Apparently cups of this sort are not safe to hold hot
water and the only alternative was the purchase – for €3[2] – of a poly-
styrene cup. Not surprisingly the passenger found this rather excessive.
What was more surprising was his response – he proceeded to cross-
examine the flight attendant in an increasingly aggressive manner,
applying the kind of ruthless logic that would not have been out of place
in a courtroom.

The flight attendant did his best. He remained polite, consistent and
managed not to react to the escalating tone of complaint and anger that
he was subjected to. He had a kind of party line that he could fall back
on: 'Sorry sir, this is company policy, I am not allowed to give you this
cup,' and so on. After some time he managed to get away and push his
trolley on to the next customer. As he came past me our eyes met and he
gave me a rather desperate look. Although unflinchingly professional,
the flight attendant adopted the slightly world-weary attitude of someone who has seen and heard the full range of human unreasonableness
in their time, and who feels that their job does not carry the appropriate
reward in either status or payment to demonstrate an acceptable appreciation of what they suffer. It did not occur to him to put himself in the
shoes of the disgruntled passenger.

I happened to be one of the last off the plane and exchanged a few words
with the flight attendant. Remembering my look of sympathy he asked
me what I thought of the sort of thing they had to put up with. During
our short conversation my earlier hunch was confirmed – when dealing
with a stressful situation he relied on his determination to stay professional, rather than adopting any strategy to manage his stress. Instead
of de-hyping the situation for himself and easing the strain he was feeling, he took up the burden as a way of demonstrating to himself how

efficient he was at enduring one of the downsides of his job. The tension he was holding looked like it was heading towards a stiff drink and a good moan – not so bad in small doses, but not a good long-term strategy for stress reduction.

If we compare this to Simon's approach that we looked at earlier, we can see that he was able to reduce his feelings of stress simply by seeing the situation from another person's point of view. Simon also saw that defending a stance had the long-term effect of undermining his relationships with other people and that people responded well when they felt that he was trying to see things from their angle. The flight attendant did not have to see the passenger again, so he did not have to build a relationship with him, but he did have himself to take care of. His approach depended on his defending his position as a representative of the airline and by so doing overcoming the objections of the passenger. It all relied on effort of will, rather than empathy. Although he was not rude in any way, he made the passenger feel not heard and not understood by sticking so faithfully to the party line – which is probably why the passenger became more and more agitated. By trying to see the situation from the passenger's point of view, the flight attendant could have injected a little humour, and a little warmth, which would have given the passenger the sense of being a person being communicated with by another person. It would also have helped the flight attendant to relax and be less defensive, which would have meant he felt much less depleted by the whole exchange.

In chapter 11 we looked at an exercise for reducing stress and anxiety in which we used the in-breath and out-breath as ways of working to absorb our stress and exchange it with wellbeing and healing. We can use the same principle of exchanging using the breath to do an exercise called *Tonglen*,[3] which literally means 'giving and receiving' and helps us take another step in putting ourselves in another person's shoes.

Exercise: Tonglen

Sit quietly for a few moments and watch your breath.

Remember that just as you want happiness, everyone wants happiness and that just as you wish to be free from suffering, so does everyone else.

Give yourself some time to really feel the truth of this.

Then as you breathe out, consider that you are giving happiness to everyone – if it helps you can imagine it as a bright light shining out and touching everyone.

As you breathe in, consider that you are taking in or receiving everyone's suffering – if it helps you can consider it as a smoky cloud that dissolves into you.

Continue to do the exercise using the out-breath and in-breath in this way for several minutes.

Now think of one particular person. It could be someone who is having a lot of difficulties in their life. It could be someone you find challenging and want to understand better.

Do the breathing exercise in the same way but now focusing on this one person.

As you breathe out give them happiness, wellbeing and joy.

As you breathe in take in their suffering, stress and pain.

As you do so, imagine the person receiving all this wellbeing and being freed from their suffering, see them changing and becoming lighter.

After several minutes, drop the exercise and simply watch your breath.

The thing to remember when doing this exercise is, just as with the immeasurable exercises, the good stuff never runs out – your happiness will not decrease because you want to share it with other people, there will always be enough to go around. Also, taking in other people's suffering will not increase your own suffering – wishing to take it away from another person does not mean that it becomes yours. We are simply expressing the wish that the people we have in mind be free from suffering and we use this strong image to help make it feel real. The point of an exercise like this is that is helps us to open up our willingness to respond to other people's suffering and to develop the wish to help. This enables us to feel a sense of ease because instead of defending a position we are willing to be open to others. This sense of ease helps us to overcome our own stress and contributes to our peace of mind. However, do not push yourself to do this exercise. If doing it does not feel natural, leave it for a bit and continue with the exercises on the Four Immeasurables on pages 266–82. You can always come back to it later on. Remember, there is nothing to force with compassionate mind training. The most important thing is to be able to *feel* the spirit of the exercises and use that feeling as a basis from which to continue.

Seeing Others as More Important than Yourself

This is the last of the five stages in the Buddhist approach to training in compassion. It is included here for completeness and to show just how vast our compassion can become. Although we all have the potential for compassion in our minds and hearts, it is up to each of us as to how willing and able we are to develop that potential. We need to have a fully trained mind to be able to see other people as more important than ourselves from a healthy perspective without neurosis. Most of us have felt the wish to put our loved ones' interests before our own on certain occasions and frequently we hear stories of people performing acts of tremendous bravery for strangers – rescuing people from drowning, or fire, or natural disasters. The seed is there in all of us but it takes time and practice to bring it to full maturity.

Universal Responsibility

Learning to take responsibility for oneself in a healthy and sustainable way is already a big step. Taking this further to feeling responsibility for the wellbeing of others is an even bigger step. With universal compassion we aim to remove any boundaries to our compassion and to feel a responsibility for our world and all the people in it. At each step along our exploration of developing a compassionate mind we have seen that we can build on what we have learnt to take our compassion further – once we have understood the importance of compassion for ourselves, we can learn to extend that to compassion for other people. Universal responsibility is based on our concern for other people's wellbeing in that we see that if we wish to help other people, then feeling a concern for the world at large is an important part of that wish. All our actions have the potential to affect the world in a small way. By recognizing this and trying to make it part of our lives we are engaging in compassion with a big perspective. Our world has become very complex – it is rare now for even small groups of people to be able to live independently of the rest of the world. The effect of the volcanic eruptions in Iceland in 2010 was a good example of this. Just one volcano sending out clouds of ash brought air travel in Europe virtually to a standstill for almost a week, with numerous knock-on effects on trade, commerce and politics. Here are three stories reported by CBS News about the ash cloud that are particularly poignant:

- The lack of refrigeration facilities at the airport in the capital of the West African nation of Ghana has been a big blow to pineapple and pawpaw farmers who sell to Europe because of the lack of flights.

- In Africa, a group of five people from Sierra Leone and Liberia had to abandon a fact-finding trip to the war crimes trial of former Liberian President Charles Taylor in The Hague.

- In Kenya, thousands of day labourers are out of work because produce and flowers can't be exported amid the flight cancellations. Kenya has thrown away 10 million flowers – mostly roses – since the volcano eruption. Asparagus, broccoli and green beans meant for European dinner tables are being fed to Kenyan cattle because storage facilities are filled to capacity.[4]

Indeed food distribution is a good example of how complex and interdependent the world has become. As recently as 200 years ago it is unlikely that people would have eaten any food that they did not know the origin and history of. People would have produced a range of foods themselves and then they would have probably known the butcher, baker or dairyman who supplied additional products. The choice of foods would have been much smaller than what is available to us now but the knowledge of how it was produced would have been more detailed. Nowadays – at least in the West – we have a dazzling selection of food available to tempt us but we have much less knowledge of where it comes from and how it gets from the point of origin to our plates. Supermarkets have made it possible to offer a wide choice but have tended to alienate us from its production. I remember clearly from my teaching days explaining to disbelieving nine-year-olds that their Big Mac started life as a cow! An average supermarket will stock 20,000 items – 4,000 of these are chilled and will need to be replaced within three days; the remaining 16,000 will need restocking in two weeks.[5] Half the contents of the warehouses that supply the supermarkets are always 72 hours away from being inedible. So, when there is disruption to road, rail and air travel, it only needs to last for three days and immediately large amounts of food will have to be thrown away. I happen to love strawberries – they mean summer for me – but nowadays it is possible to buy them all year round. They are imported from Spain in the spring, from Holland in early summer, from the UK in August, from California in the autumn and Israel in the winter. The catch is that there are only 96 hours available from the moment the fruit is picked until it starts to mould, so all the transport has to be by air and as fast as possible.[6]

I am not saying that I should give up my enjoyment of strawberries. In fact, such is the complexity and interconnectedness we are talking about here that if people decided to boycott out of season strawberries – because they think it is not a good use of our resources to fly them around the world – it could do more harm than good. A lot of strawberry producers would be put out of business as a result, and a lot of people and their families could suffer due to lost jobs. It is more a question of trying to see the global implications of each individual action. It is not that each of us is individually responsible for the wars, famines and squandering of resources that have such an effect on our world, but rather that we can be aware of each person's equal right to have happiness and avoid suffering. If we can see any opportunity to help others then we should take it, instead of remaining focused on our own interests alone.

If we can try to develop this kind of awareness in as many of our activities as possible it will help in the process of removing our metaphorical blindfold, enabling us to appreciate and be nourished by the big view of compassion. Looking down over a town or city from a plane can help to remind us that we are just one person going about our business among so many others. When we are on the ground it is easy to see our own problems and concerns as special and unique, whereas the chances are that there are probably many people having their own version of the same situation. As we aspire to have an attitude of universal responsibility we can try to give thought to the numerous small daily actions that we rarely pay attention to. How often do we consider the immense amount of expertise and human effort behind the simple act of switching on an electric kettle, or turning on a cold water tap in the kitchen? Numerous people have been involved in building the power stations that produce the electricity, or laying the pipes to conduct the water to our taps. Each part of the kettle or the tap and all that goes along with it has been designed and made through human effort. These apparently simple actions are only possible because of an intricate series of interconnected actions performed by a wide variety of different people – people who, just like us, want to be happy and avoid suffering and pain.

Seeing how we fit into the big picture will help us to want to ensure that it is a compassionate and beneficial one. Each one of us is helping to create the world that we are living in. It is so easy to feel that we have no say in how the world works, that there is too much suffering for us to have any effect on it at all. Worse still is to feel cynical and detached, as if it is all nothing to do with us anyway. Universal responsibility means that each one of us remains committed to trying our best to practise compassion within our own lives in the hope that its effect can reach as far as possible. We can begin by remembering that we are all the same in that we all want to be happy and to avoid pain and suffering. It makes sense to focus on our similarities rather than on our differences. If we can build bonds based on common understanding

then our individual differences can be seen as interesting and inform-
ative, rather than a source of conflict. We can look to trying to create
harmony rather than divisiveness. We all know people who are skilled
at making people feel at ease and welcome, whereas there are others
who easily get into gossiping and complaining and create an unfriendly
atmosphere.

In general our society is preoccupied with the acquisition of material
gain. Our pursuit of material wealth seems to permeate all aspects of life
and yet, as we saw in chapter 5, it does not bring us lasting happiness.
Developing a sense of contentment, an ability to savour what we have
rather than thirsting for more, is in itself an aspect of universal responsibility. Our acquisitiveness, if left to itself, can never be satisfied and can
lead to destructive competition and exploitation of natural resources as
well as the populations of poorer nations. Unlike a householder switching on her kettle with no awareness of the bigger picture, we need to see
our wish for a second car, increased air travel, or simply more choice,
in terms of its impact on other people beyond ourselves, as well as on
future generations.

If we ask ourselves what impact developing a sense of universal responsibility will have on our stress levels the answer is clear. As we have seen
throughout the book, activities such as recognizing others as the same
as ourselves and focusing on harmony between people helps to dissolve
stress. We feel much better when we are experiencing love, tolerance,
patience and compassion than when we are feeling anger and hatred.
Connecting ourselves with the bigger picture gives a sense of meaning
and purpose to our lives, and helping others nourishes us at the same
time. Contentment dissolves the stress of struggling to acquire more
things, of becoming bored with what we already have and of envying
what others have. There is a direct link between the satisfaction of using
our energy in a beneficial way to society and experiencing a reduction
in our own stress – and this link can become a spiral as we see more and
more that our wellbeing and the wellbeing of each person on the planet
is intricately connected.

KEY POINTS

- The last two stages in training the mind in compassion are:
  - Putting yourself in the other person's shoes.
  - Seeing others as more important than yourself.

- Here, we build on the work we have already done on developing compassion for others and try to see things from their perspective.

- We have not been brought up this way and society is not tuned to support us to continuously try to see things from another person's point of view, so it is understandable if we forget to do it from time to time. The thing is to understand *why* it is a good idea both for other people and as a way of reducing our own stress.

- Being able to get a sense of how other people may see us is a very effective way of putting ourselves in another person's shoes.

- Universal responsibility is based on our concern for other people's wellbeing in that we see that if we wish to help other people, then feeling a concern for the world at large is an important part of that wish.

- It is not that each of us is individually responsible for the wars, famines and squandering of resources that have such an effect on our world, but rather that we can be aware of each person's equal right to have happiness and avoid suffering.

- If we can see any opportunity to help others then we should take it, instead of remaining focused on our own interests alone.

- Seeing how we fit into the big picture will help us to want to ensure that it is a compassionate and beneficial one.

- Universal responsibility means that each one of us remains committed to trying our best to practise compassion within our own lives in the hope that its effect can reach as far as possible.

- We can begin by remembering that we are all the same in that we all want to be happy and to avoid pain and suffering. We can remember this by:
    - Focusing on our similarities rather than our differences.
    - Seeking harmony rather than divisiveness.
    - Developing contentment as an antidote to greed.

- There is a direct link between the satisfaction of using our energy in a beneficial way and experiencing a reduction in our own stress.

EXERCISES

- In this chapter we learnt two exercises: putting yourself in the other's shoes and *Tonglen*. During the next week try to practise each one at least twice.

Exercise 1

As you go about your day, choose people to 'put yourself in their shoes' and see what you discover – make notes in your notebook.

Exercise 2

Next time you are in a supermarket think about the 20,000 items stocked in it and all the people involved in getting them there.

Notice which ones you really need and which ones you buy because they are there.

Exercise 3

Choose moments in your day like switching on the kettle – or a light, or your computer, or TV – and think about all the activities and people involved in your being able to do that.

Conclusion:
Making the Compassionate Mind Approach
to Reducing Stress Part of Our Lives

Changing our habits is not easy. Most of us have experience of trying to give up something – like chocolate or cigarettes – and of trying to do something that is good for us – like taking more exercise or going on a diet. We start off full of enthusiasm and hope for change but after a while our old ways creep back and it becomes harder and harder to stay on course. We have seen that learning to develop a compassionate mind in order to work with stress involves changing habits on several different levels and there is no doubt that it requires effort, but it does not need to go the same way as our previous attempts to change. Once we begin applying compassion to our stress we can see the benefits, and this will help us to continue to make changes step-by-step. There is no need to set big targets, or get ambitious about how you want to do this. Just start simply and build on what you can manage as you feel more familiar with the material and more confident in using it. The key thing is to make working with compassion part of your life, rather than something extra, or something you feel you *have* to do. It also helps to be able to rejoice in your progress, however small the steps you take.

In this conclusion to the book we will look at some practical points to help you get started on working with what we have covered, and then we will look at a typical example of how all this can be applied in everyday life. We will wrap up by looking at the bigger picture of how using compassion to work with stress can be used in different contexts.

Some Practical Points

The formula of this book is:

- Define the problem – in our case, stress – and view it from all angles.

- Identify a helpful way of approaching it – applying compassion – and explore it fully.

- Realize that in order to apply compassion we will need to make some changes in our habits.

- Examine how our mind works in order to understand our habits better.

- Engage with mindfulness and meditation as a means to make a space for change and developing discernment, so we can identify which are our helpful habits and which are our unhelpful habits.

- Learn compassion techniques and how they can help us with our stress – thereby replacing unhelpful habits with helpful ones.

Exercises

The key exercises are:

Which exercises should you focus on?

Chapter 8 offers practical advice on how to organize your circumstances so that you can do some meditation every day. Those points apply to all the exercises, so you might like to look them over again. And then, here are a few practical tips:

Decide how much time you can spend each day sitting down to do these exercises.

Spend at least half that time on meditation.

Choose another exercise to do in the remainder of your time – you may like to try one for a week, and then move on to another one and try that for a week until you have been through all the exercises.

Once you are familiar with them all and you have decided which habits you want to focus on, you may decide to try a particular exercise for a longer period, such as a month or six weeks, until you feel some change happening.

Choose a few of the exercises to try out at different times during the day. You could change these each week until you feel familiar with them all and can decide which ones help you most.

Bringing it all together

In order to bring all that we have learnt together, let's take an imaginary scenario of moving house and see how we could put some of this into action. This could help us to see how to make all we have learnt part of our everyday lives. Everybody moves house at some time or other and as it is considered to be on a par with divorce and bereavement in terms of stress it gives us quite a bit of ground to cover.

Background

In this scenario we will be looking at moving house through the eyes of Kate, who is married to Keith and has two children aged nine and eleven. Kate runs her own website-design business from home. We could easily run into her at the supermarket we visited at the beginning of the book! This move is special in that the family is buying their first home and is moving from a rented flat into a house of their own. Let's say that she read this book about six months ago and has been using it to work with her stress levels. Kate was drawn to the book because she was finding herself getting irritable easily and felt it was impacting on her family life. The information on the fight-or-flight response made sense to her and helped her to see that her stress response was indeed becoming over-activated, and leading her to more easily become stressed. Using compassion as a way to address this seemed very attractive because it helps a person develop as a human being and, at the same time, it helps other people while helping you – this appealed to Kate. When it came to the second part of the book and identifying habits, Kate realized that she is a bit of a perfectionist and that this can lead her to be quite judgemental of other people and even to treat them rather harshly. At the same time she is also hard on herself – even though she is highly efficient and capable, she can drive herself too hard. This manifests in the making of endless lists and of her becoming quite hyper, which makes her tired and can leave her with a feeling that no one else – her husband and children included – are trying as hard as she is.

Using the book to prepare for the move

Kate spent some time identifying her layers of stress so that she could be aware of them and therefore more likely to catch them before they became a problem. In terms of the stressful aspects of her world – the first layer – she felt there was plenty to work with: her children needing to change school, her husband needing to adjust to a different commute to work, keeping her business together as they packed up the house and so on. She could see that all this was predictable, which helped, but that her habit would be to try and control everything to make it work. Pain settling in her neck helped Kate to notice that she was becoming stressed and she identified one of her stress alerts as being over-tired and feeling that things were getting on top of her. She decided to stop packing and preparing half an hour earlier than she been doing each day, in order not to let her tiredness build up and become a problem.

Over the six months since reading the book, Kate has been trying out mindfulness techniques and now tries to use them as she is packing up the flat. She finds that if she can focus her attention on the acts of collecting and sorting items and packing them into boxes her energy lasts much longer than if she worries about cooking dinner, how the new school will work for the children or how much the move is costing at the same time. She has also reflected a lot on how she is spending energy in hoping the new house will work well for them and fearing that something might go wrong. Applying what she has read in chapters 5 and 6 about happiness and suffering, Kate tries to remember that, while the new house will be a big improvement, it cannot be the answer to all the family's needs and that problems and difficulties will arise as a normal part of the life they will lead there. This helps her feel more settled and less anxious as she realizes that levels of happiness are not just about how hard she works and how perfectly she arranges everything but simply the ups and downs of life. It is not all down to her! She is also aware that if she gets hyper and over-efficient she will affect the whole family and they will feel more anxious and stressed, whereas when she can manage to be patient and kind to herself everyone feels the benefit.

Since reading this book, Kate has been trying to do some meditation for ten minutes every morning before the children wake up. It is still early days but already she is getting a sense of what it means to see her thoughts and emotions from the perspective of the space and calm that she sometimes feels in meditation, rather than from the perspective of the hustle and bustle of her daily life. She feels that she has been able to take a step back from her thoughts and emotions and can notice more how they affect her. She has chosen to work with her habit of being too perfectionist and its subsequent effect of making her judgemental of others and hard on herself. Kate has taken on board that there has been research into neuroplasticity, which confirms that she can indeed change these habits.

In the weeks immediately before the move, Kate has tried to add another five minutes to her morning meditation time. She feels that allowing this time for herself each morning is a way of showing kindness to herself, which eases her tendency to be self-critical. Along with sitting meditation she sometimes does the exercise for working with stress and anxiety as she finds it helps her deal with her wish to get everything right. On some mornings she combines meditation with the Loving Kindness meditation in which she includes all the other people involved in the move – the estate agent, the solicitors, the removal company, electricians, phone technicians and so on. She finds it helps her remember they are all human beings just trying their best and also reduces her irritation with them. Her husband has a much more relaxed attitude to the move than she does, trusting everything will work out for the best. Sometimes Kate finds this very reassuring but when she is tired – a trigger of stress for her – it can really annoy her. She has been using the Don't Go There! exercise to help with this. Whenever she feels the possibility of getting irritated with her husband she just says to herself, 'I am not going there!'

The day of the move

When the day of the move comes, Kate has a sense that she has made some progress with her habits of irritation and control. Her family seem excited and relaxed and she herself feels that she has been less bossy with them and a bit kinder to herself. Of course, her habits have not just disappeared overnight – she still has lists for everything – but all the signs are that it is workable and she is able to make real progress. Over breakfast she asks her husband and children to each name one thing about their present home that they have really appreciated as a memory to take with them – this works really well and provides a pleasant way of saying goodbye to the flat.

When the removal men arrive everything is ready. Kate finds one of the men a bit irritating. He is opinionated and loud and seems to have a comment to make about everything. Remembering her loving kindness meditation, Kate tries to repeat the phrases, 'May you be happy, may you be well,' in her mind to help her transform her irritation. While she is appreciating that this seems to be working, her husband's mobile rings. It's the carpet people who are laying carpet at the new house. They were supposed to have finished the evening before but fell behind schedule and still have one of the children's bedrooms to do. This is a potential disaster, as they will be in the way of the removal men when they arrive. For a moment Kate forgets all her good work and simply gives in to frustration and irritation. Overhearing the conversation the annoying removal man comes up with a great solution – they will pack the van with all the items for the bedroom that needs carpet at the front of the van. That way, these things will be unloaded last by which time the carpet people have promised to be finished. This solution is accepted by everyone and gives Kate a chance to reflect on what has happened and her reaction. She tries to think of the carpet people as being just like her – people who are trying to do their best but sometimes cannot get things completely right. This helps the stress reaction from her earlier outburst subside a bit and helps her to feel more relaxed. She is also struck by how wrongly she had judged the removal man as being annoying, when in fact he just has lots of spare energy and more intelligence than the job demands of him, so his running commentary is a way of entertaining himself and not intended to harm anyone.

The next obstacle comes when the van is almost loaded but not completely finished. The people who are due to move into Kate's flat arrive early with all their furniture! For an instant Kate feels that this is all her fault and that her organization has somehow been incomplete, but she quickly catches herself and realizes that the other family have simply decided to turn up early and nothing she could have done could have prevented it. She tries to catch her anxiety on her breath and to breathe it down into her belly so it can dissolve. This helps to calm her down and she simply puts on the kettle to make tea for everyone while the new family wait for their turn to unload. She lets go of her wish to give the whole flat another clean – it's no longer possible and actually she wanted it for herself most of all, as the whole place will get disturbed by all the unpacking to come. As she hands out cups of tea she looks at the young couple and their baby who will live in her old home, and for a moment she is able to put herself in their shoes and see how excited they are to be moving in and how they simply forgot the time and got carried away. They had not intended to cause any trouble at all.

Eventually everything is ready. The removal van moves off and Kate's family follow in their car. On the short journey Kate takes a moment to think about all the other people who might be moving house that day and sends them a silent good luck wish. She starts to play a game with her husband and children to make a list of all the people who have made it possible for them to live in their new house – the list gets very long and takes up the whole journey. Just as they arrive at their new home they say a big 'thank you' to all these people – most of whom they will never meet. For Kate it helps to connect with the bigger picture and takes some of the pressure off her own personal situation.

As they all get out of the car at the new house, Kate thinks ahead to all the work that needs to happen for everything to be in order but decides not to go there and instead tries to be mindful of one task at a time. She feels that so far the move has gone well and she has managed to work with her triggers and reactions to stress quite well. This increases her confidence in the techniques she is working with and helps her to feel that change is happening. She feels less stressed than she expected to feel and does not feel overwhelmed about what is to come. She knows that it will take time for her new habits to feel like second nature but if she has been able to work with them during such a demanding time as the family has just gone through, she feels that the outlook is good.

Using Compassion to Work With Stress in Different Contexts

This book has been written from the perspective of an individual person who wishes to use compassion to work with their stress. However, because these techniques are learnable skills, they can be applied in a variety of settings.

When Barack Obama was on his way to the White House in 2008 he spoke about the importance of developing empathy and in his first year of office as president of the United States he named it as one of the guiding principles in his life. It was to become an enduring feature of his terms of office. As the world becomes more complex, and even confusing at times, there is a definite turning towards the understanding and benefits of compassion, and an interest in applying these benefits in different areas of society.

Karen Armstrong, British author and theologian and founder of the Charter for Compassion, which was mentioned in chapter 3, has stressed the importance of educating children in compassion as part of their school curriculum. Simon Baron Cohen, professor of psychopathology at Cambridge University, who says that empathy is one of the most valuable resources in our world, backs her up. Vinciane Rycroft has set up an organization called Mind with Heart, a charity and network of educators, which focuses on training teachers, as well as offering educational materials for teenagers, on empathy and compassion. In 2010 over 10,000 art students in the Appleton Area School district in the USA were given a six-inch square art panel to draw or paint their idea of compassion.[1] The project was inspired by brain researcher Richard Davidson who also believes that children should be trained in compassion as part of their education. The results were exhibited in the Trout Museum of Art galleries the following year.

Stanford University in the United States has established The Center for Compassion and Altruism Research and Education (CCARE), which is striving to create a community of scholars and researchers, including neuroscientists, psychologists, educators and philosophical and contemplative thinkers, around the study of compassion. It runs regular training programmes designed to develop the qualities of compassion, empathy and kindness for oneself and for others.

The writings of Daniel Goleman, author of *Emotional Intelligence*, have led to empathy being accepted as a foundation skill for social competency in the workplace. There is a growing understanding that compassion can help raise levels of wellbeing and thereby improve the functioning of a work environment. This is my main area of work and it is fascinating to see just how quickly people can learn to use compassion techniques to deal with the challenges of their work environment. It is still early days – a tension remains between meeting targets and budget constraints and providing training for staff in how to approach their job from a compassionate standpoint. Not surprisingly, it is the caring professions that are most open to this kind of work. Here there is an obvious benefit in learning to apply compassion to the clients receiving care and support, but increasingly I see the need for the staff themselves to have guidance in how to manage burnout and compassion fatigue. If investment in staff is to be effective then it is vital that people have an opportunity to learn how to use their own resources to the fullest extent while as the same time understanding how to care for themselves in order to be able to keep doing their job.

Where individuals have tried these techniques and found them helpful it is possible to establish programmes within the business world. Chade-Meng Tan has established the Search Inside Yourself programme[2] at Google in order to offer something back for the success and prosperity he has gained as a member of the company. Focusing on teaching mindfulness and emotional intelligence, the programme is available for all Google employees, whose inspiration for taking the course is to make the world a better place. It is now part of Google University, which also includes a course on the neuroscience of empathy.

There is also a growing interest in how these skills can become part of training for leadership. A short time ago I had the opportunity to be part of a team offering an eighteen-month course on leadership for CEOs in the third sector in Nottinghamshire. My job was to offer the modules on meditation and compassion. Participants started out by appreciating the qualities that I was presenting to them but at the same time feeling that it was a challenge to see how these could become part of everyday working life. Gradually, over the eighteen-month period, as people began to try out the techniques and gradually apply them to their leadership roles, they were able to see their practical application. The fact that the group had the support of a course over such a long period of time, combined with a committed set of peers to share with, helped allow this process to happen effectively. This kind of work needs support in order to address old habits and try out new approaches. It is not a quick-fix solution but when the change does take place it is sustainable.

We can see that whatever our starting point is for wanting to understand our minds better and to develop compassion – whether it is wanting to overcome a problem we have, such as stress; offering the best opportunities for our children and their future; wanting more meaning in our working life; or simply wanting to make the world a better place – the work that starts with each of us as individuals is a thread that can stretch from us to our family and workplace, to our community, and eventually the benefit of our whole world. Each one of us can indeed make a difference.

Appendix: A Selection of Helpful Compassionate Mind Exercises

A FURTHER EXERCISE FOR CHAPTER 8

Exercise: Mindful breathing

To start with, find a place where you can sit comfortably and won't be disturbed. Keeping your back straight, place both feet flat on the floor about shoulder width apart and rest your hands comfortably on your knees or in your lap. If you're sitting on the floor or on a small meditation stool, you may like to have your legs crossed. Try and find a position that's comfortable for you but don't slouch – your back should be straight. Sometimes lying flat on the floor can be helpful if that's the most comfortable position for you to start your work. The idea is not to relax so much that you become sleepy but to develop a certain type of alert focus and awareness.

Now just gently focus on your breathing. Breathe through your nose, and as you breathe in, let the air reach down to your diaphragm – that's just at the bottom of your rib cage, in the upside-down 'V'. Place a hand on your diaphragm with the thumb pointing upwards and notice how your hand lifts and falls with your breath. Feel your diaphragm (i.e. the area just below your ribs) move as you breathe in and out. Do this for a few breaths until you feel comfortable with it and it seems natural and easy to you.

Next, place your hands on either side of your rib cage. This is slightly more awkward because your elbows will be pointing outwards. Now breathe gently. Notice how your rib cage expands out against your hands, your lungs acting like bellows. This is the movement of the breathing you're interested in – you feel your lungs expanding around you. So basically you want a breath to come in and down while expanding your rib cage at the sides. Your breathing should feel comfortable to you and not forced. As a rough guide, it's about three seconds on the in-breath, a slight pause, then three seconds on the out-breath. But you must find the *rhythm that suits you*. As you practise, try to replenish the air in your lungs but not in a forced way.

Now just notice your breathing and experiment with it. Breathe a little faster or a little slower until you find a pattern that, for you, seems to be your own *soothing rhythm*, which feels natural to you. As you engage with it, you'll feel your body slowing down. It's as if you're checking into and linking up with the rhythm. You're letting your body set the rhythm, breathe for you, and you're paying attention to it.

Rest your eyes so that they're looking down at an angle of about 45 degrees. You may wish to close them but be careful – you may become very sleepy. Now spend 30 seconds or so focusing on your breathing, just noticing the breath coming through your nose, down into your diaphragm, your diaphragm lifting, your ribs gently expanding side-ways, and then the air moving out, through your nose. You can check on this by, first, putting a hand on your diaphragm and feeling it lifting and falling with your breathing. Next, put your hands on each side of your lower ribs and feel them being pushed apart as you breathe. Notice the difference. It's an 'all-round experience' of the breath coming into your lungs and expanding them. Notice the sensations in your body as the air flows in and out through your nose. Just focus on that for 30 seconds (longer if you like) and sense a slight slowing of your breathing ... Feel your body slowing down as you find and slip into your soothing rhythm.

The important thing is to find your own rhythm rather than imposing one on yourself. As for a focus for your attention, once you're comfortable with your breathing, you can bring your attention to the inside of the tip of your nose. Try it and see how useful it is as a focal point for you.

Assuming all went well, what did you notice during the breathing exercise? You might have been aware of how your body responds to the breathing, with feelings of slowing and being slightly heavier, and of how your chair is holding you up. You may also have noticed that, although it was only thirty seconds or so, your mind wandered. You may have had thoughts like 'What's this about? Will this help me? Did I do my job correctly yesterday? Where did that pain in my leg come from?' If you practise breathing for any length of time, distracting discomforts are very common. Your attention may have been drawn to the sound of letters being pushed through the letterbox, the traffic outside or whatever. The point is that our minds are very unruly, and the more you practise this breathing exercise and the longer you extend it, the more you'll notice how much your mind simply bops about all over the place. When you first do this kind of mindful breathing and focusing, it can be quite surprising just how much your mind does shift from one thing to another. This is all very normal, natural and to be expected.[1]

FURTHER EXERCISES FOR CHAPTER 11

Exercise: The art of appreciation

If we can direct our attention to where we want it to be, to the top of our head or to a big toe or to the plants sitting on the windowsill, why not use this ability to stimulate some of our positive emotions? There's an old saying about a glass being seen either as half-full or as half-empty. When feeling depressed, we see it as half-empty; when we feel good, the glass is half-full. We know that our moods shift our attention. The glass is the same whatever we do – it doesn't change, only our feelings towards it and perceptions of it do. But we can practise learning to shift our attention to the things that we appreciate, that stimulate pleasure and other nice feelings in us; we can practise directing our attention to the half-full bit of the glass. Here's how.

Each day when you wake up, focus on the things that you like or give you just a smidgen of pleasure. For example, you may like being in a warm bed. So rather than focusing on how having to get out of bed is annoying, smile to yourself at the enjoyment you've had in being comfortable and warm and how, in just sixteen hours or so, you can return there. Think about how you'll enjoy taking a shower, drinking your first cup of tea, tasting your breakfast or looking at the paper. When you make your tea and toast, try doing it mindfully. Pay attention to the water, that life-giving fluid, and how the hot water on your tea bag gradually produces a swirl of brown liquid. As for your toast, focus on the taste and feel. Imagine that you're an ant crawling over your toast – it would be a lunar landscape. When was the last time you really tasted fresh toast and butter – I mean, *really* tasted it? Are you aware of what the air of a new spring day *really* smells like? Do you ever take time to really breathe it, notice it and appreciate it? If we're honest, we're so preoccupied thinking ahead to all the issues of the day that all these simple pleasures simply pass us by.

Even when doing something as mundane as the washing up, notice the warm feeling of the water and the bubbles and the way in which you can almost see rainbows in them. We lose our fascination for these everyday things because we, as a species, easily get used to things and always want something new. We're also always thinking about so many other things, one of which is how it's such a drag to have to do the washing up when we're tired and we want to do so much else – get back to that warm bed for one. But learning to *notice*, to feel and to see, can stimulate our brain in new ways.

Do you take time to appreciate what people do for you? Choose a day and spend time focusing only on the things that you like and appreciate in people, letting go of the things that you don't like. Think about how all of us are so dependent on each other. People have been up since about four o'clock in the morning so that we can have fresh milk, bread and newspapers. And every day they do the same. What about the people you work with – what are their good points? How often do you really focus on those? How often do you make a point of telling them that you appreciate them?

What you're doing in these exercises is practising overruling your threat/ self-protection system, which is determined to focus you on the glass as half-empty. Its job is to warn you that you might run out of water or to make you exclaim: 'Hey, what happened to the other half? Some bugger drank it!' It's what it's designed to do, and you could let it do that. But let's start to take control of our feelings and *deliberately* use our attention to practise stimulating emotion systems that give rise to brain patterns that create good feelings. Appreciation is one way of practising doing this.[2]

Exercise: Using memory to create compassionate feelings

As with all these exercises, sit comfortably with a good straight posture, engage with your soothing breathing rhythm for a short while and then engage with the exercise when you feel you can attend to it. Start by trying to recall someone who was caring, kind and warm towards you. Try to imagine a specific event and then focus on the *details* of that – what was happening? Don't pick something that was very distressing for you because then your attention will be focused on the upset caused by the difficulties that you experienced. The purpose of this exercise is to recall how you felt when you experienced the kindness of another. So focus on the kind person's facial expressions, his/her voice tones and general manner. Focus on as much *specific detail* that you remember as you can. What feelings were being directed at you? Could you sense those coming from the kind person? Explore your feelings about receiving kindness. Can you sense them in your body? You're exploring from memory feelings of kindness and compassion *flowing into* yourself. When you've finished, you may want to note down your thoughts and feelings in your journal – maybe note the memory itself and what it felt like going into it again.

The second memory exercise is to focus on compassion as 'arising within the self' and *flowing out*. Recall a time or times when you have felt kind, warm and caring towards another person (an adult or child or even towards an animal) who was in some distress. Again, don't recall times when you were trying to help others in major distress because of problems, traumas or accidents, or if you had heightened anxious and 'need to rescue' feelings. If you do, you might be reminded of feeling alarmed and unsure whether you could help that individual or becoming upset by their upset. It's not the 'distress of the other' that we want to bring to mind; rather, the focus should be on your feelings of warmth, understanding and kindness. So it's better to start with gentle(ish) feelings of wanting others to experience wellbeing. It is the warmth and kindness that is *flowing from you* to the other person that is important here.

So, again, engage your soothing breathing rhythm, close your eyes or look down and really try to bring a memory to mind in all its *sensory* details. Recognize these memories and what it *feels* like when you focus on warmth and kindness for others. Again, jot down your reflections in your journal. Which exercise did you find easier – compassion flowing in or compassion flowing out?[3]

Exercise: The desire for others to be happy

So far we have reflected on our feelings when we recalled being kind to another adult, child or animal in the past, but you can extend this in an imagery exercise to the here and now. Imagine directing kindness towards people you care about. Bring them to mind, see their faces and how they move, what it is you love about them, remembering that in mental imagery you usually only get fleeting impressions, not clear pictures. Now explore the feelings emerging from this desire for them to be happy, peaceful and content. You might repeat in your mind the Buddhist statements: 'May you be well. May you be happy. May you be free from suffering.' They, like you, have simply found themselves here in this world and are doing the best they can. Sometimes this realization might make you sad because you're actually rather worried about them. Or it might make you tearful as your emotions overflow with the desire for good things to happen to them. Or perhaps you just experience a gentle sense of warmth for them. Note these experiences; you can later reflect on them as stimulating specific brain patterns within you. Keep in mind that thinking of them as brain patterns is not in any way to reduce these feelings or explain them away. They are important, meaningful experiences in the flow of life.

Now our feelings are likely to be strongest towards those we are attached to, have shared our lives with and are genetically related to. Nonetheless, it's useful to begin to widen the circle of people to whom you direct compassionate feelings. First, imagine directing towards your friends your desire for them to be happy, content, peaceful and free from suffering. See them in your mind's eye as best you can. Imagine that you truly wish for their contentedness and happiness. Don't rush through this – allow time for things to emerge in your mind. See your friends actually smiling and becoming happy and free from suffering.

When you're ready to move on, focus on people you don't know very well and, as before, think about your desire for them to be peaceful, content and happy. They, too, have just found themselves here and want to be happy and free from suffering. Then you can imagine directing kindness towards all your neighbours and those in your local area (okay, yes, and to your local football team, who you hope will do well today).

Keep extending this desire for others to be content, peaceful and happy to your city, to your country and to the world. You'll end up wishing for all living things in the flow of life to flourish and be free from suffering. You can extend this through time so that your desire for warmth, contentment and peacefulness is not just for people and things living now but for all living things to come in the future. In studies of the effects on brain physiology of having compassion for others, this was the exercise used where an 'unconditional feeling of loving kindness and compassion pervades the whole mind as a way of being with no other consideration or discursive thoughts'.

At some point, you may realize that, by extending your desire for others to be content, peaceful and happy, you're going to have to include people you don't particularly like, those who have done you harm and even your enemies. Although it's a bit trickier, extending your desire for contentment, peace and happiness to these people can be a very useful exercise if you've built up to it. You have to remember that none of us has chosen to be here in this life, nor did we choose the genes that we were born with or the archetypes that can so easily set one against another, or the conditioning we were given. We're all actors in the flow of life. We hurt each other because we're ignorant and because it's so difficult for us to be truly and fully in control of our own mind.[4]

Exercise: Compassion for our distress and threat feelings

As we have seen, our threat/self-protection system, which gives us feelings of anger, anxiety, disgust and other unpleasant things, can get very worked up.

If you've experienced difficult feelings or become upset about something, here's an exercise that can be helpful. Sit quietly in a chair or in your compassion posture, engage in your soothing breathing rhythm and then focus on becoming a compassionate self. Imagine that you *are* a deeply compassionate person, who never condemns and who possesses wisdom and great warmth.

Now imagine that the angry, anxious or upset part of you is in front of you as the deeply compassionate you. Look at your facial expressions and behaviour. Imagine what that part of you is feeling and thinking.

Now simply send compassion to that part of yourself. Try to really feel compassion for it. Don't try to change anything – just sit looking at that part and feel compassion. You recognize these emotions are from the threat system and are related to fears and upsets.

If you practise holding your compassionate position and looking at your upset, anxious or angry self, you may notice that different feelings and thoughts come to mind that are helpful to you. Give it a try and see how you do.[5]

A FURTHER EXERCISE FOR CHAPTER 12

Exercise: Limiting your criticism of others

Research suggests that some self-critics are also quite critical of other people. Try to monitor how often you have critical thoughts or say critical things about others, either directly to them or behind their back, or if you simply ruminate on these thoughts. Don't be self-critical about this: observe that it happens and think to yourself: What is that about? Why did I need to do that? Where is the fear and vulnerability in me?

Treat your criticism of others compassionately, and avoid shaming yourself for it because then it will be difficult to work with. At the same time, ask yourself if you want to be different. One of the problems with living in a world in which you're critical of others is that you'll constantly be stimulating your threat/self-protection system. As we can create in ourselves feelings of compassion and loving kindness for others, this action stimulates our brains in a different and positive way. So even if you feel justified in being critical of others, you're still far better off practising generating compassion for others.[6]

References

Introduction

1 Gilbert, P., *The Compassionate Mind* (Constable, 2009) 38

2 Gilbert, P., *Compassion-Focused Therapy* (Routledge, 2010) 14

3 Rinpoche, S., *The Tibetan Book of Living and Dying* (Rider, rev. 2002)

4 www.awarenessinaction.org

5 If you are interested in learning more about secular ethics you could look into:

   HH the Dalai Lama, *Ancient Wisdom, Modern World: Ethics for the New Millennium* (Little, Brown, 1999) and HH the Dalai Lama, *Beyond Religion: Ethics for a Whole World* (Rider, 2011)

6 In 2005 the Dalai Lama published his book entitled *The Universe in a Single Atom* (Broadway Books, 2005) which documents his lifelong interest in science and the beneficial role he believes a dialogue between science and spirituality has to play

7 www.mindandlife.org

8 Davidson, R., with Begley, S., *The Emotional Life of your Brain* (Hodder & Stoughton, 2012)

Chapter 1

1 Cannon, W., *Bodily Changes in Pain, Hunger, Fear and Rage* (D. Appleton & Co., 1929)

2 Cannon, W., *The Wisdom of the Body* (W. W. Norton, 1932)

3 Selye gained a medical degree and Ph.D. from a German university

in Prague and a D.Sc. from McGill University in Montreal. He is the author of 38 books and 1,600 technical articles

4   Sapolsky, R., *Why Zebras Don't Get Ulcers* (St Martin's Press, third edn 2004) 13, italics mine

5   Professor emeritus of psychology at the University of California, Berkeley

6   Lazarus, R., and Folkman, S., *Stress, Appraisal, and Coping* (Springer Publishing, 1984) 19, italics mine

7   Ibid., 141

8   The Sainsbury's Centre for Mental Health, 'Policy Paper 8: Mental Health at Work: Developing the Business Case' (December 2007) 1

9   A survey carried out for the US National Institute for Occupational Safety and Health by Northwestern National Life found that 40 per cent of workers reported their job to be 'very or extremely stressful'. Quoted in Patmore, A., *The Truth about Stress* (Atlantic Books, 2006) 36

Chapter 2

1   Sapolsky, R., *Why Zebras Don't Get Ulcers* (St Martin's Press, third edn 2004)

2   Diagram adapted from Gilbert, P., *The Compassionate Mind* (Constable, 2009), reprinted with permission from Constable & Robinson Ltd

3   Adrenaline and noradrenaline are the terms used in the UK. In the USA the terms used are epinephrine and norepinephrine

4   Sapolsky, R., *Why Zebras Don't Get Ulcers*, 16

5   A key factor was the work of Redford Williams of Duke University, who declared himself to be a Type A Personality. Realizing the destructive potential of Type A characteristics both from a social and health point of view, Williams set out to try and understand the

pattern more deeply. He identified hostility as the key factor in the list of Type A symptoms. Williams wrote a book, *Anger Kills* (Harper Perennial, 1993), with his wife, who was an important influence in helping him overcome his own hostile behaviour as a way of safe-guarding his marriage

Chapter 3

1 Davidson, R. J., and Harrington, A., (eds), *Visions of Compassion* (Oxford University Press, 2002) 68

2 The Chinese sage Confucius is thought to have been the first to formulate the Golden Rule but references can be found in many religious and ethical writings including the New Testament, the Talmud and the Koran, as well as the Analects of Confucius

3 Or conversely: *Do not treat others as you would not like them to treat you*

4 Matthew 7:12, Matthew 22:39, Luke 6:31

5 Drafted by representatives with different legal and cultural backgrounds from all regions of the world, the Declaration was proclaimed by the United Nations General Assembly in Paris on 10 December 1948

6 Carl Rogers (1902–87) was an influential American psychologist and among the founders of the humanistic approach to psychology

7 This wish is what is known as *bodhicitta* in Sanskrit – *bodhi* is enlight-ened essence; *citta* is heart, or mind. The Buddhist teachings on compassion are often referred to as Bodhicitta teachings. There are two aspects to the practice of Bodhicitta – absolute and relative. Absolute bodhicitta is the direct insight into the true nature of mind, and the realization of our fundamental nature. For most of us, this is not something that can be easily accomplished and so there is the more gradual path of relative bodhicitta

8   Gilbert, P., 'Introducing Compassion Focused Therapy', *Advances in Psychiatric Treatment* online magazine, 2009, http://apt.rcpsych.org/content/15/3/199.full

9   HH the Dalai Lama, *Ancient Wisdom, Modern World, Ethics for the New Millennium* (Little, Brown, 1999) 24

10 http://charterforcompassion.org

11 Tutu, D., 'Truth and Reconciliation', included in Keltner D., Marsh, J., and Smith, J. A., (eds), *The Compassionate Instinct* (W. W. Norton, 2010)

Chapter 4

1   Sapolsky, R., *Why Zebras Don't Get Ulcers* (St Martin's Press, third edn 2004) 116

2   1809–82

3   1820–1903

4   More detail on this can be found in Gilbert, P., *The Compassionate Mind* (Constable, 2009)

5   HH the Dalai Lama, *Ancient Wisdom, Modern World, Ethics for the New Millennium* (Little, Brown, 1999) 72

6   Experiment carried out by Jack Nitschke at the University of Wisconsin

7   Carried out by James Rilling and Gregory Berns at Emory University, Atlanta

8   Harrington, A., and Zajonc, A., *The Dalai Lama at MIT* (Harvard University Press, 2008)

9   If you are interested in reading the details of Keltner's work, consult his book *Born to be Good* (W. W. Norton, 2009)

10 Keltner, D., Marsh J., and Smith, J. A., (eds), *The Compassionate Instinct* (W. W. Norton, 2010) 11

11   Quoted in 'Hope on the Battlefield' by Dave Grossman in Keltner, Marsh and Smith, ibid., 41

12   Charlotte van Oyen Witvliet

13   British researchers Peter Woodruff and Tom Farrow from Sheffield University have collaborated on developing a functional MRI protocol to measure forgivability. Their findings suggest that the areas of the brain associated with forgiveness are to be found deep in the emotional centres of the brain, in the region known as the limbic system, rather than in the areas of the cortex usually associated with reason. Altering deep emotional patterns imprinted on to our limbic system does not happen easily and can take considerable time, but research is also showing that forgiveness can be learnt. Robert Enright, a professor of Educational Psychology at the University of Wisconsin-Madison, has developed a twenty-step intervention that is showing encouraging results. For example, men who experienced pain and hurt at their partner's decision to undergo an abortion went through twelve ninety-minute weekly sessions designed to help them forgive, resulting in a decrease in their levels of anxiety, fear and grief and an increase in their levels of forgiveness. This research is still in its early stages but there is plenty of evidence to support the beneficial effects of forgiveness.

14   Haidt, J., 'Wired to be inspired', in Keltner, Marsh and Smith, (eds), *The Compassionate Instinct* op. cit., 91

Chapter 5

1   From a public talk given by the Dalai Lama to an audience in Arizona, USA in 1993.
    HH the Dalai Lama and Cutler, H., *The Art of Happiness: A Handbook for Living* (Hodder & Stoughton, 1998)

2   To learn more about this view, see Achor, S., *The Happiness Advantage* (Virgin Books, 2010)

3   Schwartz, B., *The Paradox of Choice* (Ecco, 2003)

4   *Online NewsHour* with Paul Solman, 26 December 2003
    http://www.pbs.org/newshour/bb/economy/july-dec03/para-
    dox_12-26.html

5   Delingpole, J., 'The tyranny of choice', *Mail Online*, 5 July 2007

6   Definition of flow: 'A sense that one's skills are adequate to cope with
    the challenges at hand in a goal directed, rule bound action system
    that provides clear clues as to how one is performing. Concentration
    is so intense that there is no attention left over to think about any-
    thing irrelevant or to worry about problems. Self-consciousness
    disappears, and the sense of time becomes distorted. An activity that
    produces such experiences is so gratifying that people are willing to
    do it for its own sake, with little concern for what they will get out
    of it, even when it is difficult or dangerous.' Csikszentmihalyi, M.,
    Flow: The Psychology of Optimal Experience (Harper & Row, 1990)

7   M.E.P. Seligman Ph.D., *Authentic Happiness* (Simon & Schuster, 2002)
    46

8   Sonja Lyubomirsky in her book *The How of Happiness* (Penguin Press,
    2007) uses the same format but calls it the Subjective Happiness
    Scale

9   This was established by Dr Ruut Veenhoven, who is also one of the
    editors of a trade journal, the *Journal of Happiness Studies*, which
    began publication in 2000

10 Definition of Hedonic Psychology from Kahneman, D., Diener,
    E., and Schwarz, N., (eds), *Well-Being: Foundations of Hedonic
    Psychology* (Russell Sage Foundation, 1999) ix

11 Layard, R., *Happiness: Lessons from a New Science* (Allen Lane, 2005).
    Layard dedicated his book to Daniel Kahneman

12 ibid., 233

13 www.grossnationalhappiness.org

14   The 5th International Gross National Happiness Conference was held in December 2009

15   Article by Brickman and Campbell 1971 from Kahneman, Diener, and Schwarz (eds), *Well-Being: Foundations of Hedonic Psychology* op. cit., ix

16   Gilbert, D., *Stumbling on Happiness* (Alfred A. Knopf, 2006)

17   Richard Easterlin's study of the hedonic treadmill, published in Easterlin, R. A., 'Does Economic Growth Improve the Human Lot?' in David, P. A., and Reder, M. W., (eds.), *Nations and Households in Economic Growth: Essays in Honor of Moses Abramovitz* (Academic Press, 1974)

18   Seligman, *Authentic Happiness*, op. cit., 70

19   Solnick, S. J., and Hemenway, D., 'Is more always better?', *Journal of Economic Behavior & Organization*, 37: 3 (1998), 373–83

20   Medvec et al, 'When less is more: Counterfactual thinking and satisfaction among Olympic athletes', Journal of Personality and Social Psychology, 69: 4 (October 1995), 603–10

21   Layard, R., *Happiness: Lessons from a New Science*, op. cit., 49

22   Kahneman, Frederickson, Schreiber and Redelmeier, 1993

23   TheHappinessFormula,http://news.bbc.co.uk/2/hi/programmes/happiness_formula/default.stm

24   Lyubomirsky, *The How of Happiness*, op. cit.

25   Harvard Science section, *Harvard Gazette*, 15 February 2012 http://news.harvard.edu/gazette/story/2010/11/wandering-mind-not-a-happy-mind/

26   Gilbert, D., *Stumbling on Happiness*, op. cit.

27   Kahneman, Frederickson, Schreiber and Redelmeier, 1993

Chapter 6

1   Gilbert, P., *The Compassionate Mind* (Constable, 2009) 64

2   When the Buddha realized fundamental awareness and woke up to his own nature and the nature of everyone, he wanted to share what he had learnt in order to help others. In his very first teaching he chose to talk about suffering – not happiness, not liberation, not about how to become like him – but the reality of suffering as something that is part of the way we live our lives. These teachings became known as the Four Noble Truths – the truth of suffering, the truth of the causes of suffering, the truth of the cessation of suffering and the truth of the path that leads away from suffering. This detailed examination of suffering remains a kind of blueprint for all the Buddha's teachings, providing an understanding of our basic problem, along with an analysis of why we have it, a view of how we can overcome it and the methods to be able to bring this about.

3   There is a traditional Buddhist story of a young mother, Krishna Gotomi, who lived at the time of the Buddha. Tragically her only son died when he was just one year old and she was driven mad with grief and despair. She went from one person to another, carrying the body of her son and begging for help to bring him back to her. Finally someone sent her to see the Buddha to ask him for help. When the Buddha heard her story and her frantic plea to have her son restored to her he told her that indeed the boy could be brought back to life if she would collect some mustard seed from a house that had never known death and bring it to the Buddha. Delighted, Krishna Gotomi set off to the nearest house to ask for mustard seed only to find that the mother of the house had died the previous year. She went to the next house but there a brother had died. So it went on from house to house – there was none that had not experienced death. Quietly she returned to the Buddha and gave up her son's body for burial. The Buddha asked her what had changed and she explained that she understood that death comes to everyone; it was not just her own personal suffering.

Chapter 7

1   Milton, J., 'Paradise Lost' (1667)

2   Kahneman, D., The Riddle of Experience vs Memory, TED lecture (February 2010) video at http://www.ted.com/talks/daniel_kahneman_the_riddle_of_experience_vs_memory.html

3   Frankl, V. E., Man's Search for Meaning (Rider, new edn 2004)

4   Germer, C. K., The Mindful Path to Self-Compassion: Freeing Yourself from Destructive Thoughts and Emotions (Guilford Press, 2009) 31

5   Goleman, D., with Boyatzis, R. and McKee, A., The New Leaders (Little, Brown, 2002) 202

6   Adapted from ibid., 201

Chapter 8

1   Salzberg, S., A Heart as Wide as the World: Stories on the Path of Loving Kindness (Shambhala Publications, 1999)

2   According to the Buddhist teachings these are known as the Four Foundations of Mindfulness. An account of them is given in the Satipatthana Sutta. You can read about them in Goenka, S. N., Satipatthana Sutta Discourses (Vipassana Research Publications, 1998)

3   This exercise is a simplified version of: Williams, M., Teasdale, J., Segal, Z., and Kabat-Zinn, J., The Mindful Way through Depression (Guilford Press, 2007) 104–6

4   Michie, D., Hurry Up and Meditate (Snow Lion Publications, 2008) 82

5   Rinpoche, S., The Tibetan Book of Living and Dying (Rider, rev. 2002) 63

6   Lutz, A., Ricard, M., and Davidson, R. J., 'Long-term meditators self-induce high-amplitude gamma synchrony during mental practice', Proceedings of the National Academy of Sciences 101: 46 (2004), and for

a detailed account of this study see Kabat-Zinn, J., *Coming to Our Senses* (Hyperion, 2005) 368–74

7 www.cultivatingemotionalbalance.org

8 For a detailed account of this study see Kabat-Zinn, *Coming to Our Senses*, op. cit., 359–365

9 Kaufman, M., 'Meditation Gives Brain a Charge, Study Finds' in the *Washington Post* (3 January 2005) A05

Chapter 9

1 Foley, M., *The Age of Absurdity* (Simon & Schuster, 2010) 36

2 James, O., *Affluenza* (Vermilion, 2007) vii

3 Sapolsky, R., *Why Zebras Don't Get Ulcers* (St Martin's Press, third edn 2004) 260

4 HH the Dalai Lama and Cutler, H., *The Art of Happiness: A Handbook for Living* (Hodder & Stoughton, 1998)

5 The 'third sector' is the term used to describe the range of organizations that are neither public sector nor private sector. It includes voluntary and community organizations (both registered charities and other organizations such as associations, self-help groups and community groups, social enterprises, mutuals and cooperatives). Definition from the National Audit Office

6 Kabat-Zinn, J., *Coming to Our Senses* (Piatkus, 2005) 74

7 Gilbert, P., *The Compassionate Mind* (Constable, 2009) 38

8 Hanson, R., with Mendius, R., *Buddha's Brain* (New Harbinger Publications Inc, 2009) 55

Chapter 10

1　King, Jr., Dr. M. L., 'Christmas Sermon on Peace', CBC Massey Lectures (1967)

2　Rinpoche, Y. M., *Joyful Wisdom* (Harmony Books, 2009) 55

3　Adapted from ibid., 59

4　Cosley, B. J., McCoy, S. K., Saslow, L. R., and Epel, E. S., 'Is Compassion for Others Stress Buffering? Consequences of Compassion and Social Support for Physiological Reactivity to Stress', *Journal of Experimental Social Psychology*, 46: 5 (September 2010), 816–23

5　Luks, A., and Payne, P., *The Healing Power of Doing Good* (iUniverse.com, 1991, 2001)

6　Sobel, D., and Ornstein, R., *Healthy Pleasures* (Addison-Wesley Publishing, 1989) 235, quoted in Luks and Payne, ibid., 115

7　Begley, S., *Train Your Mind, Change Your Brain* (Ballatine Books, 2007) 9

8　ibid., 24–5

9　Begley, S., 'How the Brain Rewires itself', TIME Magazine (19 January 2007), article at http://www.time.com/time/magazine/article/0,9171,1580438,00.html

10　Quoted in Begley, S., *Train Your Mind, Change Your Brain* (Ballantine Books, 2007) 242

Chapter 11

1　The Buddha said that if you searched the whole world for someone more worthy of love than yourself you would not find anyone – just as everyone else in the world is worthy of love, so are we.

2　Germer, C. K., *The Mindful Path to Self-Compassion* (The Guilford Press, 2009) 84

3   Neff, K., *Self Compassion* (Hodder & Stoughton, 2011) 41

4   ibid., 47–8

5   Kabat-Zinn, J., and Davidson, R., with Houshmand, Z., (ed), *The Mind's Own Physician* (New Harbinger Publications, 2011) 50

6   Sonja Lyubomirsky defines these three categories of social support in her book *The How of Happiness* (The Penguin Press, 2007) 139

Chapter 12

1   Armstrong, K., quoted on Bill Moyers Journal PBS (13 March 2009), transcript at http://www.pbs.org/moyers/journal/03132009/transcript3.html

2   Kabat-Zinn, J., and Davidson, R., with Houshmand, Z., (ed), *The Mind's Own Physician* (New Harbinger Publications, 2011) 50–1

3   Albert Schweitzer (1875–1965), philosopher, physician, Nobel Peace Prize winner

4   Scherwitz, L., Graham II, L. E., and Ornish, D., 'Self-involvement and the risk factors for coronary heart disease', *Advances*, 2: 2 (Spring 1985), 6–18

5   Luks, A., and Payne, P., *The Healing Power of Doing Good* (iUniverse. com, 1991, 2001) 96

6   Goleman, D., *Social Intelligence* (Bantam Books, 2006) 308

7   Abuelaish, I., *I Shall Not Hate* (Bloomsbury, 2011)

8   Haidt, J., *The Happiness Hypothesis* (Arrow, 2007)

9   Joseph Campbell (1904–87), American mythologist and author

10 Based on the work of Paul Ekman, psychologist. Explained by Daniel Goleman in Keltner, D., Marsh, J., and Smith, J. A., (eds), *The Compassionate Instinct* (W. W. Norton, 2010) 172–3

Chapter 13

1   Sogyal Rinpoche, *The Tibetan Book of Living and Dying* (Rider, rev. 2002) 367

2   Approximately £2.50 at the time of writing

3   *Tonglen* is a Tibetan Buddhist practice that can be practised in many ways and at many levels. If you would like to learn more about it you could look at Rinpoche, *The Tibetan Book of Living and Dying*, op.cit., 206–11

4   'Volcano Ash Cloud Sets Off Global Domino Effect', CBS News (20 April 2010, 21.38)

5   de Botton, A., *The Pleasures and Sorrows of Work* (Penguin, 2009) 41

6   ibid., 42

Conclusion

1   www.appletoncompassion.org

2   Tan, C. M., *Search Inside Yourself* (HarperCollins, 2012)

Appendix

1   Adapted from 'Mindful breathing' exercise in Gilbert, P., *The Compassionate Mind* (Constable, 2009), 225

2   Adapted from 'The art of appreciation' exercise, ibid., 236–8

3   Adapted from 'Using memory to create compassionate feelings' exercise, ibid., 246–7

4   Adapted from 'The desire for others to be happy' exercise, ibid., 248–9

5   Adapted from 'Compassion for our distress and threat feelings' exercise, ibid., 264

6   Adapted from 'Limiting your criticism of others' exercise, ibid., 346–7

Useful Resources

If you are interested in finding out more about the work of *Awareness in Action* you could:

- Check out our website www.awarenessinaction.org

- Find us on Facebook www.facebook.com/awarenessinaction

- Or talk to us on Twitter @awareinaction

Books

Other books in The Compassionate Mind series:

The Compassionate Mind, Paul Gilbert (Constable, 2009)

The Compassionate Mind Approach to Beating Overeating: Using Compassion Focused Therapy, K. Ross (Robinson, 2011)

The Compassionate Mind Approach to Building Self-Confidence, M. Welford (Robinson, 2012)

The Compassionate Mind Approach to Managing Your Anger, R. Kolts (Robinson, 2012)

The Compassionate Mind Approach to Overcoming Anxiety Using Compassion Focused Therapy, D. Tirch (Robinson, 2012)

The Compassionate Mind Approach to Recovering from Trauma Using Compassion Focused Therapy, D. Lee with S. James (Robinson, 2012)

Improving Social Confidence and Reducing Shyness using Compassion Focused Therapy, L. Henderson (Robinson, 2010)

Other useful books:

365 Thank Yous: The Year a Simple Act of Daily Gratitude Changed My Life, J. Kralik (Hyperion Books, 2010)

Affluenza, O. James (Vermilion, 2007)

The Age of Absurdity: Why Modern Life Makes it Hard to be Happy, M. Foley (Simon & Schuster, 2010)

The Age of Empathy: Nature's Lessons for a Kinder Society, F. De Waal (Souvenir Press, 2011)

Ancient Wisdom, Modern World: Ethics for the New Millennium, HH the Dalai Lama (Little, Brown, 1999)

Anger Kills: Seventeen Strategies for Controlling the Hostility that Can Harm Your Health, R. Williams and V. Williams (Harper Perennial, 1993)

The Art of Happiness at Work, HH the Dalai Lama and H. Cutler (Hodder & Stoughton, 1998)

The Art of Happiness: A Handbook for Living, HH the Dalai Lama and H. Cutler (Hodder & Stoughton, 1998)

Authentic Happiness: Using the New Positive Psychology to Realise Your Potential for Lasting Fulfilment, M. E. P. Seligman Ph.D. (Simon & Schuster, 2004)

Awakening the Kind Heart: How to Meditate on Compassion, K. McDonald (Wisdom Publications, 2010)

Beyond Religion: Ethics for a Whole World, HH the Dalai Lama (Rider, 2012)

Boeddhisme in een notendop, B. van Baar (Uitgeverij Bert Bakker, 2006)

Born to be Good: The Science of a Meaningful Life, D. Keltner (W. W. Norton, 2009)

Boundless Heart: The Cultivation of the Four Immeasurables, B. A. Wallace (Snow Lion Publications, 1999)

The Brain that Changes Itself: Stories of Personal Triumph from the Frontiers of Brain Science, N. Doidge (Penguin, 2008)

Buddha's Brain: The Practical Neuroscience of Happiness, Love and Wisdom, R. Hanson and R. Mendius (New Harbinger Publications, 2009)

Coming to Our Senses: Healing Ourselves and the World through Mindfulness, J. Kabat-Zinn (Piatkus, 2005)

Compassion Focused Therapy, P. Gilbert (Routledge, 2010)

The Compassionate Brain: How Empathy Creates Intelligence, G. Huther (Shambhala Publications, 2006)

The Compassionate Instinct: The Science of Human Goodness, D. Keltner, J. Marsh and J. A. Smith (eds) (W. W. Norton, 2010)

Dalai Lama, wijze van deze tijd, B. van Baar (Uitgeverij Bert Bakker, 2009)

The Emotional Life of your Brain, R. Davidson and S. Begley (Hodder & Stoughton, 2012)

Full Catastrophe Living: How to Cope with Stress, Pain and Illness using Mindfulness Meditation, J. Kabat-Zinn (Piatkus, 2001)

The Geography of Bliss, E. Weiner (Black Swan, 2008)

The Happiness Advantage: The Seven Principles of Positive Psychology that Fuel Success and Performance at Work, S. Achor (Virgin Books, 2010)

Happiness: A Guide to Developing Life's Most Important Skill, M. Ricard (Atlantic Books, 2007)

Happiness: Lessons from a New Science, R. Layard (Allen Lane, 2005)

The Happiness Project: Or, Why I Spent A Year Trying To Sing in the Morning, Clean My Closets, Fight Right, Read Aristotle and Generally Have More Fun, G. Rubin (HarperPaperbacks, 2011)

The Healing Power of Doing Good, A. Luks and P. Payne (iUniverse.com, 1991, 2001)

The How of Happiness: A Practical Guide to Getting the Life You Want, S. Lyubomirsky (Penguin Press, 2007)

Hurry Up and Meditate: Your Starter Kit for Inner Peace and Better Health, D. Michie (Snow Lion Publications, 2008)

I Shall Not Hate: A Gaza Doctor's Journey on the Road to Peace and Human Dignity, I. Abuelaish (Bloomsbury, 2011)

The Joy of Living: Unlocking the Secret and Science of Happiness, Yongey Mingyur Rinpoche (Bantam, 2009)

Joyful Wisdom, Yongey Mingyur Rinpoche (Harmony Books, 2009)

The Mind's Own Physician: A Scientific Dialogue with the Dalai Lama on the Healing Power of Meditation, J. Kabat-Zinn, R. Davidson and Z. Houshmand (New Harbinger Publications, 2011)

The Mindful Way through Depression: Freeing Yourself from Chronic Unhappiness, M. Williams, J. Teasdale, Z. Segal and J. Kabat-Zinn (The Guilford Press, 2007)

The New Leaders: Transforming the Art of Leadership, D. Goleman, R. Boyatzis and A. McKee (Little, Brown, 2002)

One City: A Declaration of Interdependence, E. Nichtern (Wisdom Publications, 2007)

The Paradox of Choice: Why More is Less, B. Schwartz (HarperCollins, 2005)

The Path is the Goal: A Basic Handbook of Buddhist Meditation, Chogyam Trungpa (Shambhala Publications, 1995)

The Plastic Mind, S. Begley (Constable & Robinson, 2009)

The Pleasures and Sorrows of Work, A. de Botton (Penguin, 2009)

Real Happiness: The Power of Meditation, S. Salzberg (Hay House, 2011)

Religion for Atheists: A Non-Believer's Guide to the Uses of Religion, A. de Botton (Hamish Hamilton, 2012)

Search Inside Yourself: Increase Productivity, Creativity and Happiness, D. Goleman, J. Kabat-Zinn and Chade-Meng Tan, (HarperCollins, 2012)

Self Compassion, K. Neff (Hodder & Stoughton, 2011)

Smile or Die: How Positive Thinking Fooled America and the World, B. Ehrenreich (Granta Books, 2010)

Social Intelligence: the New Science of Human Relationships, D. Goleman (Bantam, 2006)

Stress and Emotion: A New Synthesis, R. S. Lazarus (Springer, 1999)

The Stress of Life, H. Selye (McGraw Hill, 1978)

Stress: Myth, Theory and Research, Dr F. Jones and Dr J. Bright (Pearson Education, 2001)

Stumbling on Happiness, D. Gilbert (Alfred A. Knopf, 2006)

The Tibetan Book of Living and Dying, Sogyal Rinpoche (Rider, rev. 2002)

Train Your Mind, Change Your Brain: How a New Science Reveals Our Extraordinary Potential to Transform Ourselves, S. Begley (Ballantine Books, 2007)

The Truth about Stress, A. Patmore (Atlantic Books, 2006)

The Truth Of Suffering and the Path of Liberation, Chogyam Trungpa (Shambhala Publications, 2009)

Twelve Steps to a Compassionate Life, K. Armstrong (The Bodley Head, 2011)

The Universe in a Single Atom: How Science and Spirituality can Serve Our World, HH the Dalai Lama (Abacus, 2005)

Visions of Compassion: Western Scientists and Tibetan Buddhists Examine Human Nature, R. J. Davidson and A. Harrington (eds) (Oxford University Press, 2002)

Why Kindness Is Good For You, D. R. Hamilton (Hay House, 2010)

Why Zebras Don't Get Ulcers, R. M. Sapolsky (St Martin's Press, third edn 2004)

Organizations

UK/Europe

Awareness in Action was founded by Maureen Cooper in 2004. We offer workshops on applying the approach and techniques shared in this book in the modern workplace.

www.awarenessinaction.org

The Compassionate Mind Foundation

Set up in 2006 the Foundation aims to promote wellbeing through the scientific understanding and application of compassion.

PO Box 7505, Derby, DE1 0LT

www.compassionatemind.co.uk

Mind with Heart

Mind with Heart is a charity dedicated to equipping young people with the social and emotional skills necessary to their wellbeing and to building a more sustainable society.

4 Sanford Walk, London N16 7LB

www.mind-with-heart.blogspot.co.uk

Rigpa

Rigpa aims to present the Buddhist tradition of Tibet in a way that is both completely authentic, and as relevant as possible to the lives and needs of modern men and women. Rigpa has more than 130 centres in 41 countries all over the world, including three retreat centres dedicated to providing secluded and inspiring environments in which people can study and practise the Buddhist teachings: Lerab Lingin France, Dzogchen Beara in Ireland and the Tongnyi Nyingjé Ling in the USA. Rigpa also runs the Dechen Shying Spiritual Care Centre in Ireland. For people who do not live close to a centre, Rigpa offers a full curriculum of courses in Buddhism, meditation and compassion online at www.rigpa-onlinecourses.org.

www.rigpa.org

What Meditation Really Is

What Meditation Really Is has been developed by Sogyal Rinpoche after many years of teaching in the West, and with the support of some of his most experienced students. Sogyal Rinpoche is one of the best-known meditation teachers of our time and has a remarkable gift for presenting meditation in a way that is authentic, accessible and relevant to modern men and women. Drawing on the profound experience of the Tibetan tradition, he offers a powerful glimpse of the transformative potential of meditation, and addresses the challenges of life with humour and insight. This unique programme is based on the wisdom of the Tibetan Buddhist tradition, making the benefits of meditation available to everybody. The What Meditation Really Is website features regular, thought provoking articles by meditation practitioners and teachers as well as a wealth of videos, a place to ask questions and the 'Dare to Meditate' 10 step video guide.

www.whatmeditationreallyis.com

USA

The Center for Compassion and Altruism Research and Education

The Center for Compassion and Altruism Research and Education (CCARE) at Stanford University School of Medicine was founded in 2008 with the explicit goal of promoting, supporting and conducting rigorous scientific studies of compassion and altruistic behaviour. Founded and directed by Dr James Doty, Clinical Professor of Neurosurgery, CCARE is established within the Institute for Neuro-Innovation and Translational Neurosciences.

Stanford University, 1070 Arastradero Road, 2nd Floor, Palo Alto, CA 94304 (650) 721-6142

http://www.stanford.edu/group/ccare/cgi-bin/wordpress/

Center for Investigating Healthy Minds

The Center for Investigating Healthy Minds (CIHM) conducts rigorous interdisciplinary research on healthy qualities of mind such as kindness, compassion, forgiveness and mindfulness. Scientists at CIHM represent an integrated team with a broad array of research methodologies from behavioural to neuroscientific. The CIHM engages in translational research and outreach with the goal of cultivating healthy qualities of the mind at the individual, community and global levels.

Waisman Center, Suite S119, University of Wisconsin-Madison, 1500 Highland Avenue, Madison, WI 53705-2280

www.investigatinghealthyminds.org

Charter for Compassion

The Charter for Compassion is a document that transcends religious, ideological and national differences. Supported by leading thinkers from many traditions, the Charter activates the Golden Rule around the world. The Charter for Compassion is a cooperative effort to restore not only compassionate thinking but, more importantly, compassionate action to the centre of religious, moral and political life. Compassion is the principled determination to put ourselves in the shoes of the other, and lies at the heart of all religious and ethical systems.

4669 Eastern Avenue N., Seattle, WA 98103

www.charterforcompassion.org

The Greater Good

The Greater Good Science Center studies the psychology, sociology and neuroscience of wellbeing, and teaches skills that foster a thriving, resilient and compassionate society.

Greater Good Science Center, University of California, Berkeley, 2425 Atherton Street, #6070, Berkeley, CA 94720-6070

http://greatergood.berkeley.edu/

Mind & Life Institute

The Mind & Life Institute is a non-profit organization that seeks to understand the human mind and the benefits of contemplative practices through an integrated mode of knowing that combines first person knowledge from the world's contemplative traditions with methods and findings from contemporary scientific enquiry. Ultimately, our goal is to relieve human suffering and advance wellbeing.

Mind & Life Institute, 4 Bay Road, Hadley, MA 01035 (413) 387-0710

www.mindandlife.org

Index

exercise 243–4
exercises xxxii-xxxiii, 18-20, 40-1, 63-4,
    80, 120-1, 141-2, 207-8, 226, 254-5,
    305-6, 308-10
  adaptation 106
  anticipating what will make us
    happy 107
  applying mindfulness to a life
    situation 156-7
  art of appreciation 322-3
  avoiding harm 287
  be accepting of everything that
    comes to you 105
  cloakroom meditation 181-3
  comparison 106
  compassion for our distress and
    threat feelings 327–8
  compassion meditation 277–8
  cutting the commentary 181
  developing compassion 287
  developing equanimity 267-8
  developing gratitude and
    appreciation 288
  developing kindness 287
  don't go there – recognizing what
    will undo your composure 248–50
  everybody wants happiness and to
    avoid suffering 105
  extending mindfulness 149–53
  fundamental wholeness 64
  Golden Rule 63
  happy, the desire for others to be
    325–7
  how to meditate 161-2
  identifying your early warning
    signs of stress 265
  identifying your emotional triggers
    257
  interconnection and 64
  key 308-9
  learning to pay attention to our
    breath 147-8
  limiting your criticism of others 328
  loving kindness meditation 272-4
  meditation on joy 280-2
  meditation using a candle 163-4
  mindful breathing 319–21
  a mindful cup of coffee 154-5
  putting things right – for when
    you've lost it 251–3
  putting yourself in the other's shoes
    292–6

  reflecting on how you react to stress
    202-4
  reflection on the changes in your
    body 213
  seeing another person is just like
    you 284, 288
  seeing our pain as it is, a
    tremendous help 120
  seeing thoughts from the
    perspective of the sky 166-9
  a selection of helpful compassionate
    mind exercises 319–28
  switching off the autopilot 180
  Tonglen 296, 297–9
  transforming destructive emotions
    288
  using memory to create
    compassionate feelings 324–5
  using the breath – for when our
    sense of calm is disturbed 250–1
  wandering mind experiment 97–8
  'watching' our mind 126–7
  watching the news 217–18
  which exercises should you focus on
    310
  working with stress and anxiety
    241–2
experiencing aspect of the mind
    128–9, 139
'experiencing self' 129, 139, 145, 236

'fight-or-fight response' 6, 7, 8, 9, 17, 32,
    33, 67, 200, 238, 253, 262, 270, 311
'flow' 85
fMRI (functional magnetic resonance
    imaging) 175
forgiveness xxxviii, 60, 61–2, 76–7, 80,
    197, 218, 252, 260, 271, 286, 294, 333
Four Immeasurables 57, 58, 265, 266,
    283, 286, 298
Frankl, Viktor 131
Friedman, Meyer 37
functional analysis 24
fundamental wholeness 50–5, 62, 129,
    241, 260

gamma wave activity 176, 224
General Adaptation Syndrome, The
    8–9, 17
General Happiness Scale 85
Germer, Christopher 132, 238, 240
Gilbert, Daniel 88, 95, 96

The Compassionate Mind

by Paul Gilbert

ISBN 978-1-84901-098-6 (paperback)
ISBN 978-1-84901-248-5 (ebook)
Price: £9.99

'As one of Britain's most insightful psychologists Gilbert illuminates the power of compassion in our lives.'
Oliver James, author of *Affluenza*

In societies that encourage us to compete with each other, compassion is often seen as a weakness. Striving to get ahead, self-criticism, fear, and hostility towards others seem to come more naturally to us.

The Compassionate Mind explains the evolutionary and social reasons why our brains react so readily to threats – and reveals how our brains are also hardwired to respond to kindness and compassion.

Research has shown that developing kindness and compassion for ourselves and others builds our confidence, helps us create meaningful, caring relationships and promotes physical and mental health. Far from fostering emotional weakness, practical exercises focusing on developing compassion have been found to subdue our anger and increase our courage and resilience to depression and anxiety.

The Compassionate Mind Approach to Managing Your Anger

by Russell Kolts

ISBN 978-1-84901-559-2 (paperback)

ISBN 978-1-78033-083-9 (ebook)

Price: £15

An invaluable self-help guide for recognising personal anger problems, what lies behind that anger and how to deal with it using Compassion Focused Therapy (CFT).

We can all get angry from time to time but when it gets out of hand it can have a serious impact on many aspects of our lives. As well as damaging our physical and mental health and our ability to engage in healthy relationships, it can also potentially have an enormous impact on society.

Mounting evidence suggests that all this anger can be harmful to us in a number of different ways. As well as the harmful effect chronic anger can have on our relationships with other people, it is linked to health problems such as cardiovascular disease and irritable bowel syndrome (IBS) and mental illnesses such as depression and post-traumatic stress disorder (PTSD).

This invaluable self-help guide will enable the reader to recognise their personal anger problems, gain an understanding of what lies behind their anger, and use techniques based on CFT to deal with their anger more effectively.

The Compassionate Mind Approach to Overcoming Anxiety

by Dennis Tirch

ISBN 978-1-84901-513-4 (paperback)
ISBN 978-1-84901-960-6 (ebook)
Price: £15

An accessible self-help guide, which provides a clear understanding of how problem anxiety develops, the kinds of problems it causes and sets out ground-breaking Compassion Focused Therapy (CFT) techniques to overcome that anxiety.

We know what it's like to worry from time to time, but for some of us, our worrying can take over and have a serious impact on our lives. When our anxiety gets out of hand and starts to dominate our lives, affecting how we function and our general sense of wellbeing, it's time to do something about it.

Anxiety is a universal emotion but understanding what causes it to become a problem is the first step towards overcoming it. Recent research has shown that developing compassion towards ourselves and others gives us the courage to take steps to overcome our difficulties and tackle anxiety head-on.

The Compassionate Mind Approach to Building Self-Confidence

by Mary Welford

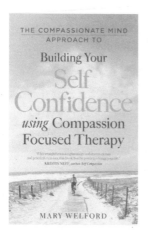

ISBN 978-1-78033-032-7 (paperback)
ISBN 978-1-78033-133-1 (ebook)
Price: £15

Written by a leading expert in the field, this self-help book sets out to help the reader to recognize the ways in which they are self-critical and to understand the impact this may be having on their life.

Based on Compassion Focused Therapy (CFT), the reader will learn proven techniques that will help them to improve their self confidence and fulfill their goals and aspirations.

Consistent with the ethos of the Compassionate Mind Approach, and the needs of the reader, this book includes findings from the latest scientific research on self-confidence and self-esteem, practical advice and a wealth of exercises.

The Compassionate Mind Approach to Recovering from Trauma

by Deborah Lee with Sophie James

ISBN 978-1-84901-320-8 (paperback)
ISBN 978-1-84901-945-3 (ebook)
Price: £15

Terrible events are very hard to deal with and those who go through a trauma often feel permanently changed by it. Grief, numbness, anger, anxiety and shame are all very common emotional reactions to traumatic incidents such as an accident or death of a loved one, and ongoing traumatic events such as domestic abuse.

How we deal with the aftermath of trauma and our own emotional response can determine how quickly we are able to 'move on' and get back to 'normality' once more. An integral part of the recovery process is not only recognising and accepting how our lives may have been changed but also learning to deal with feelings of shame – an extremely common reaction to trauma.

This book uses the groundbreaking Compassion Focused Therapy to help the reader to not only develop a fuller understanding of how we react to trauma, but also to deal with any feelings of shame and start to overcome any trauma-related difficulties.